CHANOYU

和敬清寂

CHANOYU

The Urasenke Tradition of Tea

edited by Sōshitsu Sen XV
translated by Alfred Birnbaum

New York · WEATHERHILL · *Tokyo*

This book is a translation of selected chapters from the six-volume *Chadō no Genryū* (The Source of the Way of Tea), published in Japanese by the Kyoto-based publisher Tankosha in 1983.

FIRST EDITION, 1988

Published by John Weatherhill, Inc., of New York and Tokyo, with editorial offices at 7–6–13 Roppongi, Minato-ku, Tokyo 106, Japan. Copyright © 1983 by Tankosha, 1988 by Sōshitsu Sen; all rights reserved. Printed in Japan.

Library of Congress Cataloging in Publication Data: Chadō no genryū. English. Selections. / Chanoyu: the Urasenke tradition of tea. / Selected translation: Chadō no genryū. / 1. Japanese tea ceremony—Ura Senke school. / I. Sen, Sōshitsu, 1923–   .   II. Birnbaum, Alfred.   III. Title.   IV. Title: Cha no yu. / GT2912.U7C482513   1987   394.1′2 86-32503 / ISBN 0-8348-0212-0

Contents

	Preface, *by Sōshitsu Sen XV*	*vii*
1	A Brief History of Tea in Japan *by Yasuhiko Murai*	*3*
2	Lives of the Urasenke Grand Masters *by Sōshitsu Sen XV*	*35*
3	The Master's Taste: Tea Utensils *by Sōshun Hamamoto*	*52*
4	The Master's Touch: Tea Scoops and Scrolls *by Hiroichi Tsutsui*	*77*
5	Urasenke Tearooms and Their Settings *by Masao Nakamura*	*96*
6	Midday Tea in the Urasenke Manner *by Sōbin Kawashima*	*120*
	Appendix: Documents on the Urasenke Grand Masters *by Akio Tanihata*	*142*
	Index	*163*
	A Note on Japanese Usage	*170*

Preface

The Book of Tea, published in 1906, first brought *chadō,* or the way of tea, to the attention of the English-speaking world. Its author, the noted art historian and connoisseur Kakuzō Okakura (1862–1913), approached his subject with the avowed purpose of contrasting East and West by placing tea within the larger continuum of Oriental thought as a key to Japanese culture. *The Book of Tea* was an overview of the philosophical basis of Japan's unique tradition of tea; it was not, strictly speaking, an introduction to *chadō,* nor was Okakura himself a tea master. This is not to discredit his achievement, for *The Book of Tea* remains a classic. After nearly a century, it still serves as one of the best introductions to Japanese culture.

Important as this work is, however, understanding between East and West needs a more solid basis. Time and distance have been compressed to the point where we are living in each other's back yard, as it were, subject to the same conditions of the modern age. The view from afar is no longer enough. Accelerated international exchange—not without occasional intercultural friction—has brought us to the point where knowledge in depth is essential.

In addressing a Victorian audience far removed from the exotic Far East, Okakura gave tea the flavor of a curious and mystical phenomenon. Many passages in his book strike us today as anachronistic. One of the main reasons for writing the present book was to bring *chadō* into clear focus through a comprehensive examination of its historical development as well as of its practice today.

In a sense, I have waited all my life for this opportunity to provide people overseas with a truly in-depth, concrete introduction to *chadō.* It is my conviction that a real understanding of the living way of tea can do much to bridge cultural differences. Toward that end, this book was conceived as the first authentic primer of the Urasenke tradition of *chadō.* Perhaps this is too much to expect of one book, given the sheer volume of material to be covered. Yet every attempt has been made to touch upon all aspects of Urasenke, from the grand masters' biographies, favorite tea utensils, and calligraphy to a description of a tea gathering.

It is my sincere hope that this introductory work on *chadō* will help promote a true meeting of hearts and minds the world over.

SŌSHITSU SEN XV

CHANOYU

CHAPTER ONE

A Brief History of Tea in Japan

by Yasuhiko Murai

The Origin of Japan's Tea Culture

People had long been drinking tea when the eighth-century Chinese sage Lu Yu wrote the *Cha Jing* (Classic of Tea). Cultivation of the tea plant, a shrub belonging to the camellia family, is thought to have begun well over two millennia ago in the so-called East Asian Crescent, which stretches from Yunnan in southern China to Assam at the eastern edge of India, whence it spread via trade routes to all surrounding areas. By the Former Han dynasty (206 B.C.–A.D. 8), according to Lu Yu, Chinese in every part of the empire were drinking of the "esteemed plant from the south."

Tea cultivation and drinking continued to spread, each new culture varying the method of preparing the tea leaves and serving the beverage to suit local tastes. The tea plant itself remained the same; the difference between black tea and green tea depended simply on whether the leaves were fermented to make black tea or steamed to make green tea. The culture of black tea took root in India and points west—the Middle East, North Africa, and Europe. Green tea predominated throughout East Asia, including Japan.

Leaving aside speculation that the tea plant may also have been native to Japan, the first mention of tea drinking in Japanese records occurs early in the Heian period (794–1185), when Saichō, Kūkai, and other Buddhist monks went to China to study. These official envoys of scholar-monks played an important role in popularizing tea at the Japanese court. The Tang-dynasty (618–907) manner of preparing and drinking tea, known as *dancha*—tea leaves pressed into bricks that were shaved directly into a kettle of boiling water—soon gained popularity at the Japanese court in Kyoto. Tea was drunk at poetry gatherings, and such imperially sponsored verse anthologies as the *Ryōun Shū* (814), the *Bunka Shurei Shū* (818), and the *Keikoku Shū* (827) included tea-inspired pieces.

Eventually the Tang dynasty began to decline, and after Japan stopped sending official envoys to China in 894, the Heian aristocracy lost interest in tea and other things Chinese. Tea drinking did not die out, however; it was taken up by Buddhist monks, who found the medicinal properties of tea an aid to digestion and to alertness in meditation (Fig. 1). The priest Seihō (832–909), founder of Daigoji temple southeast of Kyoto, is said to have always had a bowl of tea by his side while chanting the sutras when he was training at Tōdaiji temple in Nara. Likewise, Yakuōji, a temple founded by the priest Gyōki (668–749) in what is now Aichi Prefecture, had tea and herb gardens in its grounds.

In the Heian period and early Kamakura period (1185–1336), tea was also served at the formal banquets, called *naorai,* held after religious ceremonies. On the grandest of these occasions, the spring and autumn imperial sutra-chanting ceremonies, a hundred or more priests from various temples would gather at the imperial palace to pray for the well-being of the nation and the emperor, whereupon the imperial household would "bestow tea" *(incha)* upon them. This tea, served in plain earthenware bowls, was flavored with ginger and potent herbs. In the latter half of the tenth century, Ryōgen (912–85), head priest of the powerful Enryakuji temple near Kyoto, forbade drinking tea to excess at the Enryakuji ceremonies held in the sixth and eleventh months, an indication of the importance tea had assumed at formal banquets. One form of *naorai* that continues to this day, the twice-yearly serving of the *ōchamori,* or "great tea bowl," to worshipers at Saidaiji temple in Nara (Fig. 2), dates from when Eison (1201–90) shared the tea remaining from an offering to Chinju Hachimangū shrine with his fellow monks.

A new era in tea culture began with the introduction of powdered tea *(matcha)* by Eisai (1141–1215), founder of the Rinzai sect of Zen Buddhism in Japan, on his return from China in 1191. An enthusiastic advocate of tea, Eisai wrote the two-

1. Tea drinking at Kiyomizudera in a building adjacent to the main worhip hall. From the Kiyomizudera Engi Emaki (History of Kiyomizudera Picture Scroll).

2. Ōchamori tea service at Saidaiji, Nara.

volume treatise *Kissa Yōjō Ki* (Preservation of Health Through Drinking Tea), of which two slightly different copies are extant. The first volume extols the virtues of tea, and the second explains tea cultivation in addition to offering further comments on the drink itself. Eisai is said to have presented a copy of the *Kissa Yōjō Ki* to the shogun Minamoto Sanetomo (1192–1219), advising him that tea would cure hangovers.

"Tea is an elixir for preserving life, a subtle art for extending one's years," the text begins. The bitter element in tea was believed to harmonize the "five internal organs" and strengthen the heart. How did Eisai recommend that powdered tea be prepared? "Pick tea leaves in the morning and steam them immediately. Start drying them the same day and roast them overnight. If you put them in a good-quality jar sealed with bamboo leaves, they will keep for years with no change in quality." He also writes, "Tea is best prepared with very hot, pure water, using two to three spoonfuls [of tea] the size of a one-*mon* coin per serving, although the amount may be varied somewhat as desired."

Eisai is also reputed to have brought tea seeds back from China, presenting some to temples in the northern part of Kyushu, the southernmost of Japan's four main islands, before returning to Kyoto, where he persuaded the priest Myōe (1173–1232) to plant them at his temple, Kōzanji, in the hills of Toganoo, northwest of the capital. The small tea container known as "Chinese Persimmon Stem" *(aya kaki no heta chaire)*, in the collection of Kōzanji, has not been conclusively identified as the container in which Eisai gave three tea seeds to Myōe, but an authenticated letter in Myōe's hand states clearly that tea was being cultivated at Toganoo. In fact, by the end of the Kamakura period the Toganoo produce, called "true tea" *(honcha)*, was favored over the "lesser tea" *(hicha)* grown elsewhere. In another letter, Lord Kanazawa (Hōjō) Sadaaki (1278–1333) writes with great pleasure that his son, a monk at Ninnaji temple in northwestern Kyoto, not far from Toganoo, had managed to acquire some of the prized Toganoo tea for him.

Myōe is said to have provided the powerful Konoe clan with tea seeds for planting on its land in Uji, southeast of Kyoto. This was the origin of Uji tea, which eventually overshadowed that of Toganoo. Meanwhile, tea drinking and cultivation continued to spread, so that by the Northern and Southern Courts period (1336–92) not only temples but even local farmers had land planted in tea. A manuscript of the period, *Isei Teikin Ōrai* (Different Instructive Passages), includes the following passage in praise of Toganoo:

> Toganoo is first among the renowned plantations of our realm. Those of Ninnaji, Daigo, Uji, Hamuro, Hannyaji, and Kamioji are close rivals. Aside from these, places worthy of note for their tea are Murō in Yamato, Hattori in Iga, Kawai in Ise, Kiyomi in Suruga, and Kawagoe in Musashi. Compared with Ninnaji and such famous sites as those in Yamato and Iga, other localities are like bits of tile or mere pebbles next to agate. And even Ninnaji and Daigo are as lead and iron compared with the gold of Toganoo.

Tea drinking was no longer limited to the nobility, clergy, and warrior-class aristocracy but had filtered down to some commoners. A letter from the priest Junnin of Gokurakuji temple in Kamakura to the priest Myōnin of Shōmyōji temple in the province of Musashi (the present-day Tokyo area) confirms that tea plantations were flourishing throughout the land: "Most gratefully I received the parcel of new tea from your temple. Now that tea plantations everywhere are at their peak, new tea reaches far and wide."

By the fourteenth century the spread of tea had prompted a new vogue. In addition to *renga,* or "linked verse," poetry gatherings, aesthetes began to amuse themselves with tea-tasting competitions *(tōcha),* laying wagers as to who could identify teas from different growing areas. Indeed, tea and *renga* together typify the cultivated pastimes of medieval Japan.

The Foundations of Chanoyu

Once tea cultivation and the custom of tea drinking were well established in Japan, two more factors contributed to the birth of chanoyu, the consummate practice of tea connoisseurship: *sarei,* the code of "tea etiquette," and *cha suki,* "tea taste." Both grew out of the Zen tradition.

The formal rules that distinguish chanoyu from mere tea drinking derive from the guidelines for communal tea ceremonies included in the monastic codes observed in Chinese Zen temples. The first such code to be widely incorporated in the Chinese Zen temples was the *Chanyuan Qinggui* (Zen Garden Monastic Code) of the Song-dynasty (960–1279) master Zongze. Although Eisai is said to have shown an interest in this code, there is no record of him promulgating it when he transmitted Rinzai Zen to Japan. It was the Zen priest Dōgen (1200–53), transmitter of the Sōtō sect to

3. Four-headed tea service at Kenninji, Kyoto.

Japan, who drew up what was probably the first monastic code in Japan, the *Eihei Shingi*, for his monastery Eiheiji in what is now Fukui Prefecture. When the Zen priest Enji Ben'en (1202–80) returned from China in 1241 and founded Tōfukuji temple in southeastern Kyoto, he based that temple's rules of conduct on the *Chanyuan Qinggui* (Jap., *Zen'on Shigi*). He was followed in 1246 by the Chinese Zen priest Lanqi Daolong (1213–78), who further promulgated Song guidelines in Japan. In 1326 another Chinese priest, Qingzhuo Zhengcheng (1274–1339), went to Japan, where he wrote the *Daikan Shingi* (Great Mirror of Monastic Codes) to bring Japanese monastic codes into line with Chinese models.

In time, the tea ceremony procedure prescribed by these monastic codes reached the samurai and other lay classes. The fourteenth-century *Kissa Ōrai* (Letter on Tea Drinking) describes the secular tea-making procedure of the period—which closely resembled that of the monasteries—as follows:

1. The son of the host offers tea sweets to those gathered.
2. Next a comely youth hands a Jian ware [Jap., *temmoku*] tea bowl to each participant.
3. This being done, the youth, carrying a vessel of hot water in his left hand and a tea whisk in his right, prepares tea [for those gathered], beginning with the most honored guest.

At such a ceremony there would be four main participants: the host, the host's counterpart, the guest, and the guest's counterpart, each of whom might have further guests. Thus the tea gatherings of this period were called "four-headed" tea gatherings (*yotsugashira no chakai*; Fig. 3). The fourteenth-century war tale *Taihei Ki* (Chronicle of the Great Peace) mentions just such an arrangement, "four main persons, each seated at the head of a line." Host and guests alike would be given Chinese Jian ware tea bowls, which already contained a measured amount of powdered tea. Each person would then hold out his bowl, and a servant would prepare the beverage by pouring hot water over the tea and whisking the mixture. Sometimes everyone would be seated in chairs throughout the tea service.

According to the example in *Kissa Ōrai,* the guests partook of a light meal with sakè and tea in a "meeting room" (*kaisho*), then strolled in the garden before going to a "pavilion for tea-drinking" for the full tea function. This arrangement—initial refreshments, intermission, and formal tea—resembles the structure of the typical midday tea function practiced today (see chapter 6) and thus deserves note as a major transitional step between temple tea ceremonies and chanoyu. Here the resemblance ends, however, because once the four-headed tea service was over, host and guests would engage in a tea-tasting competition followed by a banquet.

Such early exercises in tea connoisseurship helped stimulate an interest in tea utensils and settings as embodiments of *cha suki,* the refined taste that was to become synonymous with chanoyu itself. At the time of which we are speaking, hosts displayed only Chinese paintings and used only Chinese wares. This taste for things continental (*karamono suki*) obviously owed a great deal to the Chinese background of the formal tea service at Zen temples, and especially the travels of Zen monks between Japan and China in the Southern Song period (1127–1279). Active sea trade between Japan and China continued in the Yuan dynasty (1279–1368) despite two attempted invasions of Japan.

Objects originally taken to Japan by Zen monks for religious purposes—portraits and calligraphy of high priests, monochrome ink landscapes infused with Zen spirit, *temmoku* tea bowls and other ceremonial articles, and altar fittings—became objects of aesthetic appreciation in themselves and were much in demand by connoisseurs. The official register of the vast holdings of Butsunichian, a subtemple of Enkakuji temple in Kamakura, gives some idea of the wealth of Chinese artifacts then in the possession of Zen temples. The above-mentioned letter by Kanazawa Sadaaki comments that "things continental [*karamono*], so much in vogue with tea, grow ever more popular," a further indication of the vital role that the late-Kamakura taste for art objects from the Asian continent played in the development of the tea aesthetic.

The early rooms where these treasured Chinese artifacts were displayed and tea gatherings, as well as *waka* (thirty-one-syllable poems in vernacular Japanese) and *renga* gatherings, took place were known simply as *kaisho,* or "meeting places." These were usually the large banquet halls of villas and palatial residences (Fig. 4). The *Taihei Ki* reports that when the incense connoisseur Sasaki Dōyo (1296–1373) was to leave the capital, he decorated the *kaisho* of his villa with his best Chinese artworks for a banquet. The elite devoted increasing sums to creating showplaces of culture: the third Ashikaga shogun, Yoshimitsu (1358–1408), had two *kaisho* on his Sanjō Bōmonden estate, although one was actually built by his brother Yoshinori (1394–1441), the sixth shogun, who also built three on his Muromachidono estate. Each hall was more sumptuous than the last, reflecting the lengths to which the leaders of the day pursued things Chinese as much as the need for official functions and ceremonies.

4. *A waka poetry gathering depicted in the* Boki Ekotoba *picture scroll. 1351. Nishi Honganji, Kyoto.*

5. *The* shoin *of Yoshimizu Shrine, Nara Prefecture. This is the oldest extant shoin-style room, dating from the early Muromachi period.*

The early part of the Muromachi period (1336–1568) saw the development of *oshi ita* (inset display boards), *chigaidana* (ornamental staggered shelves), and *tsukeshoin* (a window with a deep sill used as a writing desk) as elements of the type of *kaisho* interior that came to be called the *shoin* style (Fig. 5). It was at this time that tatami mats came to be used as wall-to-wall floor coverings. More important, however, the search for a formal space for arranging Chinese art objects eventually led to the development of the display alcove known as the tokonoma. The tea practice that developed in these new surroundings was known, naturally enough, as *shoin*-style chanoyu.

The *Shoin* Style of Chanoyu

The synthesis of the formal tea etiquette based on the rules of tea service in Zen temples, the taste for Chinese utensils, and *shoin*-style interiors yielded the oldest and most formal style of chanoyu, *shoin*-style chanoyu, practiced by the warrior-class aristocracy at gatherings mainly held on the estates of the Ashikaga shoguns.

Collections of treasures from the continent became so large, and the task of keeping an ordered, changing, room display (*zashiki kazari*; Fig. 6) so demanding, that soon official advisers called *dōbōshū* (Fig. 7) were hired by the shogunal household as purveyors and evaluators of art. Holders of this hereditary position were allowed to add the suffix *ami* (from Amida, the Japanese pronunciation of the name of the Buddha Amitābha) to their names, as in the case of the famous three-generation lineage of Nōami (1397–1471), Geiami (1431–85), and Sōami (1445?–1525). The number and responsibilities of *dōbōshū* grew under each successive shogun. By the time of the eighth Ashikaga shogun, Yoshimasa (1436–90), the duties of the *dōbōshū* included the acquisition, cataloguing, handling, storage, mounting, day-to-day selection, and display of Chinese artworks.

Nōami and Sōami devised a ranking of Chinese masterpieces, along with detailed rules for their display, which they set forth in the *Kundaikan Sōchō Ki,* a descriptive catalogue of the shogun's collection. This work, arguably the first treatise on interior decoration, is divided into three parts. The first lists about one hundred fifty Song and Yuan painters by ability and subject specialty. The second part treats the proper decoration of rooms, with diagrams showing examples of artwork displays for the tokonoma, *tsukeshoin,* and *chigaidana*. The third part discusses ceramics and lacquerware in detail with the help of illustrations. The act of appreciation had become the focus for the selective exhibition of artworks in an architectural environment specifically designed for display.

Instructions in the book foreshadowed many later practices. Examples of the proper display of flowers before the Buddhist altar formed the basis for the sixteenth-century *rikka* style of flower arrangement. The lineage of *dōbōshū* who went by the name Ritsuami was adept at arranging flowers. The Sen'ami lineage was adept at preparing tea and incense, a combination that was reflected in the chanoyu of Sen Rikyū, who is reputed to have been the grandson of the Sen'ami who served Yoshimasa.

In *shoin*-style chanoyu, tea was prepared in an adjoining area and carried by a *dōbōshū* or servant to where the host and guests sat waiting. This was known as *tatedashi,* or tea "served already whisked." According to a 1437 entry in the *Eikyō Gyōkō Ki,* a record of events in the Eikyō era (1429–41), when Yoshinori invited the emperor Gohanazono to his Muromachidono estate, there was a set of shelves for the tea implements (*ochanoyudana*) in the adjacent service area (*oyudono no jo*). On its top shelf were a *temmoku* tea bowl, a tea caddy, a tea whisk, a tea scoop, and a tray of other utensils; below were a bronze brazier and a silver kettle. This set of shelves was probably portable. Other records show that Yoshimasa had three separate tea-preparation rooms (*chanoyudokoro*) in different wings of his Higashiyama

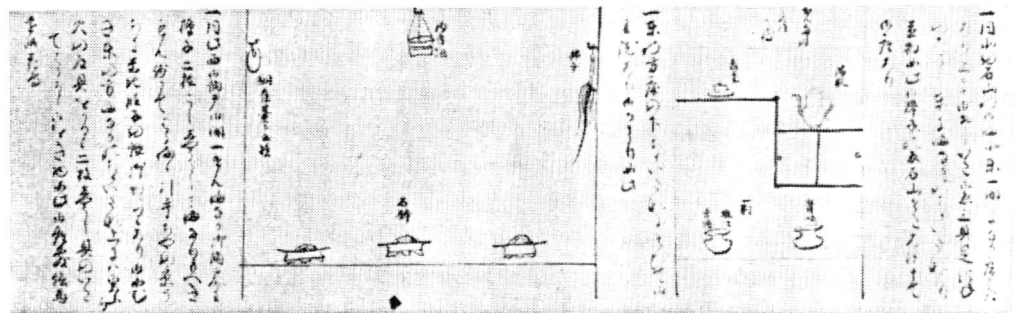

6. Sketch showing the display scheme for the tsukeshoin and chigaidana of the Saga no Ma, a room in the kaisho of Ashikaga Yoshimasa's Higashiyama villa. Tokugawa Art Museum, Nagoya.

7. Ashikaga Yoshimochi and his dōbōshū, detail of Wakamiya Hachimangū Yashiromairi no Zu Emaki *(Pilgrimage to Wakamiya Hachiman Shrine Picture Scroll)*. Yoshimochi, wearing a ceremonial eboshi hat, is second from the left. He is accompanied by three dōbōshū with shaved heads.

villa. The *Kissa Ōrai*, however, mentions another practice in which tea was prepared in the room in which it was served. One corner of the room was screened off for a small brazier; opposite sat two decorative stands laden with sweets. The practice of *daisu* tea, in which a Chinese-style lacquered tea-preparation stand called a *daisu* was brought out for serving tea and displaying tea utensils, apparently dates back to the beginning of the Muromachi period, though probably not codified by Noami as some scholars have claimed. Later generations came to identify *shoin*-style chanoyu with *daisu* tea, and to this day the *daisu* is used in the most formal tea service.

As *shoin*-style chanoyu still lacked a hearth *(ro)* in the room, the designation of the brazier *(furo)* for summer tea service and the hearth for winter—presently set at May to October and November to April, respectively—did not yet exist. Round hearths called *ganro* were used for heating water in the preparation room (Fig. 8), but it was only with the advent of the more informal *sōan*, or "thatched hut," style of tea later in the Muromachi period that a square hearth was actually set into the floor of the

8. Ganro, *"round hearths."*
Jishōin, Shōkokuji, Kyoto.

tearoom. *Shoin*-style chanoyu still had a somewhat impromptu character; the *shoin* was not really a tearoom but merely a room where tea could be served. The transition to the *sōan* style thus entailed a conscious restructuring of chanoyu.

Toward the *Sōan* Style of Chanoyu

An interesting glimpse of the aesthetic shift toward the tea of the "thatched hut" is afforded by the mid-fifteenth-century *Shōtetsu Monogatari* (Tale of Shōtetsu), a poetic treatise by the *waka* poet-priest Seigan Shōtetsu (1381–1459). In the following passage he compares poets to tea practitioners:

> Many are the aficionados of verse. Of all kinds, too, are the connoisseurs of tea. By "tea connoisseurs" *(cha no suki)* should be understood those who, taken with the beauty of tea utensils, are wont to possess as many different *temmoku* bowls, tea kettles, fresh-water jars, and the like as they fancy. Poets whose taste runs to beautiful ink stones, writing stands, and *tanzaku* and *kaishi* papers, and who can always be counted on to give at least one recitation at any gathering, are akin to such connoisseurs of tea.

In another passage Shōtetsu remarks that those who can tell good tea from bad but show no particular interest in tea utensils are merely "tea drinkers" *(cha nomi)*, while those who gulp down huge bowls of tea regardless of the quality of the brew are "tea fools" *(cha kurai)*. Shōtetsu's observations attest to the continued popularity of both tea competitions and the taste for things Chinese.

Not much later, however, there is evidence that the tea aesthetic was undergoing considerable change. The famous *Kokoro no Fumi* (Letter of the Mind), written

9. *"Tortoise shell"* temmoku *tea bowl and a carved lacquer stand. Private collection.*

by the tea master Murata Shukō (1423–1502), a pupil of Nōami's, to his disciple Furuichi Chōin (1459–1508), an influential figure in Nara, marks a major turning point in the concept of chanoyu:

> Nothing will hinder you more in your practice of tea than feelings of self-satisfaction or self-attachment. It is utterly wrong to envy the skillful man his attainments or to look down upon the beginner. One must venture into the company of the truly accomplished and know the need for their guidance, and also take it upon oneself somehow to help the initiate.
>
> The matter of greatest importance in tea is the merging of things native and Chinese. This is essential, and you should give every attention to it.
>
> Nevertheless, these days there are people who, while utter beginners, purchase Bizen and Shigaraki pieces because they hear that such wares are "chill and withered," and without the approval of anyone they take on the airs of that which is "advanced and deepening"; it is unspeakably absurd. By "withered" is meant having good utensils and being capable of appreciating them thoroughly; and at the depths of the heart and mind advancing and deepening past fullness, chill and meagre to the very end. It is this that has character. Those who are simply unable[,] though, should not be overly concerned about owning utensils. And however dexterous your manner may be, a painful awareness of your shortcomings is essential. Just remember that self satisfaction and self-attachment are obstructions. But it is also harmful to be without a certain self-satisfaction. An old master made this statement on practice: "School your heart and mind; do not be schooled by them."*

* Dennis Hirota, "In Practice of the Way: *Sasmamegoto*, An Instruction Book in Linked Verse," *Chanoyu Quarterly*, No. 19 (1977), p. 28.

10. Dōjinsai tearoom. Tōgudō, Ginkakuji, Kyoto.

With this teaching, the way of tea had truly become a discipline, its aesthetic embracing both Chinese and Japanese wares. Furthermore, judging from the admonition against uninformed infatuation with rustic Bizen and Shigaraki ceramics, it is not hard to imagine that the trend of the time was away from the love of ornate continental wares and toward an appreciation of the understated, half-hidden beauty of simple objects. This *wabi* aesthetic is perhaps best summed up in Shukō's aphorism, "Even the moon is displeasing without clouds." Quoted by one of his pupils, Komparu Zempō (1454–1532), in *Zempō Zatsudan* (Zempō's Miscellany), Shukō goes on to remark that "used in interesting ways [domestic wares] surpass [continental wares]." The key was that utensils were to be "used in interesting ways." No longer was tea taste simply a matter of acquiring expensive foreign artifacts; inventiveness *(sakui)* and tasteful combinations *(toriawase)* of utensils now took precedence among connoisseurs.

This new taste in tea utensils was paralleled by a growing preference for small retreats over formal *shoin*-style meeting places. Traditionally, the change has been traced to Dōjinsai (Fig. 10), a room of four and a half tatami mats (about 2.7 square meters) in the Tōgudō hall of Yoshimasa's Higashiyama villa, now part of Ginkakuji temple. Yoshimasa, whose rule saw Kyoto virtually reduced to ruins by the Ōnin wars (1467–79), built the Tōgudō in the eastern hills of Kyoto—hence the name Tōgudō, or Hall Facing East, away from the turmoil of the capital. Even more significant at a time when *shoin*-style architecture was growing larger in scale, with separate rooms for people of higher and lower social status, Dōjinsai (Sanctuary of Equal Benevolence) rejected the prevailing hierarchy. The room itself was designed in a simplified *shoin* style, with *chigaidana* and a *tsukeshoin* but no tokonoma. Recently, however, when the room was dismantled for repairs, the inscription "Room with Hearth" was found on one of the ceiling panels. If Yoshimasa's original plans did indeed include a sunken hearth, in the fashion of later tearooms, this would place the room between the *shoin* and *sōan* styles.

Dōjinsai was only the first of many four-and-a-half-mat rooms built at the end of the fifteenth century and in the early sixteenth century. In 1502 the courtier Sanjōnishi Sanetaka (1455–1537), an associate of Yoshimasa's and a major cultural figure of the time, bought a six-mat hut and had it remodeled to four and a half mats when it was moved to his Mushanokōji estate in central Kyoto. There he held *waka* and *renga* sessions to which he invited other poetry enthusiasts. One of these, the courtier Toyohara Sumiaki, followed suit, building the four-and-a-half-mat Yamazatoan (Mountain Village Hut) under a large pine tree on his estate and composing this verse, found in the poetry anthology *Sekireki Shū*:

> When even in the mountains
> Sorrows encroach,
> This hut beneath a pine
> In the midst of the capital
> Shall be my hermitage.

The intention here is clear: the rustic four-and-a-half-mat room was a refuge from worldly concerns, effectively bringing a mountain retreat into the heart of the city.

This peculiarly urban ideal became more pronounced in the "city hermitage" of Murata Sōshu, Shukō's successor. Living in the bustling Shimogyō commercial district of Kyoto, the "Shimogyō tea master" was regarded as something of an eccentric but was praised for his taste. A 1532 entry in the *Nisui Ki* (Diary of Two Waters) by Washio Takayasu tells of a visit to Sōshu's home, finding him "very much the mountain hermit, living a true life of seclusion in the midst of the city—an exemplar of the taste of the times." Other Shimogyō "hermits" of the period included Jūshiya Sōgo, a pupil of Shukō's and the mentor of the tea master Takeno Jōō (1502–55; Fig. 11), as well as Jōō's first teacher, Fujita Sōri.

The urban pastoral aesthetic was not limited to Kyoto. Many wealthy merchants in the booming port city of Sakai, near present-day Osaka, fancied the life of the hermit. When the Portuguese Jesuit João Rodrigues (1561?–1633) set down his observations on Japan in his *História da Igreja do Japão* (History of the Church of Japan), this aspect of Sakai tea circles caught his attention:

> Certain Sakai men versed in *cha-no-yu* built the *cha* house in another way. It was smaller and set among some small trees planted for the purpose, and it represented, as far as the small site allowed, the style of lonely houses which are found in the countryside, or like the cells of solitaries who dwell in hermitages far removed from people and give themselves over to the contemplation of the things of nature and its First Cause. . . . In order that the furnishings might be in keeping with the smaller hut, they did away with many of the utensils and items required by *cha-no-yu,* together with the order and arrangement of these things, and in everything they did what seemed most fitting and appropriate for their purpose.

11. Portrait of Takeno Jōō. Takeno collection, Nagoya.

12. Detail of the Fukutomi Zōshi *picture scroll showing the "good life" in the fifteenth century. Note the tatami mats, numerous furnishings, and tea utensils on a display shelf. Shumpoin, Myōshinji, Kyoto.*

So they entertained each other with *cha* in these small huts within the city itself and in this way they made up for the lack of refreshing and lonely places around the city; indeed, to a certain extent this way was better than real solitude because they obtained and enjoyed it in the middle of the city itself. They called this in their language *shichū no sankyo,* meaning a lonely hermitage found in the middle of the public square.*

Chanoyu in the Temmon Era

The transition from *shoin* to *sōan* aesthetics had begun by the latter half of the fifteenth century, a time characterized by the "Higashiyama culture" of Yoshimasa and other aristocrats. In the early sixteenth century the new aesthetic filtered down to affluent townspeople (Fig. 12). By the Temmon era (1532–55) *sōan*-style chanoyu had developed an even wider base. This era was characterized by the development of urban culture on the one hand and of provincial culture on the other. It was the height of the so-called age of the warring provinces (1482–1558), and castle towns proliferated. Many local lords, known as daimyo, modeled their castle towns on Kyoto, thus encouraging the spread of the sophisticated culture of the capital. *Renga* poets and *biwa hōshi,* blind monks who were itinerant minstrels, also played a significant role in bringing the sophisticated culture of Kyoto to the provinces. The daimyo took up *renga* and chanoyu and built up sizable collections of both Japanese and continental tea utensils. Excavation of the Asakura-clan estate in Echizen (pres-

---

* Michael Cooper, trans. and ed., *This Island of Japon: João Rodrigues' Account of 16th-century Japan* (Tokyo and New York: Kodansha International, 1973), pp. 275–76.

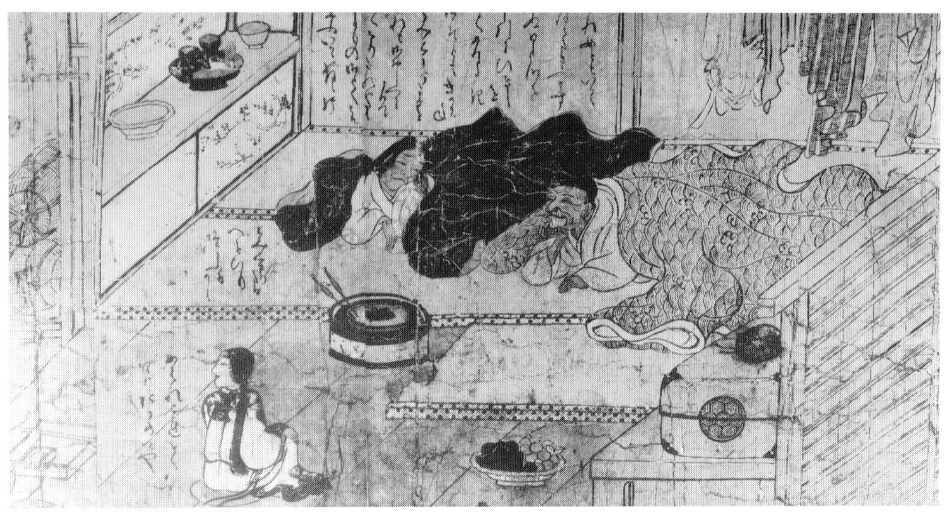

ent-day Fukui Prefecture) has yielded quantities of tea-bowl shards, as well as the remains of what is thought to have been a tearoom. There were no doubt other tearooms built by daimyo on their estates.

Further clues to the spread of chanoyu are found in the records of tea gatherings (*kaiki*) that began to be kept around the Temmon era. The *Matsuya Kaiki,* begun in 1533 and covering three generations of the Matsuya family of Nara; the *Tennōjiya Kaiki,* begun in 1548 and covering three generations of the Tsuda family of Sakai; and the *Imai Sōkyū Chanoyu Nikki Kakinuki* (Selections from the Tea Diary of Imai Sōkyū), begun in 1554 by the Imai family, also of Sakai—known collectively as the *Temmon Cha Kaiki*—are especially useful in documenting the development of the *chaji,* or "tea function." Records of these functions list the tearoom, host, guests, artworks displayed, and utensils used, as well as the refreshments served. In the first entry in the *Matsuya Kaiki,* for example, Matsuya Hisamasa (d. 1598) outlines a tea function held by the priest Shiseibō of Tōdaiji in 1533:

> Twentieth day of third month.
> Went to Shiseibō's [unaccompanied].
> Small horizontal river landscape by Muqi in tokonoma. Broad kettle displayed on *oshi ita*. Next to it, an Ishibana incense burner. In cabinet, crane-neck tea caddy on tray, large lidded fresh-water container, shallow tea bowl, broad metal waste-water receptacle.
> After tea, *sōmen* noodles were served.

One of the things that these records provide insight into is the character of the meals that were served following the tea. Although tea drinking and eating had long been informally connected, as indicated by the *naorai* banquets of the Heian and Kamakura periods and the meal recorded in the *Kissa Ōrai,* by the Temmon era the meals

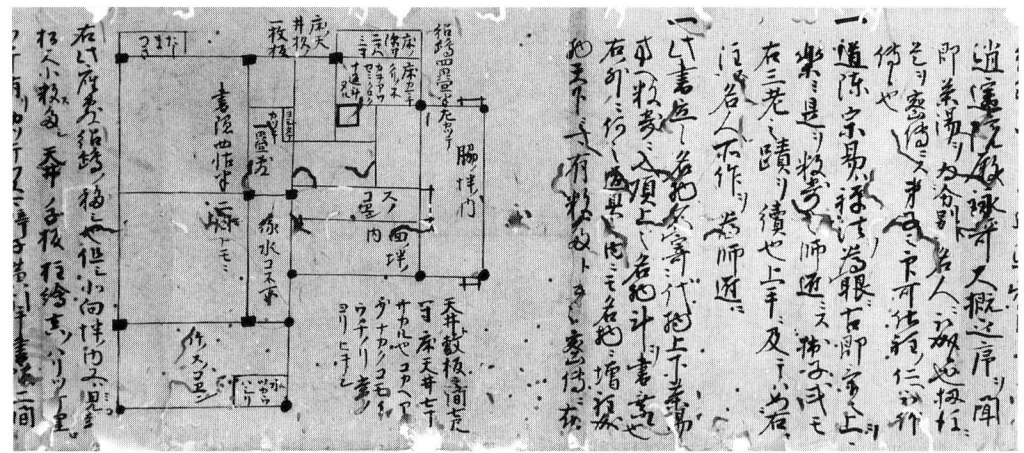

13. Part of the Yamanoue Sōji Ki. *Fushin'an, Omotesenke, Kyoto.*

had assumed a different character. From relatively early on, tea practitioners recognized that the two most fundamental facets of a tea function—the host's hospitality (*furumai*) and the atmosphere of artistic refinement (*suki*)—were most clearly embodied, respectively, in the meal portion of the function and in the tea portion. That the meals were called *kaiseki ryōri*, or "cuisine for a gathering," and that the term "*furumai*," or "hospitality," was considered synonymous to this, reflect this idea; that is, that the meals were looked upon as the very embodiment of hospitality.

Eventually, the meal came to be considered as integral a part of the "tea experience" as the serving of the tea. As such, not only the selection and combination of ingredients but also the entertainment of those partaking of the meal required serious consideration. The tea practitioner Yamanoue Sōji (1544–90) had this to say on the subject in his famous *Yamanoue Sōji Ki* (Commentary of Yamanoue Sōji; Fig. 13).

> Each gathering occasions a different kind of meal. The orthodox manner is thus subject to variation day by day, unusual methods being used perhaps one or two times in ten, though a master who possesses celebrated items may use such methods three or four times [in ten] for the sake of young disciples. What is important is to do everything in a manner that appears natural and unpretentious. Inventiveness [*sakui*] in chanoyu means [inventiveness] first in the meal [and] second in the array of utensils. . . . Never rely on others' inventions.

Thus, through the influence of the tea aesthetic, food preparation and service grew increasingly refined.

Furthermore, during this era the spirit of communion among participants, host and guests fusing their sensibilities for that one sitting (*ichiza*), became more pronounced. The *Yamanoue Sōji Ki* states:

Toward the constructive realization of that one sitting, . . . even if the participants are old friends who meet daily, and not only on the occasion of bringing out newly acquired utensils or opening the new year's tea jar—that goes without saying—but even at an ordinary chanoyu gathering, [guests] must behave with awe and reverence toward their host from the time they enter the garden until the time they leave, as befits this unique encounter [*ichiza*]. . . . The host [likewise] must act with due reverence toward the guests.

Only through mutual awe and reverence could there be a harmonious meeting of the minds of host and guests. The formulation of the principle of "one time, one meeting" *(ichigo ichie)*—the awareness that this particular meeting in the tearoom is unique and unrepeatable, that here and now the participants are as one despite their different identities and that they will never again come together in exactly the same way—completed the conceptual framework of *sōan*-style chanoyu.

Sen Rikyū and His Times

By the mid-sixteenth century chanoyu had achieved mass appeal and tea practitioners were numerous. Meanwhile, at the upper end of the scale, chanoyu was rapidly becoming an esoteric art, and the more accomplished "men of tea" *(chajin)*, true masters. Where the fifteenth-century *Shōtetsu Monogatari* had needed only to distinguish "tea connoisseurs," "tea drinkers," and "tea fools," the *Yamanoue Sōji Ki* sought to establish more precise categories of evaluation, naming figures representative of each.

Chanoyu adepts *(chanoyusha)* were "those who can discriminate among utensils, are skilled in tea etiquette, and make a living teaching tea." Two men designated as adepts were the affluent merchants Matsumoto Juhō and Shino Dōji. *Wabi* aesthetes *(wabi sukisha)* were "those who own no outstanding utensils but embody the three qualities of aspiration, creativity, and achievement," people like Awataguchi Zempō. The category of master *(meijin)* was reserved for "those of profound awareness who possess continental wares, a discriminating eye, and skill at chanoyu," such as Murata Shukō, Torii Insetsu, and Takeno Jōō. Two interesting sidelights on the age that emerge from these evaluations are that a need to discriminate among the vast quantities of tea utensils flooding the market in the wake of the popularization of chanoyu was clearly felt, and that the possibility of making a living by teaching tea had arisen. These were major developments in the course of only a century.

Japan entered the Momoyama period (1568–1603) when the warlord Oda Nobunaga (1534–82) conquered Kyoto in 1568 and toppled the Ashikaga shogunate. Major changes in chanoyu were initiated when Nobunaga employed merchant-class tea masters from Sakai as resident tea advisers *(sadō;* Fig. 14). The historian may be tempted at this point to wonder what would have happened if Nobunaga had not become a tea patron. There might never have been a Sen Rikyū, let alone the Sen family lineage.

As it was, Nobunaga engaged the services of the "three Sakai masters," Imai Sōkyū

14. *A feudal lord's* sadō, *or resident tea adviser (wearing a soft cap and seated at a* daisu*), prepares tea. Detail of the* Shimba Chōkyō Zu *(Training Sacred Horses) screen. Taga Taisha shrine, Shiga Prefecture.*

(1520–93), Tsuda Sōgyū (d. 1591), and Tanaka Sōeki (1522–91), better known as Sen Rikyū. These three were given preferential treatment on four occasions between 1571 and 1574 at the tea gatherings Nobunaga held when he returned to the capital from his military campaigns. Granted, Nobunaga made use of the three merchants as part of his strategy for securing economic support in the rich autonomous port of Sakai. Nonetheless, they served the warlord for nearly a decade, until his assassination in 1582, then served his successor, Toyotomi Hideyoshi (1536–98), for almost another decade.

Many details of Rikyū's family background are subject to conjecture. Throughout the *Yamanoue Sōji Ki* he is referred to as Tanaka Sōeki, and no mention is made of the *dōbōshū* Sen'ami, his putative grandfather and the possible source of the family name Sen. Rikyu is first mentioned in an entry in the *Nembutsu Sachō Nikki* (Records of Aguchi Shrine) dated the twenty-eighth day of the fourth month of 1535. Then thirteen years old, he is listed as "Master Yoshirō, Sen." He studied tea first under the Sakai tea connoisseur Kitamuki Dōchin (1504–62) and then under Takeno Jōō. It is generally believed that he began studying under Jōō when he was eighteen years old, and that he took the name Sōeki at about this time. He first appears in the records of tea gatherings in a 1544 entry in the *Matsuya Kaiki,* where he is listed as the host to Matsuya Hisamasa and the priest Eisombō of Shōmyōji temple. Until he entered Nobunaga's service he remains a sketchy figure.

Hideyoshi met Rikyū through the auspices of Nobunaga, who, taking chanoyu as seriously as politics, often gave presents of tea utensils to his second in command, Hideyoshi, and, on one occasion (in 1582), even requested that he partake of tea with the Sakai masters. By 1582 Hideyoshi had become a tea enthusiast and a close associate of Rikyū, the two frequently exchanging gifts of tea utensils. When Hideyoshi became the de facto ruler of Japan after Nobunaga's death, he built a small group of

15. Red Raku tea bowl "Kōtō" by Chōjirō. Tekisui Art Museum, Ashiya.

16. Black Raku tea bowl "Daikoku" by Chōjirō.

17. Taian tearoom. Myōkian, Shōkokuji, Kyoto.

tearooms, which he named the Yamazatomaru (Mountain Village Compound), within Osaka Castle. This juxtaposition of palatial quarters and thatched huts, so emblematic of Momoyama culture and aesthetics, owes a great deal to Rikyū's influence and taste.

Rikyū's aesthetic sensibility reached maturity around 1582, the year of his initial collaboration with the potter Chōjirō to produce the first Red Raku-ware tea bowls (Fig. 15). In 1588 his creativity reached a new height with the Black Raku tea bowls in the style that came to be known as "Sōeki style" (Fig. 16).

At the core of Rikyū's aesthetic was the so-called small tearoom (koma no chashitsu). He was the first to create a tearoom smaller than four and a half mats, which was an important innovation. The *Yamanoue Sōji Ki* clearly states that "the first one-and-a-half-mat [tearoom] was built in Kyoto by Sōeki." This is thought to have been the famous Taian (Hut of Vigilance; Fig. 17), constructed around 1583 on the grounds of Myōkian, a subtemple of Shōkokuji temple in the Yamazaki district of Kyoto.

The *Yamanoue Sōji Ki* comments, in connection with Rikyū's 1584 tearoom in Osaka Castle's Yamazatomaru:

> The two-mat room befits the nobleman or the true *wabi* aesthete, but otherwise is of no use. . . . Though it was highly novel at the time, it is of no use to an ordinary person. Because Sōeki is a master, when he breaks the rules of chanoyu, freely turning mountains into valleys and west into east, the effect is tasteful; but if an ordinary person did the same, it would no longer be chanoyu.

Indeed, the very idea of creating interior spaces of only one and a half or two mats was so outlandish as to preclude ordinary use. This, however, must have been the effect Rikyū wished. The tiny "crawl-in entrances" *(nijiriguchi)* that formed an integral part of the architecture of these tearooms served to heighten the sense of passage out of the everyday world. Above all, Rikyū sought to mold chanoyu into a spiritual path; where the *shoin* style had been secular, his distillation of the *sōan* style was based on renunciation and spiritual values. At the same time, his radical simplification of the tearoom interior, his reduction of space to the bare minimum needed for that "one sitting," was undoubtedly the most practical way of focusing tea practice on the communion of host and guests. The combination of attention to both practical concerns and transcendental imagination indicates the great breadth of Rikyū's vision.

Rikyū's achievement represents the culmination of the *wabi* aesthetic born of the contemplative awareness of the relationship between people and things. While chanoyu necessarily involved the element of material things—without utensils there would have been no connoisseurship—the *wabi* ideal originated in the idea of negation or lack. In the first anthology of Japanese poetry, the eighth-century *Man'yōshū*, *wabi* meant simply "poverty" or "meanness." Its transmutation into a positive aesthetic came with Saigyō (1118–90) and Kamo no Chōmei (1153–1216), literati of the late Heian and early Kamakura periods. Together with the closely related term *sabi*—also originally a "lack," but of companionship—*wabi* characterized the sensibilities of many poets represented in the *Shin Kokin Waka Shū* poetry anthology of the early thirteenth century. Rikyū himself cited two poems from this collection as exemplifying his *wabi* aesthetic. One, a favorite of Takeno Jōō's, is by Fujiwara Teika (1162–1241):

> Casting wide my gaze,
> Neither flowers
> Nor scarlet leaves:
> A bayside hovel of reeds
> In the autumn dusk.

The other, in which Rikyū himself found particular appeal, is by Fujiwara Ietaka (1158–1237):

> Show them who wait
> Only for flowers
> There in the mountain villages:
> Grass peeks through the snow,
> And with it, spring.

Undoubtedly the greatest conceptual influence on *wabi* chanoyu was the Muromachi-period priest and *renga* poet Shinkei (1406–75) and the poetics in his treatise *Sasamegoto* (Hushed Words; ca. 1463). The aesthetic ideal Murata Shukō expressed as "chill and withered" or "chill and lean" in his *Kokoro no Fumi* was Shinkei's. Takeno Jōō, himself a *renga* poet in his youth, was fond of quoting Shinkei's words "withered with cold" when describing the manner proper to chanoyu. Influential as he was, however, Shinkei never actually used the word *wabi*.

It was not until the middle of the sixteenth century and the *Jōō Wabi no Fumi* (Jōō's Letter on Wabi) that the term *wabi* began to be used in reference to the subtle chanoyu aesthetic of tearooms and tea utensils. With Rikyū, *wabi* took on its most profound and paradoxical meaning: a purified taste in material things as a medium for human interaction transcending materialism. Through *wabi,* Rikyū heightened the principle of "one time, one meeting" into an identification of tea and Zen (*cha Zen ichimi*).

The Chanoyu of the Warrior Class

Eventually relations between Hideyoshi and Rikyū, both strong personalities, became strained, and Hideyoshi ordered his renowned tea master to commit *seppuku,* ritual suicide by disembowelment. Banished from Jurakudai, Hideyoshi's palatial mansion in Kyoto, Rikyū left Kyoto for Sakai by boat on the thirteenth day of the second month of 1591. He was seen off by two disciples, Furuta Oribe (1544–1615; Fig. 18) and Hosokawa Sansai (1563–1645; Fig. 19). Hosokawa Yūsai (1534–1610), Sansai's father and a fellow pupil of Jōō, expressed his grief in a letter to Rikyū, as did another of Rikyū's disciples, Shibayama Kemmotsu. After about ten days' confinement in his home in Sakai, Rikyū was called back to Jurakudai, where he committed *seppuku* on the twenty-eighth day of the month. He was buried at Jukōin, a subtemple of Daitokuji.

Thus came to an end one of the most illustrious careers in tea and an era in the history of chanoyu. The other two Sakai tea masters died soon after, Tsuda Sōgyū the same year and Imai Sōkyū two years later. By the time of Hideyoshi's death in 1598, much of what Rikyū had said and done was already becoming legend.

At this point, on the threshold of the Edo period (1603–1868), the leading role in dictating tea taste and practice to the world at large was assumed by Rikyū's most favored warrior-class disciples—the so-called Seven Sages of Rikyū (Rikyū *shichitetsu*). The most active role was played by Oribe, although he was considered the least worthy when Kōshin Sōsa (1613–72), Rikyū's great-grandson and founder of the Omotesenke branch of the Sen family, passed retrospective judgment in his *Kōshin Gegaki* (Summer Writings of Kōshin; 1663):

The Seven Disciples of Rikyū included:
1. Gamō [Ujisato], Lord of Hida [Fig. 20]
2. Takayama Ukon [Nagafusa], known as Nambō

18. *Statue of Furuta Oribe. Kōshōji, Kyoto.* 19. *Portrait of Hosokawa Sansai. Kōtōin, Daitokuji, Kyoto.* 20. *Portrait of Gamō Ujisato. Ōbaiin, Daitokuji, Kyoto.*

3. Hosokawa [Tadaoki], Lord of Etchū, known as Sansai
4. Shibayama Kemmotsu [Toshikazu]
5. Seta Kamon [Masatada]
6. Makimura Hyōbudayū [Masayoshi]
7. Furuta Oribe [Shigenari]

Of these, Oribe was the most inept at chanoyu, but eventually he became a master.

Oribe is noted for his innovations. In ceramics he is credited with the creation of the distinctive "shoe-shaped tea bowl" (*kutsugata chawan*), so distorted in shape that it was sometimes called the "warped tea bowl" (*hizumi chawan*). In tearoom design he lightened the dark, austere interior with small windows, juxtaposed *sōan*- and *shoin*-style rooms, and transformed the *roji,* the path to the tearoom, into a scenic garden. If, as Rikyū reportedly said, "Taste [*suki*] consists in doing things differently," then certainly Oribe's artifice and fancy were tasteful.

Hosokawa Sansai maintained a more conservative stance that accorded with the *wabi* spirit of Rikyū's teachings. As the *Matsuya Hikki* (Matsuya Family Records) explains, "For this reason, Furuta Oribe prospered, while Hosokawa Sansai, being so close [to Rikyū's practice], could not make a name for himself." Oribe and Sansai represented the two poles of the art of chanoyu.

Oribe's fame opened doors for him. In 1605 he began teaching tea to the second Tokugawa shogun, Hidetada (1579–1632), eventually following him to the new capital of Edo (present-day Tokyo). According to a 1612 entry in the *Sumpu Ki* (Annals of Suruga), "Oribe is the master of tea [*suki*] of these times. Everyone in the shogunate reveres him. All the samurai aspire to learn chanoyu, and there are tea functions morning and night." Almost single-handedly, Oribe created a tea cult among the elite of the Edo shogunate. The government even began to dictate certain standards in tearoom architecture and tea practice, and the third Tokugawa shogun, Iemitsu (1603–51), instituted a policy of sending an envoy to Uji to obtain jars of the best tea leaves every year.

Oribe passed on the role of tea instructor to the shogunal household to his disciple Kobori Enshū (1579–1647). Well educated and, as a daimyo himself, thoroughly at home in the upper echelons of society, Enshū brought an aristocratic touch to tea with his classical names for tea utensils and his preference for *waka* poems over the eccentric calligraphy of Zen priests for the scroll hung in the tokonoma. His sensibilities were attuned to the beauties of the four seasons—spring flowers, wafting summer breezes, the autumn moon, winter snow—hence his aesthetic was called "beautiful *sabi*" *(kirei sabi)*. A synthesis of Rikyū's spiritual discipline and Oribe's fanciful innovation, this new aesthetic blended the *sōan* and *shoin* ideals so seamlessly that it underlies much of Japanese taste even today.

When Enshū died, the leadership in warrior-class tea passed to Katagiri Sekishū (1605–73). Although not a direct disciple, his study under Kuwayama Sōsen (1560–1632), a pupil of Rikyū's oldest son, Dōan (1546–1607), had exposed him to merchant-class tea as well as that practiced by the ruling class, yet his preference for Rikyū's predecessor, Takeno Jōō, seems to speak of a longing for the grandeur of *shoin*-style chanoyu. His *Sekishū Sambyakkajō* (Sekishū's Three Hundred Points on Tea), written at the behest of the fourth Tokugawa shogun, Ietsuna (1641–80), set the standards for warrior-class chanoyu and ensured the popularity of Sekishū's teachings for decades to come.

The Rise of the Sen Family

Immediately after Rikyū's death, his sons left Kyoto. It is thought that Dōan took up residence either in the mountains of Hida, northeast of Kyoto, or in the province of Awa on the island of Shikoku. Rikyū's adopted second son, Shōan (1546–1614), was granted refuge by Rikyū's disciple Gamō Ujisato (1556–95) in the town of Aizu Wakamatsu in northern Japan. But eventually Hideyoshi pardoned Rikyū's sons, and when Dōan and Shōan returned to the capital, Hideyoshi even engaged Dōan's services as his tea instructor. According to the *Chawa Shigetsu Shū* (Collection of Directly Transmitted Tea Tales) by Kusumi Soan (1636–1728), Hideyoshi found Dōan's tea service "very much like Rikyū's." Expectations were high that Dōan would succeed his father as the leader of the Sen tradition. However, with Hideyoshi's sudden death at his residence in Fushimi, near Kyoto, in 1598, Dōan was left without a patron and returned to the family home in Sakai, where he died nine years later.

Shōan chose to remain in Kyoto, living near Hompōji temple. The son of Rikyū's second wife, a widow, by her first marriage, Shōan had never been on good terms with Dōan. Although Shōan showed more talent for tea and was Rikyū's favorite, it was Dōan who had helped Rikyū draw up his will (Fig. 21) during his confinement

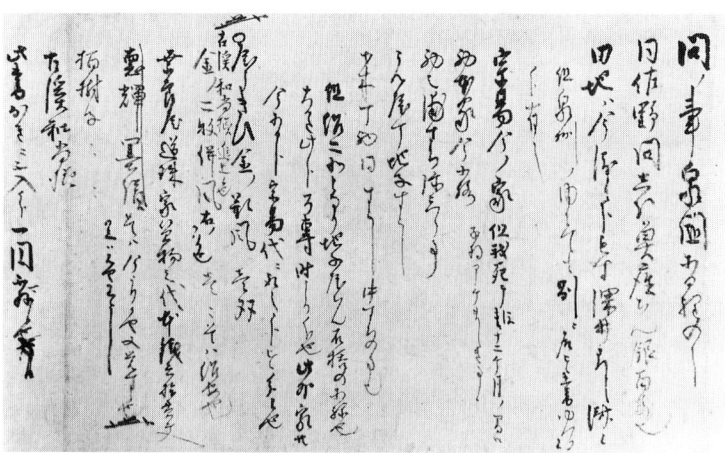

21. Rikyū's will. Mori collection, Aichi Prefecture.

in Sakai and who, as the first son (though he and Shōan were actually the same age), inherited all the Sen family holdings in Sakai.

When Shōan died seven years after Dōan, the full responsibility of carrying on the Sen name and tea teachings fell to Shōan's oldest son, Sōtan (1578–1658), though he had been named the titular head of the family some years earlier. Times were hard. When Dōan had served as tea adviser to Hideyoshi and there had been no prospects for Shōan's side of the family, Sōtan had taken the tonsure and become a Zen priest at Daitokuji. Later, when his father became the Sen heir, Sōtan returned to secular life. He had no patron, however. The wealth of Rikyū's day had faded to a distant memory, along with the role of tea master to the ruler. Sōtan was forced to borrow money from the priest Hōrin of Kinkakuji temple and other friends. His sons urged him to make his way to Edo and take an advisory post there for the family's sake, but to no avail. It was small wonder that the chanoyu of "beggar Sōtan" (*kojiki* Sōtan), as he was known, was so deeply steeped in the austerity of *wabi*.

The *Chawa Shigetsu Shū* emphasizes the Zen flavor of Sōtan's tea:

> Rikyū's grandson Gempaku Sōtan has never chased after fame and fortune but seventy-odd years now has always hung a bamboo blind in his window to lend a note of purity. On snowy mornings or moonlit nights, when he pleases he invites his tea friends; when the mood strikes him he sits alone. And if by chance someone should happen by to inquire about the Way, he answers that since chanoyu originally derives from Zen, there is no new Way to teach.

The description of Sōtan as a beggar is not complete, however; Sōtan also had occasion to associate with the nobility. He is known to have exchanged gifts with the empress Tōfukumon'in (1607–78; Fig. 22), daughter of Tokugawa Hidetada and wife of the emperor Gomizunoo (1596–1680; Fig. 23), presenting the

22. Statue of the empress Tōfuku-mon'in. Kōunji, Kyoto.

23. Statue of the emperor Go-mizunoo. Enshōji, Nara.

empress with a *daisu* and a full set of tea utensils and in return receiving a scroll by the empress portraying the woman poet Ono no Komachi, as well as various decorative furnishings. As the founder of the Edosenke tea tradition, Kawakami Fuhaku (1716–1807), remarked in his *Fuhaku Hikki* (Notes by Fuhaku), "Sōtan should not be regarded as such an austere *wabi* figure"; his restrained style was, rather, a reflection of the difficult circumstances forced on him by changes in society at large.

The next generation sought to better the Sen family's lot. Whether because of the family's financial straits or because of the increased interest various daimyo were showing in chanoyu, Noh drama, and other arts now that the nation was at peace, Sōtan's sons took an active interest in propagating the *wabi* aesthetic among people of influence. Eventually three of Sōtan's four sons secured positions with warrior-class households. Sōtan divided the Kyoto Sen family holdings—a small property on Mushanokōji Street and the front *(omote)* and back *(ura)* halves of the main property on Ogawa Street—among these three sons. This marked the beginning of the Mushanokōjisenke, Omotesenke, and Urasenke traditions of chanoyu.

The oldest son, Sōsetsu (d. 1652), gained an introduction to the powerful Maeda clan of Kaga (present-day Kanazawa Prefecture) through the good offices of Gyokushū (1600–1668), head priest of Daitokuji, but for some reason was soon dismissed. Next he managed to have the famous swordsman Yagyū Munenori (1571–1646) put in a word for him with the branch of the Tokugawa clan based in Kii (present-day Wakayama Prefecture) and Lord Inaba Masanori of Odawara Castle, near Edo, but nothing came of it. His inability to establish himself anywhere drove a wedge between him and his father, and he left the family, first becoming a hanger-on of the Kyoto physician Noma Gentaku and eventually ending his days at Shōdenji temple in the Nishigamo district of Kyoto.

The second son, Sōshu (1593–1675), was adopted into the Yoshioka family of lacquer craftsmen but by the late 1640s had decided to concentrate on chanoyu. Sōtan requested one of his pupils, the wealthy Kyoto merchant Gotō Shōsai, to help Sōshu buy membership in a silver guild in Edo, but whether anything came of this is not known. In 1666 Sōshu gained an appointment as tea adviser to the Matsudaira clan of Takamatsu, in Sanuki (present-day Kagawa Prefecture) on the island of Shikoku, though he resigned his post the following year.

Sōtan's third and fourth sons, Sōsa (1613–72) and Sensō (1622–97), were the issue of a second marriage and were almost a generation younger than his first two sons. In 1633 Sōsa became tea adviser to Lord Terazawa Hirotaka of Karatsu Castle in Hizen (present-day Nagasaki Prefecture) but lost the position when the 1637 Shimabara Rebellion undermined political authority in the domain. Two years later, through the good offices of Gyokushū, he found employment with Lord Ikoma Takatoshi of Takamatsu Castle, but a clan feud cost him his patron. In 1642 Yagyū Munenori commended him to the Kii branch of the Tokugawa clan, which he served as tea master in residence for the rest of his life. In 1653, when clan historians were compiling the official biography of the first Tokugawa shogun, Ieyasu (1542–1616), who had been a general under Hideyoshi and thus had known Rikyū, they turned to Sōsa for information on his venerable great-grandfather. The result was recorded as the *Sen Rikyū Yuishogaki* (Matters Relating to Sen Rikyū).

Sensō, the fourth son, was apprenticed to the physician Noma Gentaku, but when Gentaku died in 1646, Sensō returned to the Sen household and the life of tea. In 1652 he became tea adviser to the Maeda clan and was granted a villa on the grounds of Komatsu Castle in Kaga by the retired daimyo Maeda Toshitsune (1593–1658). When he moved there, he was accompanied by the Raku potter Chōzaemon and the kettle maker Miyazaki Kanchi, who set up the still-extant Ōhi kiln and Kanchi foundry, respectively.

Although Sōtan was reluctant to seek a paid position, many people from all walks of life came to him seeking instruction. Four disciples in particular stood out, the so-called Sōtan Shitennō (Sōtan's Four Deva Kings): Fujimura Yōken (1613–99; Fig. 24), Yamada Sōhen (1627–1708), Sugiki Fusai (1628–1706; Fig. 26), and Kusumi Soan. Some sources list two other students, Matsuo Sōji (1579–1658) and Miyake Bōyō (1580–1649; Fig. 25), among the Shitennō, but being of the same generation as Sōtan himself, they should not be seen in the same light as the younger four.

Yamada Sōhen, the learned head priest of Chōtokuji temple, had begun his tea studies under Sōtan at the age of seventeen. Completely initiated into the secrets of chanoyu at the age of twenty-five, he relinquished his priestly duties to his father and decided to dedicate the rest of his life to tea—apparently at Sōtan's urging—whereupon he built the tearoom Yohōan (Hut of the Four Directions) on the grounds of Sambōji temple in Kyoto's western Narutaki district. In 1655 he accepted a prestigious position in Sōtan's stead as resident tea adviser to Lord Ogasawara Tadatomo of Yoshida Castle in Mikawa (present-day Aichi Prefecture). Sōtan even granted Sōhen permission to make use of the names of two Sen family tearooms,

24. Portrait of Fujimura Yōken. Saiōin, Konkaikōmyōji, Kyoto.

25. Portrait of Miyake Bōyō. Tada collection, Tokyo.

26. Portrait of Sugiki Fusai.

Rikyū's Fushin'an (Hut of Uncertainty) and Sōtan's own Konnichian (Hut of This Day), indicating not only that Sōtan trusted his pupil implicitly but also that Fushin'an and Konnichian had not yet become synonymous with the schools of Omotesenke and Urasenke, respectively.

Sōhen spent about fifty years in the service of the Ogasawara clan. When the fief changed hands, he moved to Edo, where he spent his last years. He wrote several books on chanoyu, including the *Chadō Bemmō Shō* (The Way of Tea at a Glance; 1690), the *Chadō Yōroku* (An Outline of the Way of Tea; 1691), and the *Rikyū Chadōgu Zue* (Illustrations of Rikyū's Tea Utensils; 1701).

Sugiki Fusai's career was the antithesis of Sōhen's. Instructed first by Sōtan, then after Sōtan's death by Sōshu and Sōsa, he never settled in one post, nor did he enter government service, like Sōhen. Born into a family of *onshi*, low-ranking Shintō priests connected with Ise Grand Shrine whose duties entailed frequent travel, he is known to have journeyed as far as Kyushu. There also exist several letters of certification granted by Fusai to the Sasaki family, prosperous merchants in Harima (present-day Hyōgo Prefecture). Fusai was undoubtedly one of the first tea teachers to make a practice of certifying disciples and swearing them to secrecy on the "inner teachings"; it is thought that he took this upon himself as a mission in order to preserve the authentic tradition of Rikyū. He also appended a commentary to Sōhen's *Chadō Bemmō Shō* that offers a wholly different perspective from Sōhen's on the teachings both men received from Sōtan.

Older than these two was Fujimura Yōken, a well-to-do kimono merchant. Having first had close contact with many other tea masters, including Kobori Enshū, he went to Sōtan to round out his tea education and was initiated into all the Sen family's practices. Yōken borrowed freely from both the *sōan* and the *shoin* styles. He was also a poet of some accomplishment; his *Yōken Shi Shū* (Collected Poems of Yōken) was published posthumously.

Yōken's adopted son-in-law, Kusumi Soan, was a disciple of Sōtan's very last years. Soan credited his *Chawa Shigetsu Shū* entirely to Sōtan: "Gempaku Sōtan . . . merely said that it was up to the student to gain his own understanding from the tea anecdotes of earlier masters that he told over the course of his life as a means of pointing the way." This approach epitomizes the tea literature stemming from the early Sen family teachings.

The Uptown and Downtown Schools of Chanoyu

Although the three Sen families (*san Senke*)—Mushanokōjisenke, Omotesenke, and Urasenke—are descended from Sōtan's sons Sōshu, Sōsa, and Sensō, respectively, for most of the Edo period little emphasis was placed on creating distinct teachings or lineages. If anything, the contrast was between Kyoto's so-called "uptown" (*kamiryū*) and "downtown" (*shimoryū*) schools; the former included all branches of the Sen family in the north of the city, and the latter was identified with the Yabunouchi family in the south.

In many ways the Yabunouchi tradition paralleled that of the Sen family. It was founded by Yabunouchi Kenchū Jōchi (1536–1627), a disciple of Takeno Jōō's at the same time as Rikyū. Jōchi's skill in tea was such that Jōō conferred upon him the character *jō* from his own name and presented him with a complete set of tea utensils. Rikyū also held Jōchi in great esteem and especially admired his decision not to use tea as a means of making a living. After entering Hideyoshi's employ, Rikyū once sent Jōchi a letter expressing his displeasure with "the worldly life" and saying how much he envied Jōchi his detachment. The *Yamanoue Sōji Ki* echoes this sentiment in a famous passage: "Ever since Sōeki [Rikyū], we use chanoyu for our livelihood. This is most regrettable." Nonetheless, at one point Jōchi was summoned to Hideyoshi's Jurakudai mansion as a tea adviser after Rikyū's death.

The genealogy of the Yabunouchi family before Jōchi's time is unclear, but apparently Jōchi was the adopted son of the third in a line of tea practitioners. Jōchi married Furuta Oribe's younger sister and was given Oribe's tearoom En'an (Sparrow Hut). Jōchi's son Shin'ō (1580–1655) taught tea to Ryōjo, head priest of Nishi Honganji temple, and was granted the property on Nishinotōin Street that the Yabunouchi household still occupies today.

Yabunouchi Shin'ō's sons offered their services to various landholding clans; the second son was engaged by the Sōma clan of Nambu in Kai (present-day Yamanashi Prefecture), and the fourth son by the Hosokawa clan of Kumamoto in Kyushu. The next generation continued to propagate tea to members of the upper echelons of the warrior class; the second son of Ken'ō (1603–74), Shin'ō's oldest son, received a stipend from the Nabeshima clan of Saga, also in Kyushu. By the fourth and fifth generations, led by Kenkei (1654–1712) and Chikushin (1678–1745), respectively, chanoyu had spread among the merchants of Kyoto. It was around this time that people began to speak of "uptown" and "downtown" schools of tea.

In the *Genryū Chawa* (Tales of the Original Way of Tea), one of many writings by Chikushin, the fifth-generation tea master points out that chanoyu had strayed far from Rikyū's path, taking on the Neo-Confucian ethics of the Chinese philosopher Zhu Xi and emphasizing the moral virtues of "true" tea practice. Chikushin's virtual sanctification of Rikyū's memory, in addition to indicating that the distance separating schools of tea was still not great, was entirely in keeping with the "Rikyū revival" that marked the centennial of the death of the Sen family's founding father.

One Hundred Years After Rikyu

In 1690, the hundredth year after his now-legendary great-grandfather's death, Sensō, the fourth-generation grand master of the Urasenke tradition, returned to Kyoto from Kaga to dedicate the Rikyūdō, a shrine to Rikyū in the family residence complete with a statue of the master. That year the renowned haiku poet Matsuo Bashō (1644–94) mentioned Rikyū in a passage in the *Genjūan Ki* (Prose Poem on the Unreal Dwelling) that was later included in the *Oi no Kobumi* (The Records of a Travel-Worn Satchel): "One essence runs through the *waka* of Saigyō, the *renga* of Sōgi, the paintings of Sesshū, and the tea of Rikyū." In only a century Rikyū's fame had spread beyond the world of tea. Many works had elevated him to the status of the great codifier of chanoyu and consummate authority in matters of taste.

One seminal work, the *Nampō Roku* (Record of the South; Fig. 27), so named in allusion to Lu Yu's comment in the *Cha Jing* that tea originally came from the south, became a virtual bible to followers of Rikyū's chanoyu. A collection of Rikyū's teachings set down by one of his disciples, the priest Nambō Sōkei, six of the work's seven sections are known to have borne Rikyū's seal, certifying his personal approval of the contents. Only the final section, the "posthumous addendum" *(metsugo)* of 1593, was written after Rikyū's death. The work as it exists today was compiled by the tea enthusiast Tachibana Jitsuzan (1655–1708), a retainer of the Kuroda clan in

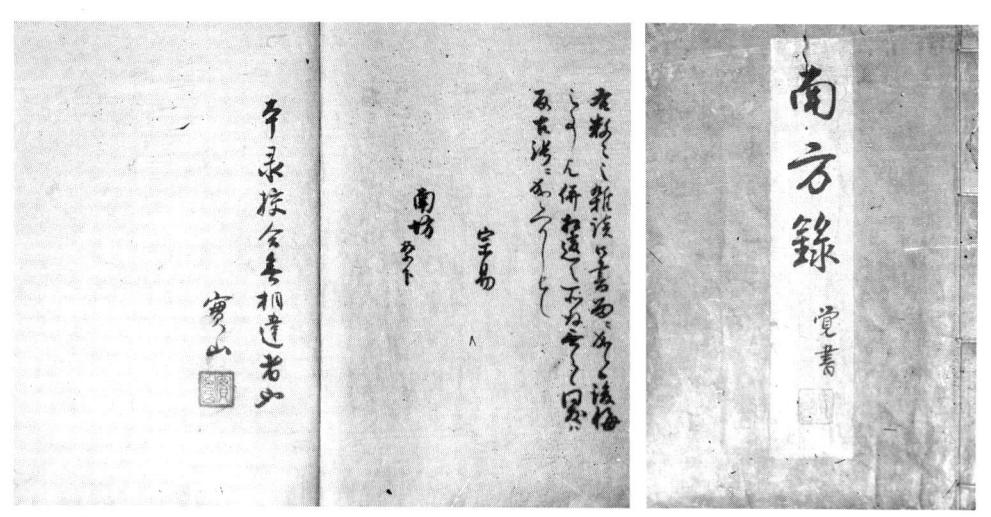

27. Cover (right) of the earliest extant copy (1690) of the Nampō Roku and the last pages of the first section, "Oboegaki" (Memorandum of the words of Rikyū), bearing the seal of Tachibana Jitsuzan and indicating where the seals of Sōeki (Rikyū) and Nambō (Sōkei) were placed in the original. Engakuji, Kita Kyushu.

Chikuzen (present-day Fukuoka Prefecture), who obtained copies of five of the sections in 1686 from a source in Kyoto and copies of the remaining two sections in 1690 from Naya Sōsetsu of Sakai, who possessed some of Nambō's effects. In his memoirs, the *Kiro Bengi* (Deliberations at a Fork in the Road; 1700), Jitsuzan records his amazement at the way in which the whole work came together miraculously on the centennial of Rikyū's death, though scholars today tend to think that the timing was part of a conscious attempt by Kuroda tea practitioners to reinstate Rikyū's tradition of chanoyu.

The number of popular treatises on tea published around 1690 is astounding. The earliest work on chanoyu intended for a general readership is probably the *Sōjimboku* (Grass, Man, Tree; Fig. 28), written in 1626. Yet the real upsurge came half a century later with Endō Genkan's *Chanoyu Sanden Shū* (Collected Transmissions of Three Men of Chanoyu; 1691), *Chanoyu Hyōrin* (Appreciations of Chanoyu; 1697), and *Chanoyu Rokusō Shō* (Transmissions of Six Masters of Chanoyu; 1702), which focused on such figures as Murata Shukō, Takeno Jōō, and Sen Rikyū. There were also more comprehensive surveys, such as Kurezome Sanrokuan's *Kokin Chadō Zensho* (Complete Writings Old and New on the Way of Tea) of 1695 and Genkan's *Kokin Chadō Daizen* (Omnibus of the Way of Tea Old and New) of 1702.

To some extent the Rikyū revival was a coincidental product of the emergence of a broad-based popular culture. The merchant class was flourishing, and by the Genroku era (1688–1704) the arts were gaining much of their support from townspeople. Many publications on flower arrangement and Noh, other accomplishments

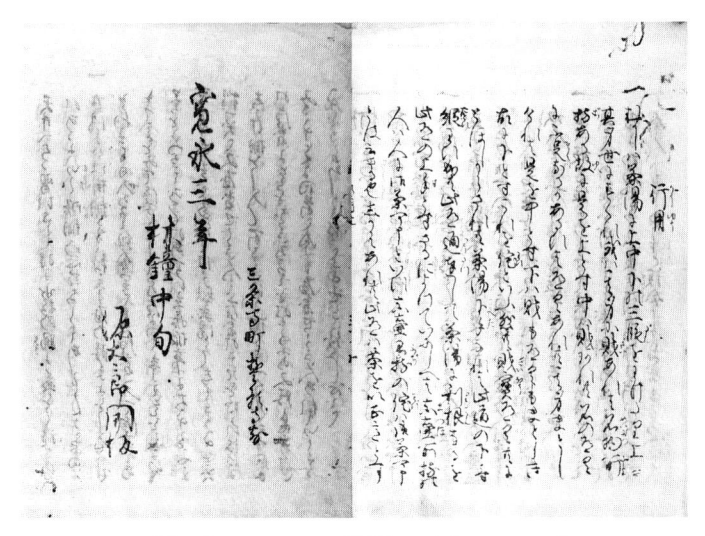

28. Opening page (left) and last page of the Sōjimboku. *Urasenke, Kyoto.*

expected of the man of culture, appeared around this time. The Neo-Confucian scholar Kaibara Ekiken (1630–1714) writes in the *Sanrei Kōketsu* (Secrets of the Three Social Graces), a popular text on calligraphy, cooking, and tea:

> No matter how accomplished you may be at anything else, unless you know the proper etiquette you will do the wrong thing when invited to a banquet and will only make a shameful and unsightly spectacle of yourself. Here, in one volume, are the secrets of tea etiquette, the procedure of tea drinking presented exactly as transmitted. While it may be difficult to avoid the censure of those truly learned in the art, may [this work] serve in some small way as a primer.

Obviously, a wide cross section of Japanese society had made chanoyu a pastime. While in part this was merely the cumulative effect of the ongoing historical process by which culture filtered down from the ruling class to the common people, it was more directly attributable to the systematization of tea teaching into a program of certification by rank. Distinct schools of tea developed, each a vast hierarchy under its *iemoto,* or hereditary grand master, who reserved the privilege of certification and of authorizing teachers nationwide to instruct on his behalf. The *iemoto* system greatly increased the spread of tea among the burgeoning merchant class from the mid-seventeenth century on, allowing the development of a huge new market in a way that the earlier one-to-one master-apprentice system could never have done.

The *iemoto* system broke down the walls of secrecy that had been built up around chanoyu and other arts. It is largely thanks to this very Japanese solution to the problem of simultaneously preserving and disseminating the tea tradition that chanoyu has survived to the present. The Urasenke tradition has led the way in this endeavor, and today there are practitioners of authentic chanoyu the world over.

CHAPTER TWO

Lives of the Urasenke Grand Masters

by Sōshitsu Sen XV

First-Generation Grand Master
Rikyū Sōeki (1522–91)

Rikyū (Pl. 1) was born in 1522 to Tanaka Yohei, proprietor of a fish warehouse in the Imaichi district of Sakai; according to the *Senke Yuishogaki* (History of the Sen Family), Rikyū was "the grandson of Tanaka Yoshikiyo, who was the second son of Satomi Tarō Yoshitoshi" of the warrior-class Seiwa Genji clan. His other grandfather is reputed to have been Sen'ami, a *dōbōshū* to the shogun Ashikaga Yoshimasa and possibly the source of the family name Sen. Rikyū's childhood name was Yoshirō; at the age of eighteen he received the name Sōeki from his Zen master, the priest Dairin Sōtō. Later he also used the names Hōsensai and Fushin'an. His first tea studies, under Kitamuki Dōchin, were in the *shoin* style, but through Dōchin's introduction he apprenticed himself to Takeno Jōō and began to practice *sōan*-style chanoyu. He hosted his first tea gathering in 1537 at the age of fifteen.

Slowly Rikyū's reputation as a tea master grew until eventually, almost forty years later, his prowess attracted the attention of Oda Nobunaga, the most powerful man in Japan at the time. On the occasion of a tea gathering held at Shōkokuji temple in Kyoto on the third day of the fourth month of 1574, Rikyū and another Sakai tea master, Tsuda Sōgyū, received gifts of rare *ranjatai* incense from Nobunaga; thus it is probable that the warlord had already retained Rikyū as a tea adviser. On the twenty-eighth day of the tenth month of the following year, Rikyū served tea at a gathering hosted by Oda Nobunaga at Myōkōji temple in Kyoto.

Rikyū's fortunes continued to improve. Even the assassination of his patron, Nobunaga, in 1582 was not a setback; his services were promptly engaged by Nobunaga's successor, Toyotomi Hideyoshi. Hideyoshi offered tea to the emperor Ōgimachi (1557–86) on the seventh day of the tenth month of 1585 in the Kikumi no Ma (Chrysanthemum-viewing Room) of the Kinri Gosho, the innermost quarters of the Imperial Palace in Kyoto, to express gratitude for having been appointed *kampaku* (regent). Rikyū's participation in this event established him as the leading figure in the world of tea, and it was on this occasion that the emperor granted the Buddhist lay name by which the master came to be known: Rikyū Koji, or "layman [*koji*] who puts keenness [*ri*] to rest [*kyū*] (Figs. 140–42).

Rikyū won ever-greater influence with Hideyoshi. In the fourth month of 1586, when the daimyo Ōtomo Sōrin (1530–87) journeyed from Kyushu to Osaka Castle for an audience with the *kampaku*, Sōrin wrote back to his senior retainer that Hideyoshi's younger brother, Hidenaga (1541–91), had told him "not to worry as long as the Lord of Mino [Hidenaga] was around. In anything that required attention, Sōeki [Rikyū] would take care of private matters and he himself would see to official matters." By that time, apparently, Rikyū was entrusted with handling Hideyoshi's personal affairs.

The next year, 1587, Hideyoshi returned triumphant from a military campaign in Kyushu to announce that he would hold the biggest tea gathering of all time in the woods outside Kitano Shrine in west-central Kyoto. Rikyū, Imai Sōkyū, and Tsuda Sōgyū were active in all phases of the Grand Kitano Tea Gathering, which was the highwater mark of Hideyoshi and Rikyū's relationship. A rift was soon to divide the two men, as signaled by their aesthetic differences on this occasion—Hideyoshi's insistence on a tearoom covered in gold leaf and the use of solid gold utensils in opposition to Rikyū's preference for a rustic two-mat hut.

By the second month of 1591 the relationship had deteriorated to such an extent that Hideyoshi suddenly accused Rikyū of lese majesty, charging that Rikyū had had a life-sized statue of himself placed in an addition to the main gate of Daitokuji that he and his family had donated, and demanding that Rikyū commit *seppuku*. The possible underlying reasons for Hideyoshi's move to rid himself of the man who had been his favorite tea master are many and complex. At the very least, it is certain that when Hideyoshi began to contemplate an invasion of Korea from Kyushu, the importance of the Sakai merchants dwindled in his eyes and he became more interested in enlisting the support of the merchants of Hakata, in northern Kyushu. Rikyū himself had just lost a major ally in Hidenaga, who had opposed the invasion plan but had died at the beginning of 1591, leaving Rikyū caught in the middle of a power struggle among Hideyoshi's advisers.

Rikyū was nearly seventy years old at the time of his death on the twenty-eighth day of the second month of 1591. He left the following death verses:

> A life of seventy years,
> Strength spent to the very last,
> With this, my jeweled sword,
> I kill both patriarchs and buddhas.
>
> I yet carry
> One article I had gained,
> The long sword

That now at this moment
I hurl to the heavens.

Second-Generation Grand Master
Shōan Sōjun (1546–1614)

Rikyū's two sons, Dōan (Fig. 144) and Shōan, were stepbrothers. Both were born in 1546. Dōan was born to Rikyū's first wife, known after her death on the sixteenth day of the seventh month of 1577 by the Buddhist name Hōshin Myōju; Shōan was the son of Rikyū's second wife, Sōon, and her first husband, the Sakai Noh teacher Miyaō Saburō Sannyū. Shōan was already married to Rikyū's daughter Okame before the second marriage. Soon thereafter he was formally adopted into the Sen family, and in 1578 his first son, Sōtan, was born.

Dōan made his first recorded appearance in Sakai tea circles at the age of twenty-two, when he was invited to a tea gathering in the company of Tsuda Sōgyū and Yamanoue Sōji on the first day of the first month of 1568. After a lengthy absence from the records, his name reappears in 1581. On the fifteenth day of the second month of 1584 he was invited to a tea gathering hosted by Hideyoshi at Osaka Castle, along with Rikyū, Tsuda Sōgyū, Imai Sōkyū, Yamanoue Sōji, Mozuya Sōan, Shige Sōho, and Sumiyoshiya Sōmu, whom the *Yamanoue Sōji Ki* refers to collectively as Hideyoshi's eight favorite men of tea *(chanoyusha hachinin shū)*. Shōan came to chanoyu somewhat later. Whereas Dōan's tea was said to have a bold, straightforward character, Shōan's tea was more tranquil and restrained. There can be little doubt that the two men were rivals for Rikyū's favor.

After Rikyū's death in 1591, Hideyoshi forced the Sen family to disband. Rikyū's disciple Gamō Ujisato gave Shōan refuge in Aizu-Wakamatsu while working with Tokugawa Ieyasu, the first Tokugawa shogun, to have the Sen family reinstated. Eventually Shōan was allowed to relocate Rikyū's tearoom Fushin'an to property near Hompōji temple in Kyoto, where he began to teach tea as the second-generation grand master in the Sen family tradition. In 1595 Shōan received a calligraphic transmission of the name Rikyū from the priest Sengaku Sōtō, abbot of Daitokuji, of whom he had inquired the "true meaning" of the lay name Rikyū Koji, an expression of Shōan's dedication to furthering the Sen tradition in chanoyu (Fig. 141). At the same time, Shōan felt that Sōtan, an actual bloodline descendant of Rikyū, should take the lead, and soon stepped down in favor of his son. In retirement he continued to practice tea, associating with Rikyū's disciple Hosokawa Sansai and with Sengaku and other noted priests, until his death at the age of sixty-eight on the seventh day of the ninth month of 1614.

Third-Generation Grand Master
Gempaku Sōtan (1578–1658)

Sōtan (Pl. 4, Fig. 29) was born in Sakai on the first day of the first month of 1578. His childhood name was Shuri. As an adult he also used the names Gempaku, Totsutotsusai, and Kan'un. In 1589, when he was eleven, he began Zen training at Daitokuji under Shun'oku Sōen, head priest of the subtemple Sangen'in, where Sōtan's main duty was the upkeep of the storehouse. When the furor over Rikyū's statue broke out only two years later, Rikyū went to Daitokuji to consult the senior priests. As the tea master was heading home by palanquin he spied his young grandson Sōtan cleaning the grounds and called out to him. According to the *Chawa Shigetsu Shū*, this was the last time Sōtan set eyes on his grandfather.

Not long after Rikyū's death and the forced dissolution of the Sen family, Rikyū's heirs were allowed to reestablish themselves in Kyoto. Sōtan left Daitokuji in either 1592 or 1593 and returned to secular life at his father's house on Ogawa Street, where he immediately began to study Rikyū's tea. On the first day of the first month of 1596 Shōan invested Sōtan, now eighteen, with leadership of the Sen family and went into retirement, possibly at Shōnantei (South Xiang Arbor) in the precinct of Saihōji temple in the Arashiyama hills of western Kyoto.

Thus fell to Sōtan the responsibility for every member of the family of the household: his grandmother Sōon; his mother, Okame; his younger brother, Sōho; and his own wife and two sons, Sōsetsu and Sōshu. It was almost too much to expect of such a young man, but he had moral support; Shun'oku bestowed on him the art name Genshuku, or "Founding Uncle," when he was only twenty-three as an expression of confidence in his ability to carry on the Sen family tradition. Over the next decade, however, many people close to Sōtan died: his grandmother, mother, and wife, his uncle Dōan, and the aged priest Shun'oku. Faced with so many deaths, at the age of thirty-three Sōtan resolved to live a life of detachment through chanoyu.

Much later, Sōtan remarried. His second wife, known only by her posthumous Buddhist name Sōken, was a lady-in-waiting of the empress Tōfukumon'in. Three children were born of this marriage: Sōtan's third son, Sōsa; a daughter, Kure; and his fourth son, Sensō. Sōtan's first son, Sōsetsu, apparently did not get along with his stepmother and left home, never to return. His lonely grave at Shōdenji temple at Nishigamo in the north of Kyoto still turns its back on the Sen family. The second son, Sōshu, was adopted into the Yoshioka family of lacquerware makers, who ran a shop called Kichimonjiya, and changed his name to Yoshioka Jin'emon. Later he would resume the family name Sen and build his own tearoom, Kankyūan (Hut of Retirement from Office), on the family's Mushanokōji Street property.

Sōtan thought little of fame and fortune and rejected frequent offers of positions as tea adviser to feudal lords in Edo. He remained based in Kyoto, perhaps wary of the fate that had befallen Rikyū because of his involvement in the world of politics. Noble as this retiring ideal was, Sōtan's children could not be expected to remain content to live in the austere fashion that this attitude necessitated. When

29. Sōtan Tossing Stones by Kanō Tan'yū. The young Kanō-school painter Tan'yū (1602–74) was decorating the paper panels of the Yūin tearoom when he noticed Sōtan out in the garden tossing pebbles to determine where to place Yūin's "Scattered Bean" stepping stones and deftly captured the scene.

Sōsa reached the age of twenty-nine, he gained a post with the Kii branch of the Tokugawa clan; interestingly enough, the sixty-four-year-old Sōtan accompanied Sōsa to Kii to offer his personal thanks for his son's appointment.

Four years later, in 1646, Sōtan transferred the Fushin'an tearoom to Sōsa's name and announced his own retirement. He then cleared a plot at the north end of the Ogawa Street property and built a small one-and-three-quarter-mat tearoom called Konnichian (Hut of This Day), a statement of his bridging of Zen and chanoyu.

Sōtan's brand of *wabi* chanoyu, steeped in the principle of identifying tea with Zen *(cha Zen ichimi)*, had considerable appeal, and many people sought him out to study under him. Among Sōtan's eminent students were Yamada Sōhen, Sugiki Fusai, Fujimura Yōken, Miyake Bōyō, Kusumi Soan, the empress Tōfukumon'in, and Lord Konoe Ōzan Nobuhiro. His philosophy of teaching is described in this verse of his:

> That which is chanoyu
> Is transmitted through the mind
> Through the eyes
> Through the ears
> With not a single written word.

Eventually Sōtan's fourth son, Sensō, found a position with the Maeda clan of

Kaga, whereupon Sōtan built more tearooms near Konnichian. With the addition of the four-and-a-half-mat Yūin (Further Retreat) and the eight-mat Kan'untei (Cold Cloud Arbor), a sizable rear *(ura)* compound took form alongside the streetfront *(omote)* house focused on Fushin'an. These two compounds, together with Kankyūan, became the headquarters of the three Sen families: Urasenke, Omotesenke, and Mushanokōjisenke, respectively.

Sōtan died on the nineteenth day of the twelfth month of 1658 at the age of eighty, leaving behind this farewell verse:

> Born out of thin air
> Void as thin air
> It comes,
> Void again, void it goes
> The sound of the bells.

Fourth-Generation Grand Master
Sensō Sōshitsu (1622–97)

Sensō (Fig. 30), born in Kyoto in 1622, was the youngest child of Sōtan, who was then forty-four years old. His childhood name was Chōkichirō. When still quite young he was apprenticed to the Kyoto physician Noma Gentaku, but on his master's untimely death Sensō returned to Sōtan's care. In 1642, after years of rigorous training in Rikyū's chanoyu, Sensō accepted a post with a 250 *koku** annual stipend as tea adviser to Lord Maeda Toshitsune of Komatsu in Kaga, much to Sōtan's pleasure. In 1651, at the age of twenty-nine, he took the name Sōshitsu and was given the tearooms Konnichian, Yūin, and Kan'untei.

Sōtan's death seven years later almost coincided with that of Sensō's patron, whereupon Sensō returned to Kyoto to head the Urasenke household. The task consumed all his energies at first, but by the time thirteenth-anniversary memorial services were held for Sōtan in 1671, he was ready to accept another post. He was now forty-nine and a widower, but his new patron, Lord Maeda Tsunatoshi of Kanazawa in Kaga, was a great patron of the arts and provided Sensō with comfortable quarters in the town of Kanazawa.

Sensō remarried soon thereafter and in 1673 fathered the son destined to become the fifth-generation grand master, Jōsō. Sensō's mother and his older brother, Sōsa, had died the previous year, and his stepbrother Sōshu died the following year; suddenly Sensō found himself the sole Sen family elder. His responsibilities kept him traveling back and forth between Kanazawa and Kyoto. For Tsunatoshi he supervised castle tea gatherings and the display of art objects in the lord's *shoin;* in Kyoto

---

* Stipends, like taxes, were paid in *koku,* a measure of volume used for rice. In the Edo period one *koku* of rice was about 0.18 cubic meter or 180.39 liters, in theory enough to feed one adult for a year.

Pl. 1. Portrait of Rikyū; a copy by Ken'ei Sōtan of a painting by Hasegawa Tōhaku.

Pl. 2. Gion Festival Scene *by Hasegawa Kyūzō, presented to Rikyū by Oda Nobunaga; colophon by Sōtan.*

Pl. 3. Rikyū's well-bucket fresh-water container, made of unfinished wood; Rikyū's seal and Sōtan's inscription, reading "As much as we have grown accustomed to its use, it remains strictly Rikyū's" on the bottom; an additional inscription by Rikkansai.

Pl. 4. *Portrait of Sōtan; inscription by Gyokushū Sōban.*

Pl. 5. Calligraphy by Sōtan, reading "This day."

Pl. 6. Sensō's gourd-shaped whirlpool-pattern fresh-water container; Ōhi ware; box inscribed "Chikusō Sōgen Sōshitsu." The whirlpool pattern, Sensō's choice for the Sen family crest, was reputedly incised by Sensō himself.

Pl. 7. Evening Bell from a Temple in the Mist *by Rikkansai.* ▶

Pl. 8. Portrait of Chikusō; *colophon by Ennōsai.*

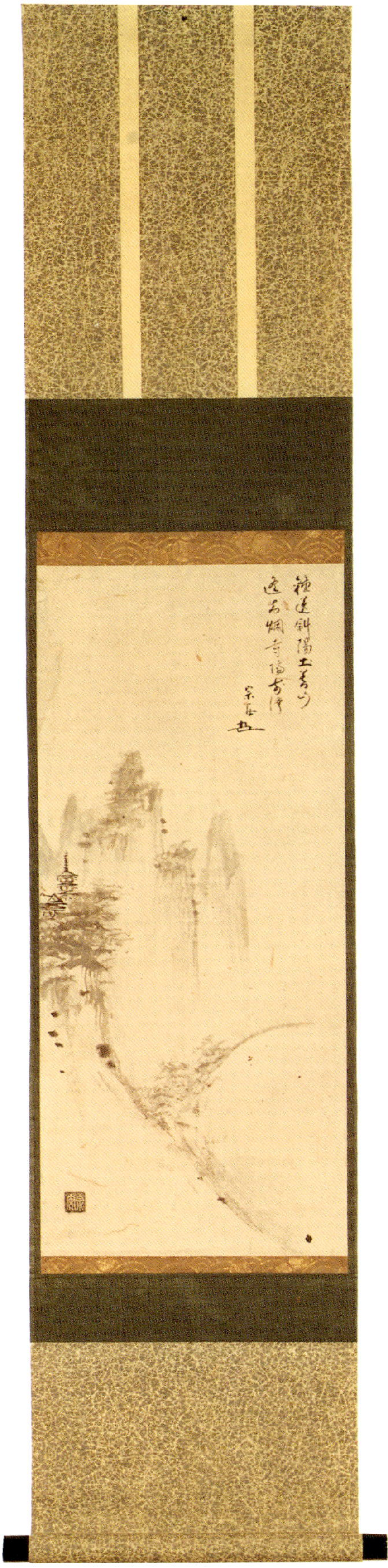
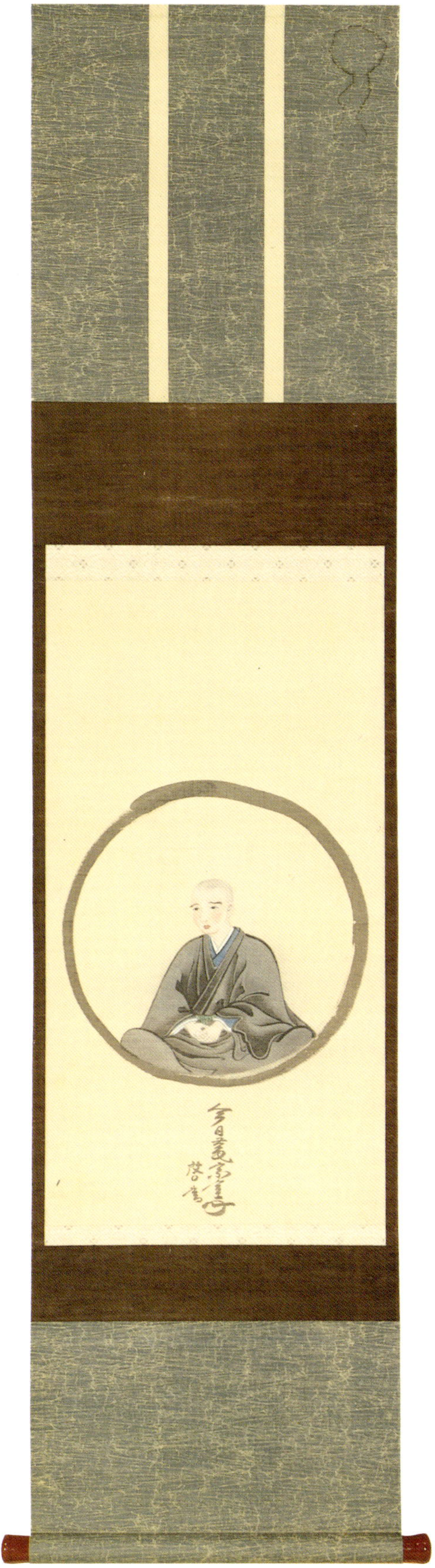

Pl. 9. Yūgensai's chrysanthemum and hailstone-pattern kettle; "Yūgensai" cast on the front; pinecone-shaped lugs.

Pl. 10. Fukensai's octagonal incense container; transparent blue-green glaze; inscribed with the character "affirmation" (kore) by Fukensai. The box inscription by Fukensai reads "Noble is the no-mind. Approved by Genshitsu [Fukensai]."

Pl. 11. Portrait of Nintokusai, inscribed by him with the character "ease" (raku).

Pl. 12. Lidded fresh-water container by Nintokusai.

Pl. 13. Red Raku tea bowl "Twin Leaves" by Gengensai.

Pl. 14. Tantansai's "Feather Cloak" incense container.

30. Portrait of Sensō; colophon by Sensō.

he hosted one hundred forty-two Sen family tea functions over a period of seven years. The pace was bound to take its toll. On the fourth day of the ninth month of 1687 Sensō petitioned Tsunatoshi to be allowed to retire to Kyoto, and on the twenty-fourth day of the ninth month of 1688, when he was sixty-six, his request was granted. Two years later, on the occasion of the centennial of Rikyū's death, Sensō dedicated the Rikyūdō family shrine, containing a statue of his great-grandfather.

Sensō made a major contribution to the art of chanoyu, particularly by taking Kyoto artisans with him to Kanazawa. His efforts enabled the Raku potter Chōzaemon to set up the Ōhi kiln and the kettle maker Miyazaki Kanchi to establish the Kanchi foundry in Kanazawa. Sensō himself designed a waiting area with a bench *(koshikake machiai)* at the entrance to Konnichian, as well as such fittings as the "Carpenter's Workbox" shelf *(kugibakodana;* Fig. 93).

The seventy-five-year-old Sensō was visiting Kanazawa when he died on the twenty-third day of the first month of 1697. He left behind this farewell verse based on the farewell verse of his father, Sōtan (Fig. 150):

> If out of thin air
> Floating on thin air
> They came forth,
> So now echo back
> The bells of dawn.

LIVES OF THE URASENKE GRAND MASTERS

Fifth-Generation Grand Master
Fukyūsai Jōsō (1673–1704)

Jōsō, born in Kanazawa in 1673, was Sensō's first son. His childhood name was Yosaburō, and he later used the names Sōan, Fukyūsai, and, after Sensō's death, Sōshitsu, establishing the precedent for the head of the Urasenke household to use that name.

He married at twenty and fathered a son the next year, the eventual sixth-generation grand master, Rikkansai. On the twenty-ninth day of the second month of 1697, a little more than a month after Sensō's death, Jōsō's familiarity with the Maeda clan of Kaga secured him the position of resident tea master at the age of twenty-four. He had not been in Kanazawa long, however, when an introduction to Lord Hisamatsu Sadanao of Matsuyama in Iyo (present-day Ehime Prefecture) on the island of Shikoku gained him another post—in fact, from then until the end of the Edo period, the Urasenke household would continue to receive a yearly stipend of 250 *koku* from the Matsuyama domain. Although the details of how this came about are lost, it is probable that Lord Maeda, seeing that Kanazawa's harsh winters did not agree with Jōsō's delicate constitution, personally recommended him to Lord Hisamatsu of southerly Shikoku, hoping that he might fare better there.

Even so, Jōsō's days were not long. He had only been serving Lord Hisamatsu five or six years when his thirty-one-year life came to an end on the fourteenth day of the fifth month of 1704. Nonetheless, his career did span the flamboyant Genroku era (1688–1704), and this is reflected in the more colorful of his favored tea utensils *(konomimono)*: the red-topped thin-tea container *(kōaka chaki;* Fig. 40) and the vermilion candle stand *(shunuri teshoku)*. In a more *wabi* key, a number of freshwater jars designed by him were made at the Raku and Ohi kilns, while his wizened calligraphy belied his youth.

Sixth-Generation Grand Master
Rikkansai Taisō (1694–1726)

When Jōsō died, his heir, Rikkansai (known as Masakichirō as a child), born in 1694, was only ten years old. At the time, the Omotesenke household was headed by the twenty-six-year-old sixth-generation grand master, Kakukakusai Gensō (1678–1730), who went out of his way to look after the boy, frequently accompanying him to tea gatherings. Some years later, on the twenty-fifth-anniversary memorial observances for the fifth-generation Omotesenke grand master, Zuiryūsai Ryōkyū (1650–91), the twenty-two-year-old Urasenke grand master, now known as Taisō Sōan, took part in rounds of *chakabuki,* "tea roles by drawing lots," held in Omotesenke's tearoom Zangetsutei (Waning Moon Arbor). In the same way, Rikkansai befriended Kakukakusai's oldest son, Yotarō, eleven years Rikkansai's junior.

Rikkansai grew into a man of learning and talent. He was tutored in the Chinese classics by the noted Neo-Confucian scholar Itō Tōgai (1670–1736), studied the classical Noh and Kyōgen drama, gained renown as a calligrapher, and skillfully fashioned his own tea bowls. All did not go smoothly in his life, however; his wife died in 1726, and the following year the heartbroken young tea master set out for Edo, intending to rest at the Edo villa of the Hisamatsu clan. Yet the grueling trip only exhausted him, and on arriving in Edo he fell ill. He died shortly after, on the twenty-eighth day of the eighth month of 1726, at the age of thirty-two and was buried under the Buddhist lay name Rikkansai Taisō Sōan Sōshitsu Koji at Tōkaiji temple in the Shinagawa district of Edo.

Seventh-Generation Grand Master
Chikusō Sōken (1709–33)

When news of Rikkansai's death in Edo reached Konnichian, his younger sister, whom he had intended to marry to Kakukakusai's second son, Chikusō (called Masanosuke as a child), was plunged into grief and took the tonsure at the Tendai-sect nunnery Saihōji. Eventually, after years of praying for the peace of her older brother's spirit, she became the thirtieth-generation abbess of the temple. Saihōji, incidentally, possesses a number of Rikyū's effects.

Rikkansai's mother took the seventeen-year-old Chikusō under her wing, and he became the seventh-generation Urasenke heir, taking the name Sōken. Kakukakusai also watched over his son, but he lived only four more years, until Chikusō reached the age of twenty-one. At that point Chikusō's older brother Sōin (1705–51; his childhood name was Yotarō, mentioned in passing above) stepped in to become Omotesenke's seventh-generation grand master, Joshinsai Tennen.

Chikusō (Pl. 8) remodeled Sensō's vestibule (*yoritsuki*) making it into a room of five mats plus a one-mat board inset, and hung a plaque there that reads, "Pines show no colors old or new," from which the room was named Mushikiken (Shelter of No Colors). This is one of the few mementos of Chikusō, also known as Saisaisai. On the second day of the third month of 1733 his brief life of twenty-four years came to an end; he was still unmarried. The young grand master was buried under the Buddhist lay name Chikusō Sōken Sōshitsu Koji.

Eighth-Generation Grand Master
Yūgensai Ittō (1719–71)

Faced with Chikusō's untimely death, Urasenke was once more at a loss for a head tea master but soon pressed Chikusō's fourteen-year-old brother Jūichirō of the Omotesenke household into the role. Proclaimed the eighth-generation grand master of the Urasenke household, Yūgensai Ittō, as he came to be known, added luster to the Urasenke name.

Joshinsai, fourteen years Ittō's senior, provided him with considerable guidance. Awakened to their spiritual responsibility to preserve the orthodox Rikyū tradition in chanoyu, together they eagerly underwent Zen training with the priests Daishin Gitō, Dairyū Sōjō, and Mugaku Sōen. Ittō then announced Urasenke's recovery from its ill fortune with a "coming out" tea gathering to which he invited the priests. The earnest cooperation of these brothers in tea led the Urasenke and Omotesenke households to formalize a program of Seven Special Tea Exercises *(shichiji shiki)* created expressly for interactive participation by having host and guests exchange roles.

Like Rikkansai before him, Ittō was an avid scholar of the Chinese classics and of Noh. He took the literary name Yūgensai from Laozi's words "darkness within darkness" *(gen yū gen;* Chinese, *xuan you xuan)* at the beginning of the *Dao De Jing* (Classic of the Way and Its Virtue), one of his favorite texts. He also used the names Futsufutsuken and Baigandō. Ittō married twice, his first wife dying when he was twenty-four. His second wife bore a son, Kumesaburō, in 1746. In 1751, when Ittō was thirty-two, his older brother Joshinsai died, leaving only a seven-year-old son, Yotarō. Up through the centennial memorial observances for Sōtan seven years later in 1758, Ittō was the pillar of both Sen families, hosting more than a hundred tea functions during that period.

Ittō's services as a tea instructor were in great demand. In addition to the continued Urasenke appointment to the Hisamatsu clan of Matsuyama, Ittō was engaged by the Hachisuka clan of Awa (present-day Tokushima Prefecture). In Edo, he gained a student in the wealthy merchant Chigara Sen'emon, and supervised the design of Sen'emon's tearoom Baian (Flowering Plum Hut). Through such activities, Ittō helped build a foundation for the Sen tradition in Edo. Ittō further helped to promote tea by sending one of his leading disciples, Kanō Sōboku, to teach in Osaka, and another, Hayami Sōtatsu, to be instructor of the Ikeda clan in Okayama. Sōtatsu in particular had a high reputation for his learning, and he was the author of many works on tea. Ittō, of course, is known for his authorship of the famous text *Hama no Masago* (Sand on the Beach).

After these glowing successes, which set the Urasenke household back on its feet, Ittō died at fifty-two on the second day of the second month of 1771. He was buried under the Buddhist lay name Yūgensai Ittō Sōshitsu Koji.

Ninth-Generation Grand Master
Fukensai Sekiō (1746–1801)

When Ittō died, his heir, Kumesaburō, was twenty-five and had already taken the adult name Genshitsu. Alternate names included Fukensai, Kan'ō, and Sekiō. In 1788, when Fukensai was forty-two, a great fire swept through Kyoto from south to north, raging for three days and nights and destroying nine-tenths of the city. Luckily, it took some time for the blaze to reach the Sen households in the north, and the families had time to gather together their priceless treasures and take shelter at Daitokuji. The monumental task of reconstructing the Urasenke household then fell to Fukensai. Repairs to the largely untouched tearoom Yūin were completed on the twenty-second day of the eighth month of the next year; work continued through the third month of the following year on the rest of the compound, the unveiling coinciding with bicentennial memorial services for Rikyū. In attendance were Lord Fujinami Hidetada and his entourage, and heads of the Omotesenke and Mushanokōjisenke households, Yabunouchi Jōchi of the Yabunouchi school of tea, third-generation Matsuo-school grand master Matsuo Sōsei, tea connoisseur Hisada Sōzen (1646–1707), eighth-generation Raku potter Tokunyū, master lacquerer Nakamura Sōtetsu, and Daitokuji priests Mugaku Sōen, Kankai Sōshun, Yūgoku Sōtsū, and Shingan Sōjō. Fukensai's oldest son, Komakichi, then nineteen, was already using the hereditary Urasenke name Sōshitsu.

The Urasenke buildings had been more or less restored to their former condition, but the statue of Rikyū in the Rikyūdō still required repair work because of damage incurred when it was submerged in the pond in front of the shrine to save it from the flames. The services of the Buddhist altar statuary sculptor Ryōkei were enlisted for the repairs, which were finished by the end of 1789. Mugaku dedicated the statue on the seventh day of the first month of 1790.

Fukensai died at the age of fifty-five on the twenty-sixth day of the ninth month of 1801 and was buried under the Buddhist lay name Fukensai Sekiō Sōshitsu Koji. His heirs included not only Komakichi, who became the tenth-generation grand master, Nintokusai, but his second son, Sōgen, and his third son, Sōjū, who became Mushanokōjisenke's sixth grand master, Kōkōsai Nin'ō (1795–1835).

Tenth-Generation Grand Master
Nintokusai Hakusō (1770–1826)

Nintokusai (Pl. 11) was known in childhood first as Yosaburō, then as Kumesaburō. He became head of the Urasenke household at thirty-four. Married young to a daughter of the prominent Zetsu family of Kibune in the north of Kyoto, his first son was born when Nintokusai was only sixteen. In 1792, when his son was six, Nintokusai sent him to Gyokurin'in, a subtemple of Daitokuji, where he was ordained as Sōichi. It was hoped that he would one day become the priest of Tokuzenji temple, but he died unexpectedly in 1811 at the age of twenty-five. Although Nintokusai fathered five other sons, none lived to adulthood. Eventually he adopted a son from the powerful Matsudaira clan of Mikawa (present-day Aichi Prefecture), and it was he who succeeded Nintokusai as the eleventh-generation master, Gengensai.

By all accounts Nintokusai was a man of stern temperament. He was strict in the demands he placed on his students—this much can be surmised from his placing his own son in a monastery at the age of six—but he was equally strict with himself. When at twenty-four he received the complete "inner transmission" of the Urasenke tradition of tea from his father, Fukensai, he memorized it and committed it to writing. When Fukensai observed this and cautioned him with Sōtan's words "That which is chanoyu is transmitted . . . with not a single written word," Nintokusai promptly burned everything he had written.

Nintokusai died at the age of fifty-six on the twenty-fourth day of the eighth month of 1826 and was buried under the Buddhist lay name Nintokusai Hakusō Sōshitsu Koji. He was survived by his wife, Sōko, who, having received training in tea from Fukensai, helped instruct the younger members of the family until her death at the age of sixty-six in 1844.

Eleventh-Generation Grand Master
Gengensai Seichū (1810–77)

Gengensai (Fig. 31) was adopted into the Sen family in 1819 and later married Nintokusai's oldest daughter, Machiko, born in 1811. By birth the son of Lord Matsudaira Noritomo of Mikawa, his childhood names were Chiyomatsu and Eigorō, but in adult life he went by the names Gengensai, Kyohakusai, and Fubō.

Nintokusai, who was forty-nine when the nine-year-old Gengensai came into the family, thought it only proper that this boy from an upper-class background be acquainted with the breadth of Japanese and Chinese high culture and embarked upon a rigorous program of education, setting him to study Noh, flower arrangement, incense connoisseurship, *waka* poetry, the Japanese and Chinese classics, and calligraphy. At the time of Nintokusai's death, Gengensai's scholarship belied his sixteen years. Bringing this learning to his new role as grand master, he made the Urasenke household the center of Kyoto culture.

From the twenty-eighth day of the ninth month of 1839 through the beginning of the next year, Gengensai prepared for a gala tea function to mark the two hundred fiftieth anniversary of Rikyū's death. Construction of additions to the Urasenke compound was undertaken. These included the main gate and entryway; the tearooms Totsutotsusai (Sanctuary of Pleasant Surprise), Dairo no Ma (Great Hearth Room), and Hōsensai (Sanctuary of the Cast Fishtrap); and a tearoom called Baishian (Plum Thread Hut), no longer extant.

The results were impressive. Indeed, Gengensai's vision represented more than Urasenke alone. Neither of the other branches of the Sen family had an experienced leader at the time: Omotesenke's tenth grand master, Kyūōsai Shōō (1817–60), was barely twenty-two, and his younger brother, tenth-generation Mushanokōjisenke grand master Ishinsai Zendō (1830–91), was only nine. Gengensai therefore handled all the arrangements for the function in the capacity of family elder. Among the notables in attendance were Imperial Regent Takatsukasa Masamichi, Minister of the Right Kujō Hisatada, and Minister of the Interior Konoe Tadahiro. Later, Urasenke received visits from Prince Chion'in, head priest Tatsujo of Higashi Hongan-ji temple, and former Minister of the Interior Tokudaiji Sanekata. Eventually, when Gengensai was forty-nine, Kujō Hisatada rewarded him with the art name Seichū.

Gengensai, himself of warrior-class origin, worked hard to build up ties with prominent samurai families. While maintaining the Urasenke appointments to the Maeda clan of Kaga and the Hisamatsu clan of Matsuyama, he was able to secure a 300 *koku* stipend from the Tokugawa clan of Owari (present-day Aichi Prefecture)

31. Portrait of Gengensai by Mitamura Sōryū; colophon by Bokusō Sōju.

and personally instructed Lord Tokugawa Naritaka in the secrets of chanoyu, including those for the most formal *shin daisu* tea procedure.

Meanwhile, Gengensai's foster mother, Sōkō, died in 1844, and his wife, Machiko, died the following year. Thereupon Gengensai married Machiko's younger sister Teruko, to whom a son was born when Gengensai was thirty-six. Unfortunately, this child, Ichinyosai, did not live past the age of sixteen, dying in 1862. In 1871 Gengensai adopted a son of the wealthy Suminokura family as a husband for his daughter Yukako.

The transition from the Edo period to the Meiji era (1868–1912) swept Japan up in rapid change. This was a difficult time for all the traditional arts: not only was patronage cut off when the feudal clans lost their fiefs, but the new government, in its enthusiastic pursuit of anything Western, summarily dismissed many "things Japanese" as anachronisms.

Few traditional arts could boast as able and knowledgeable a spokesman as Gengensai. In 1872 he submitted a formal letter of protest to the Meiji government, the *Chadō no Gen'i* (The Basic Idea of the Way of Tea; Pl. 59), objecting to the government's move to classify chanoyu as a mere "pastime" or "entertainment":

> The original intent of the Way of Tea is to instill loyalty, filial piety, and the Five Constant Virtues [benevolence, sincerity, righteousness, wisdom, and trust]; to uphold modesty, propriety, and frugality; [to encourage] the unflagging fulfillment of one's allotted role in family affairs; [to promote] service toward the peace and well-being of the realm; to have people treat one another with no distinctions of closeness or distance, wealth or poverty; and to revere divine providence for the sake of the health and longevity of generations to come. Because [tea] is a path with these tenets, strictly and formally regulated

32. Portrait of Yūmyōsai.

tea gatherings must be recognized as the sincerest form of activity that can be performed without harming the five parts of the body. The import of all these ideas is present within even the humblest thin-tea service.

> Not in clothing, food, or shelter,
> Nor in utensils or gardens—
> No excess of any kind,
> So that by sincere practice
> The taste of tea shines through.

This statement won chanoyu official recognition as a true discipline. With this achievement and the creation of the table-top *ryūrei* tea service, Gengensai paved the way for the Urasenke of today. Six years later, in 1877, the life of this forward-looking tea master came to a close at the age of sixty-seven. He was buried under the Buddhist lay name Gengensai Seichū Sōshitsu Koji.

Twelfth-Generation Grand Master
Yūmyōsai Jikisō (1852–1917)

Yūmyōsai (Fig. 32) was born into the old Kyoto family of Suminokura on the twenty-first day of the third month of 1852. At the age of nineteen he entered the Sen family as the husband of Gengensai's daughter Yukako, two years his senior. Yūmyōsai was unhappy with the demanding role of heading the Urasenke household, however, and in 1885, at the age of thirty-three, he turned over the responsibility to his oldest son, Komakichi, and sought seclusion at Myōkian temple in Yamazaki, a southwestern suburb of Kyoto. He died on December 8, 1917, at the age of sixty-five, after spending almost half his life in retirement.

Meanwhile, Yukako, known in later life as Shinseiin, became a major force in the dissemination of chanoyu among the women of Japan not only through individual instruction, although she did teach a number of noblewomen and women of the upper classes, but also through the innovative move of having tea etiquette placed on the curriculum of the newly established girls' secondary schools, a strategy whose impact is still felt today. She continued to teach until her death at the age of sixty-six on August 11, 1916.

Thirteenth-Generation Grand Master
Ennōsai Tetchū (1872–1924)

Ennōsai, the oldest son of Yūmyōsai and Yukako, was born on May 21, 1872, and was given the childhood name Komakichi. At the age of only twelve he was made grand master of the Urasenke household, and at the age of seventeen he married Tsunako, the oldest daughter of the Kuki family of Sanda in Hyōgo Prefecture.

Thinking that the world of chanoyu would now center on Tokyo, as Edo had been renamed after the Meiji Restoration of 1868, the newlyweds made their way to the new capital to explore its potential. It was there that their first son, Masanosuke, was born. Returning to Kyoto, they plunged into a busy round of activities to promote the cause of tea in the new era. Among Ennōsai's students at this time were the imperial princes Kitashirakawa and Komatsu Akihito. It was the former who bestowed upon the grand master the art name Ennōsai in the hope that he might "fully [*en*] implement his abilities [*nō*]," while the latter gave him the art name Tetchū, lauding him as "one whose metal [*tetsu*] rings truest among [*chū*] all."

Ennōsai was a liberal thinker. In 1908 he began publishing the magazine *Konnichian Geppō* (Konnichian Monthly; Fig. 160) and also systematized the guidelines for the tea etiquette courses in girls' secondary schools. In 1913 he established a regular program of summer seminars in tea. In the middle of the thirteenth annual summer seminar, on August 5, 1924, he died at the age of fifty-two. He was buried under the Buddhist lay name Ennōsai Tetchū Sōshitsu Koji.

Fourteenth-Generation Grand Master
Tantansai Sekisō (1893–1964)

Ennōsai's first son, Masanosuke, was born on September 24, 1893, and became the head of the Urasenke household upon his father's death. He underwent Zen training with Enzan Den'i, head priest of Daitokuji, and received from him the art name Mugensai. He also used the names Tantansai—bestowed by the noble Kujō family—Genkusai, and Baishian.

When the empress Teimei paid a visit to Daitokuji in 1925, Tantansai conducted

33. Matsushima Islands by Tantansai.

a formal presentation of tea in her honor. In 1953 he offered tea to the crown prince in Shōkintei (Pine Harp Arbor) at the Katsura Detached Palace in Kyoto and later presented tea to other members of the imperial household, including princes Takamatsu, Chichibu, and Mikasa. He also began the practice of offering tea at Ise Grand Shrine, the most sacred Shintō shrine in Japan, as well as at other Shintō shrines and at Buddhist temples throughout the nation.

In a career spanning the three modern eras of Meiji, Taishō (1912–26), and Shōwa (1926–), Tantansai increased the popularity of chanoyu; he encouraged the development of local tea groups, building the tearooms Tōinseki (Room in Paulownia Shade), Kan'utei (Sweet Rain Arbor), and Gyokushūan (Hut Surpassing Jewels) for such groups, and supported artisans in their efforts to create new tea utensils.

It was also Tantansai who conceived the idea of introducing chanoyu to the West, and he traveled to North America and Europe to give lectures and demonstrations. Meanwhile, within Japan, from 1940 on he worked to restructure Urasenke into an organized system of local branches under the central Urasenke organization in Kyoto. In 1946 he established the International Chadō Cultural Foundation to further the spread of chanoyu overseas, and in 1949 he founded the Urasenke Foundation and built chanoyu study centers in Kyoto and Tokyo. In 1962 he established a full-time school for the study of chanoyu.

Tantansai received many awards in recognition of his outstanding contributions to Japanese culture, including the Medal of Honor with Blue Ribbon from the emperor in February 1957 and the Medal of Honor with Purple Ribbon from the emperor in November of the same year—a first in the world of tea. In 1960 Tantansai and his wife, Kayoko, were honored with an imperial banquet.

Tantansai's death came unexpectedly on September 7, 1964, while he was on an official visit to local Urasenke tea groups on Japan's northernmost island, Hokkaido.

He was seventy. Buried under the Buddhist lay name Mugensai Sekisō Sōshitsu Koji, he was posthumously awarded the Fourth Class Order of the Rising Sun. His wife, a member of the prominent Itō family of Sendai in northern Japan, died exactly sixteen years later, on the day of his memorial services in 1980.

Fifteenth-Generation Grand Master
Hōunsai Sōshitsu (1923–   )

Born on April 19, 1923, Hōunsai studied economics at Dōshisha University in Kyoto and went on to graduate studies at the University of Hawaii. He became the fifteenth Urasenke grand master in October 1964.

CHAPTER THREE

The Master's Taste: Tea Utensils

by Sōshun Hamamoto

First-Generation Grand Master
Rikyū Sōeki

Rikyū's great achievement was the creation of the sober, meditative *sōan* style of chanoyu. Departing from the formal Muromachi-period *shoin* style of tea using the *daisu*, he advocated the simpler tea practice of the small room, steeped in the *wabi* aesthetic of simplicity and tranquility. In a famous passage from the *Nampō Roku*, Rikyū's voice is that of the true man of Zen: "Chanoyu of the small room is first of all to be taken as a discipline in accordance with the Buddha's teachings. To revel in sumptuous dwellings and delicacies is a worldly thing. It is enough if a house does not leak; food suffices if it staves off hunger." By extension, plain, frugal tea utensils were also in order.

Utensils are the minimum material requisite for the preparing and serving of tea. All are shaped to fit specific practices, while each piece selected for use embodies the individual tea practitioner's taste. With some knowledge of the utensils known to have been favored by the grand masters, we can form a picture of trends through the history of chanoyu. Thus, an examination Rikyū's preferences in tea utensils sheds much light on the master's tea.

Many pieces are credited to Rikyū: Raku-ware tea bowls, bamboo flower containers, black-lacquered *natsume* (thin-tea containers), a fresh-water container made from a well bucket (Pl. 3), bamboo tea scoops, and bamboo rests for kettle lids. Many of Rikyū's utensils were adapted from ordinary household effects—"found objects" that he appreciated and used in new ways. It is a testament to Rikyū's creative genius that many of his designs set the standard for later tea utensils.

Rikyū's "Shakuhachi" Bamboo Flower Container (Shakuhachi Take Hanaire; Pl. 15)

This bamboo flower container, one of three fashioned by Rikyū in 1590 while he was encamped with Hideyoshi at the siege of the Hōjō clan's Nirayama Castle in Izu (present-day Shizuoka Prefecture), was presented to Hideyoshi, who cherished it. The other two were the "Long Night" double-opening flower container *(yonaga nijūgiri hanaire)*, which remained in Rikyū's possession, and the "Onjoji Temple" single-opening flower container (Onjōji *ichijūgiri hanaire*), which Rikyū gave to his son Shōan. Each of the three attained renown in its own right.

The "Shakuhachi" bamboo flower container was named in reference to a poem by Ikkyū Sojun (1394–1481), renowned Zen master and forty-sixth abbot of Daitokuji. The subject of Ikkyū's verse was the traditional Japanese end-blown flute, or *shakuhachi*. Rikyu's flower container is simply an inverted section of bamboo of *shakuhachi* length—one *shaku* and eight *(hachi) sun,* or 54.5 centimeters—cut on a slight diagonal at the top and with a joint near the base. Saw marks are visible at top and bottom, and a triangular notch has been cut in the base. The graceful flow of the bamboo's grain harmonizes perfectly with the overall curve of this deservedly acclaimed *wabi* masterpiece.

Takuan Sōhō (1573–1645), one hundred fifty-fourth abbot of Daitokuji, inscribed the inner box with Ikkyū's *shakuhachi* verse:

>From both cut-off ends, past and present,
>Through a *shaku* and eight *sun* length,
>Plays the one true tune in all the impermanent world,
>Resounding beyond three thousand leagues.

An accompanying letter by Takuan repeats the poem and adds a comment: "This flower tube is called 'Shakuhachi,' in accordance with the words of Zen Master Ikkyū. Rikyū Koji said he himself had in mind, when he named it, that the music of this *shakuhachi* would resound over three thousand leagues, so I now transcribe the poem."

An outer box bears the inscription "Shakuhachi flower tube" in Kobori Enshū's hand, and inside the lid of another outer box is the inscription "Original ancestor of flower containers, one of three treasured pieces" by the ninth-generation Omotesenke grand master, Ryōryōsai Kōshuku (1775–1825). Kobori Enshū and Kōgetsu Sōgan (1574–1643), one hundred fifty-seventh abbot of Daitokuji, wrote the following verses on an accompanying scroll, beginning with Enshū's:

>Shakuhachi has but one joint [*fushi*],
>Only one refrain [*fushi*],
>Yet so familiar a ring
>It wins over successive generations
>Like an old friend.

>All day I sought some word to add to the hills and fields
>And found that what lies herein needs no words.

Rikyū's "Hundred Gatherings" Hailstone-Pattern Kettle (Arare Hyakkaigama; Pl. 16)

Long before Rikyū's time, tea connoisseurs had prized the Ashiya kettles of Chikuzen (present-day Fukuoka Prefecture) and the Temmyō kettles of Shimotsuke (present-day Tochigi Prefecture). Ashiya kettles are known for their fine texture and delicate patterns, whereas Temmyō kettles tend to be more "masculine," giving off an air of silent strength. Rikyū himself possessed a number of each, among them the Ashiya supreme treasure (*ōmeibutsu*) named the "Chrysanthemum Stream" kettle (*kikusuigama*) and such Temmyō treasures (*meibutsu*) as the "Young Maiden" kettle (*otogozegama*), "Handball" kettle (*marigama*), "Inaba Hall" kettle (*Inabadōgama*), and "Handled" kettle (*tedorigama*).

Kyoto kettle makers were also producing in quantity by the Momoyama period, in response to the spread of chanoyu. Among them was the kettle maker Tsuji Yojirō, who made a number of pieces to Rikyū's designs. Arai Isshō's *Meibutsu Kama no Ki* (Record of Treasured Kettles) lists such Rikyū-Yojirō collaborations as the "Cushion" kettle (*futongama*), "Round Hailstone 'Hundred Gatherings'" kettle (*maru arare hyakkai no kama*), "Cloud and Dragon" kettle (*unryūgama*), "Amida Hall" kettle (*Amidadōgama*), "Broad Bottom" kettle (*shiribarigama*), and "Square Body" kettle (*yohōmasugama*).

Rikyū's "Hundred Gatherings" kettle is thought to correspond to the "Round Hailstone 'Hundred Gatherings'" kettle of that text. A supplementary text identifies the kettle as Yojirō's work. It is known that Rikyū gave this kettle to Shōan, and it appears frequently in the *Rikyū Hyakkai Ki* (Record of One Hundred Tea Gatherings of Rikyū) under the description "hailstone kettle." The refined modeling of this round kettle with its sunken *ubaguchi* (hag's mouth) and spiked "hailstone" pattern characterizes it as one of Yojirō's masterpieces. The lugs are in the traditional *kimen* (demon mask) style, and the domed lid is made of bronze.

Rikyū's Bronze "Peach" Fresh-Water Container and Matching Utensils (Karakane Momo Mizusashi Kaigu; Pl. 17) The set of utensils shown in Pl. 17 actually dates only from the time of Gengensai, but, as Gengensai's inscription on the box says, is a "copy of the bronze 'Peach' fresh-water container and matching utensils owned and passed down by Rikyū." The peach-shaped knob on the lid of the fresh-water jar has two leaves and a portion of the branch attached.

Rikyū liked to use his bronze "Peach" utensils when he served tea in the "formal" manner, using a *daisu* and other Chinese items. Sōtan used the set together with a Korean-style *daisu* he was given by the king of the Ryūkyū Islands. When Gengensai, in 1839, served tea in the Hōsensai tearoom on the occasion of the two hundred fiftieth anniversary of Rikyū's death, he, too, used the "Peach" utensils together with a Korean *daisu*.

Rikyū's Small Natsume with Paulownia Crest (Kirimon Konatsume; Fig. 34) Prior to Rikyū, *natsume* had been used for thick as well as thin tea. With the spread of *wabi* chanoyu, practices changed, ceramic tea caddies coming into use for thick tea and *natsume* for thin tea, though records of Rikyū's tea gatherings show that he continued to use *natsume* for thick tea on many occasions.

34. Rikyū's small natsume with paulownia crest by Seiami, with Rikyū's cipher inside the lid.

This black-lacquered *natsume* features a paulownia crest in gold *maki-e*—the general term for gold or silver decoration on lacquer—on the lid, which bears Rikyū's calligraphic cipher on the inside. The bottom of the *natsume* carries a needle engraving of the character *sei,* the first character of the name of Rikyū's lacquer craftsman Seiami, whom Hideyoshi honored with the title *tenka ichi,* "first in the realm." *Natsume* of this type, with broad shoulders and a very slight convex curve of the lid, are also known as Seiami-style *natsume*. Other *natsume* types created by Seiami and favored by Rikyū include the so-called large *natsume* and the broad-bottom *natsume*.

Rikyū's Clamshell Incense Container with Raised Chrysanthemum Pattern (Kiku Okiage Hamaguri Kōgō; Pl. 18) A large clamshell has been surfaced inside and out with gold leaf and decorated top and bottom in a relief pattern of white chrysanthemum petals radiating from a yellow center. The inside of the lid was later signed by Ittō. Since "*natsume* with chrysanthemum crest" and "brand new kettle with chrysanthemum crest" are listed in Rikyū's own account of the imperial tea service held in the Kinri Gosho in 1585, this incense container may well date from around that time.

Second-Generation Grand Master
Shōan Sōjun

Mild-mannered Shōan held that the essence of Rikyū's tea lay in the concept of harmony: "Proper decorum in chanoyu follows the motto 'Harmony is nobility.'" Relatively few tea utensils are credited to his name, since he tended to uphold Rikyū's preferences.

35. Shōan's "Compact" chrysanthemum maki-e incense container.

Shōan's "Night Cherry Blossom" Natsume (Yozakura Natsume; Pl. 19) This *natsume*, exemplifying Shōan's chanoyu, is a masterpiece of understatement. What at first glance appears to be a plain black-lacquered *natsume* reveals, in the lamplight of a dim tearoom, a discreet black-on-black design of cherry blossoms. A special technique was used to render the design all but invisible: the flower pattern was painted in black lacquer on a black-lacquer ground and covered with another layer of black lacquer, which was then polished down to an even level. Here Shōan's introspective taste has plumbed *wabi* to the depths.

Shōan's "Compact" Chrysanthemum Maki-e Incense Container (Kiku Maki-e Tokigata Kōgō) Fig. 35) A woman's face-powder compact—and an especially small one, at that—served as the model for this incense container, finished in black lacquer and unobtrusively decorated with gold *maki-e* line drawings of chrysanthemums. The *Chadō Sentei* (Traces of the Way of Tea) describes the piece as "the Shōan-style face-powder compact, black with chrysanthemums in powdered gold outline—three on the cover and a total of seven on the lip and bottom—made by Seiami."

Third-Generation Grand Master
Gempaku Sōtan

Sōtan played a key role in the transmission of Rikyū's chanoyu; without him it is doubtful that the tradition would have survived to the present day. While Rikyū laid the spiritual foundations of tea, Sōtan was responsible for making Rikyū's tea accessible to ordinary people. Even so, discipline was the key to Sōtan's tea; though

Pl. 15. Rikyū's "Shakuhachi" bamboo flower container.

Pl. 16. Rikyū's "Hundred Gatherings" hailstone-pattern kettle by Yojirō.

Pl. 17. Rikyū's bronze "Peach" fresh-water container and matching utensils.

Pl. 18. Rikyū's clamshell incense container with raised chrysanthemum pattern.

Pl. 19. Shōan's "Night Cherry Blossom" natsume.

Pl. 20. Sōtan's bamboo natsume.

Pl. 21. Sōtan's "Peach" incense container.

Pl. 22. Sōtan's "Flower Raft" hearth frame.

Pl. 23. Sensō's "Wayfarer's Pillow" bamboo flower container.

Pl. 24. Sensō's tea bowl "Ancient Sage" by Ōhi Chōzaemon; transparent amber glaze.

Pl. 25. Sensō's "Salt-Maker's Hut" kettle by Miyazaki Kanchi.

Pl. 26. Jōsō's Red Raku broad fresh-water container.

Pl. 27. Red Raku tea bowl "White Cloud" by Rikkansai.

Pl. 28. Chikusō's "Chinese Hat" flower basket.

Pl. 29. Ittō's "Rice-Cake Mortar" fresh-water container.

Pl. 30. Ittō's "Salt Basket" charcoal basket.

Pl. 31. Fukensai's "Coiled Thread" lacquer food-service set.

Pl. 32. Nintokusai's "Ivy" natsume.

Pl. 33. Gengensai's "Feather Cloak" natsume.

Pl. 34. Gengensai's "Brushtip Persimmon" incense container.

Pl. 35. Red Raku tea bowl "Suspended Light Piebald" by Gengensai.

Pl. 36. Yūmyōsai's "Chinese Brush Basket" charcoal baskets.

Pl. 37. Ennōsai's "Yoshino" tea utensil stand.

Pl. 38. Tantansai's "Plum-Blossom Moon" natsume.

one might invite guests, the ultimate purpose of the daily practice of tea was one's own discipline. Sōtan wrote:

> Can this be chanoyu?
> I wonder: when even artlessness
> Becomes artifice,
> The show put on for others
> Shows through.

In another penetrating passage, he observed, "As scholarship follows the ability to learn, so real knowledge comes of putting studies aside and just knowing. We have ears; we can clearly tell when things fall back on practiced effect." This fully accords with Rikyū's statement that "the ultimate meaning lies in that which is not studied," that true accomplishment in tea comes from perfecting one's unique sense of *wabi,* copying no one.

Sōtan's preferences in tea utensils testify to his profound *wabi* aesthetic, which eschewed all ostentation. However, on occasion—probably when offering tea to the emperor Gomizunoo or the empress Tōfukumon'in—he did use a *natsume* with a gold *maki-e* chrysanthemum crest on its lid. On one *natsume* he painted touseled chrysanthemums in vermilion lacquer; on another he used the same vermilion lacquer to write on the lid the poem: "Chanoyu is a taste true to the heart, not to method." After his retirement he made constant use of the "Yūin" *natsume,* an ordinary black-lacquer *natsume*.

Many of Sōtan's lacquer pieces were made by the Chinese immigrant craftsman Hiki Ikkan (1578–1657) using his distinctive *ikkanbari* method of papering over the core form before lacquering, thereby reducing the number of undercoats needed. Other pieces were made by Sōchō and, occasionally, the first-generation Nakamura Sōtetsu in the orthodox manner of applying many coats of lacquer directly to the core form. Among the most *wabi* of Sōtan's lacquer pieces is a papier-mâché *natsume* made (by Sōtan himself) solely of lacquer and paper.

On the principle that nature's works are more *wabi* than any artisan's consciously conceived works, Sōtan occasionally used gourds for flower containers, such as his famous "Bodhidharma" *(Daruma hyō hanaire)* and "Face to the Wall" *(mempeki hyō hanaire)*. Many of his ceramic pieces—tea bowls, fresh-water jars, and flower vases—were of Raku ware, but almost no works by his own hand are to be found.

It should also be noted that Sōtan was the first grand master to take a special interest in smoking sets *(tabakobon)*. Tobacco had entered Japan from Portugal, along with guns, in 1543 via Tanegashima island, south of Kyushu, and in Rikyū's time it was still available only to the uppermost echelons of society. Although Hideyoshi is reported to have smoked, Rikyū himself left no smoking sets. Smoking only became popular in tea circles in the early seventeenth century, when the smoking set was regarded as an amenity to be made available to guests in the waiting room and waiting arbor. The first smoking set thought to have been favored by Sōtan is a rectangular *ikkanbari* tray, provided with a small container of tobacco and a long-stemmed pipe known as a *kiseru*.

36. Sōtan's square kettle.

Sōtan's Bamboo Natsume (Take Natsume; Pl. 20)   This rather large *natsume* is made of two sections of bamboo fitted together and lightly finished in *suri urushi,* or "rubbed-on lacquer." It bears Sōtan's calligraphic cipher inside the lid. Three metal staples were added later to reinforce a crack in the body of the *natsume,* which is a quintessential example of Sōtan's *wabi* taste. The pouch for the tea container is made of beige-colored gold brocade. The box is inscribed by the tea connoisseur Hisada Sōzen.

Sōtan's "Peach" Incense Container (Momo Kōgō; Pl. 21)   The wood grain and tool marks give textural interest to this hand-fashioned, black-lacquered piece by Hiki Ikkan, one of two Sōtan incense containers given to the Jukōin subtemple of Daitokuji. Inside the lid is Sōtan's cipher, as well as the word "Konnichian" in vermilion lacquer, reputedly written by Sensō.

Sōtan also had an *ikkanbari* peach-shaped incense container, lacquered black on the outside and vermilion on the inside and decorated with gold lines tracing the peach cleft, leaves, and a blossom. The depiction of both fruit and blossom alludes to the Chinese legend of the peach tree of immortality in the Taoist Queen Mother of the West's paradise on Mount Penglai, and more particularly to the Noh play *Seiōbo* (Queen Mother of the West), which was a favorite of Sōtan's.

Sōtan's "Flower Raft" Hearth Frame (Hanaikada Robuchi; Pl. 22)   This black-lacquered hearth frame embellished with a "flower raft" motif in vermilion and gold *maki-e* reflects the aristocratic taste of the Kan'ei era (1624–44), when Sōtan was most active. Judging from Nakamura Sōtetsu's box inscription, "Kōdaiji-style *maki-e* 'Flower Raft' hearth frame," the work may have been inspired by the famous raised-lacquer design of a swirling stream, wafting cherry-blossom petals, and rafts on the stairs of the Otamaya (spirit repository) of Kōdaiji temple in eastern Kyoto. The present hearth frame is a copy made by the seventh-generation Nakamura Sōtetsu and signed with Gengensai's cipher. One of the few examples of ornately decorated work among Sōtan's tea objects, this hearth frame may have been made for the empress Tōfukumon'in.

Sōtan's Square Kettle (Yohōgama; Fig. 36) Like Rikyū and Shōan before him, Sōtan was fond of the so-called *yohōgama* style of kettle—kettles of a square shape. It is reported that he even gave Rikyū's square kettle by Yojirō to a principal disciple, Yamada Sōhen, together with one of his own tea scoops.

Sōtan's square kettle, made by Nishimura Dōya (d. 1672) and intended for use with a portable brazier, is smaller than Shōan's and therefore is sometimes called the "small square kettle." The lugs are in the traditional "demon mask" style, and there is a slightly undercut raised lip *(kuri kuchi)* to the round mouth, which is provided with an iron lid and an alternate bronze lid.

Fourth-Generation Grand Master
Sensō Sōshitsu

The chanoyu of Sōtan's youngest son, Sensō, was deeply imbued with the *wabi* flavor of the tea of his father's later years. Most of Sensō's tea utensils were therefore understated in tone, though some more ornate pieces did reflect the general spirit of the times. Now that the nation had entered the peaceful Edo period and the common people had begun to entertain the freer ideas that come with prosperity, there was an almost irresistible trend toward lighter, more colorful designs, though even at the height of the pleasure-loving Genroku era the *wabi* style traditional to the Sen family also proved attractive to many townsfolk.

At this point, that of the separation of the Three Sen Families, three variants were created from the "spinning top" crest *(koma mon)* of the Sen family derived from the "Spinning Top" incense container *(koma kōgō)* presented to Shōan by Hideyoshi. The crest chosen for the Urasenke branch of the family was that of the spinning top viewed from directly above—a spiral. Indeed, Sensō featured spiral designs on many of his tea utensils.

Sensō designed two built-in utensil shelves of note: the "Clamshell" shelf *(hamaguridana)* in the Rikyūdō (Pl. 72) and the "Carpenter's Workbox" shelf *(kugibakodana)* in the Mushikiken (Fig. 93).

Sensō's "Wayfarer's Pillow" Bamboo Flower Container (Tabimakura Take Hanaire; Pl. 23) Every grand master from Rikyū on has made bamboo flower containers. Sensō's rough, even amateurish, touch in hewing this piece with saw and chisel imparts to it an expressive strength and honesty. The name and, in fact, the very concept of the piece stems from pilgrims' traditional practice of hacking off a length of fresh bamboo as a headrest when sleeping by the side of the road.

Sensō's Tea Bowl "Ancient Sage" by Ōhi Chōzaemon (Hijiri Chawan; Pl. 24) Hon'ami Kōetsu was the first man of tea to fashion tea bowls with his own hands. One of the earliest handmade tea bowls in the Urasenke tradition, which seems to owe a debt to Kōetsu's works, was the collaborative effort of Sensō and the Raku potter Chōzaemon, who went to Kanazawa with Sensō and there set up the Ōhi kiln, becoming the first-generation Ōhi Chōzaemon. Glazed in the transparent amber that became the trademark of Ōhi ware, this cylindrical tea bowl resembles a traveler's satchel. Combed markings sweep up under the extended lip, earning the "Ancient Sage" the alternate name "Talkative" *(oshaberi)*.

Sensō's "Salt-maker's Hut" Kettle (Shioyagama; Pl. 25) The first Miyazaki Kanchi made for Sensō such pieces as the "Oak Leaf" kettle *(kashiwagama),* "Whirlpool" kettle *(uzugama),* "Cross" kettle *(jūmonjigama),* "Rice Ball" kettle *(yakimeshigama),* and "Arrow Notch" kettle *(yahazugama).* In compliance with a request from his patron, Lord Maeda Tsunatoshi, Sensō sent Kanchi the design for the "Salt-maker's Hut" kettle in a letter that concedes the technical difficulty of the piece (Fig. 37). The lugs are shaped like miniature salt-drying huts, pierced under the eaves by holes that release thin trails of steam as if from salt-drying fires. For this reason the method for using the kettle is unique: the kettle lid is not left ajar. The cast surface decoration is the repeating "blue wave" *(seigaiha)* pattern with shells, there is a low recess between the shoulder and the raised lip, and the lid is slightly convex.

Sensō's "Flaming Jewel" Incense Container (Hōju Kōgō; Fig. 38) The central motif of this incense container resembles both a stylized rendering of the ball used in a kickball game popular among the Kyoto aristocracy since the Heian period—an auspicious New Year's motif—and the Buddhist flaming jewel, emblem of transcendental wisdom. Sensō probably had this incense container made as a gift to some member of his lord's family. The whereabouts of the original is unknown; this copy was made by the eighth-generation Nakamura Sōtetsu in Gengensai's time. The lacquered body is covered with gold leaf. The center of the lid is raised in a gold flaming-jewel design circled by five traditional treasure motifs in bright colors. The top and bottom halves feature the same pattern. The inside is finished in black lacquer.

Sensō's "Tea Measurer" Natsume (Chagō Natsume; Fig. 39) Unlike his father, Sōtan, Sensō commissioned relatively few *ikkanbari* lacquer pieces. The majority that he did have made were executed by the first-generation Nakamura Sōtetsu or, in the case of earlier pieces, by Seki Sōchō (active 1624–44). This particular tea container, like his "Moon-viewing" *natsume (mochizuki natsume),* is by Sōchō, which means that it probably dates from Sensō's early career. Modeled after the special measuring cups used when filling tea containers with powdered tea, this small *natsume* tapers down to a very small base below two indented bands and has a very shallow "medicine container lid" *(yakkibuta).* Its drawstring pouch was hand-stitched by Sensō's mother, Sōken. The container's small size suggests that it may have been originally conceived as a thick-tea container. There is no signature on the piece, but the pouch bears the inscription "Fabric favored by Sōken, made into a pouch for the 'Tea Measurer.' "

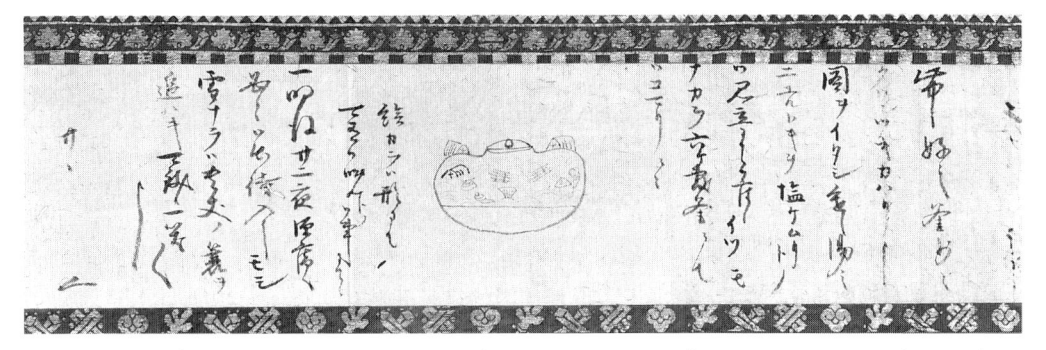

37. Design for Sensō's "Salt-maker's Hut" kettle in a letter from Sensō to Miyazaki Kanchi.

38. Sensō's "Flaming Jewel" incense container.

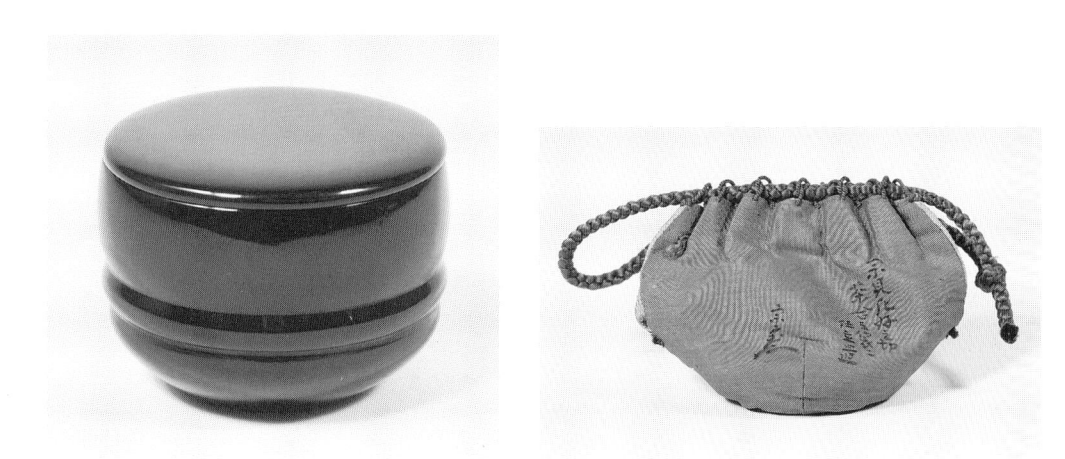

39. Sensō's "Tea Measurer" natsume and the cloth pouch made by his mother, Sōken.

THE MASTER'S TASTE: TEA UTENSILS 61

40. Jōsō's red-topped thin-tea container.

Fifth-Generation Grand Master
Fukyūsai Jōsō

Toward the end of the seventeenth century, the number of tea practitioners suddenly soared, and the services of the Sen family were in great demand. When Sensō died, the twenty-four-year-old Jōsō became Lord Maeda's tea adviser. Soon he also filled a position with the lord of Iyo, in addition to his duties at home in Kyoto. Although his short life ended at the age of thirty-one, he left behind a number of superlative tea utensils.

Jōsō's Red Raku Broad Fresh-Water Container (Aka Hira Mizusashi; Pl. 26)   This shallow fresh-water container by Ichigen, a son of Raku Dōnyū and the first-generation master of the Tamamizu branch kiln, bears Jōsō's cipher low on the side. The lid is finished in simple black lacquer *(kakiawase nuri)*. Jōsō also inscribed the box "Favored by Jōsō Sōan." Another of Jōsō's fresh-water containers is the Red Raku "Boatman" fresh-water container *(funahiki mizusashi)*, inspired by the quaint appearance of the straw raincoat-clad men who used to take boats up the Takase River in Kyoto. This piece exists now only in the form of a copy made by the eleventh-generation Raku potter Keinyū (1817–1902).

Jōsō's Red-topped Thin-Tea Container (Kōaka Chaki; Fig. 40)   This tea container is used whenever Jōsō's paulownia tea-utensil box *(kiri chabako)* and its matching set of utensils is brought out. The container seems to have been designed specially for this tea-utensil box: it is just the right size to fit in the shallow drawer at the bottom of the box. The flat-topped lid is lacquered vermilion inside and out, while the body is lacquered black inside and out. The inside of the lid is signed by Ittō.

41. Jōsō's "Jeweled Orb" kettle.

Jōsō's "Jeweled Orb" Kettle (Manjugama; Fig. 41) Two characters in Jōsō's hand, "jeweled orb" *(manju)*, are cast on the front of this subtly textured kettle. On the back is cast the character *an*, meaning "repose," as well as Jōsō's cipher. The iron lid features a raised loop grip, and the lugs on the shoulders are shaped like low, rounded hills. The box inscription by Gengensai states that the kettle is "an old work by Dōya."

Sixth-Generation Grand Master
Rikkansai Taisō

Rikkansai was still a youth when he assumed a post with Lord Hisamatsu. Since Rikkansai's father, Jōsō, died while Rikkansai was still a child, much of the young master's training in tea came from the sixth-generation Omotesenke grand master, Kakukakusai. Rikkansai's taste was further influenced by considerable contact with wealthy families, chanoyu having attained widespread appeal by the mid-Edo period, so that even within his relatively short lifetime he created a number of fine tea utensils. Among these are the many famous tea bowls made by him in 1726 and fired by the fifth-generation Raku potter Sōnyū (1685–1739). This was a fateful year: called to Edo by Lord Hisamatsu, he never returned. In traveling past Mount Fuji, he applied his gifts of painting and calligraphy for the last time in a landscape of the sacred mountain, prophetically inscribing it "He who falls away like the scattered blossoms."

Rikkansai's Red Raku Tea Bowl "White Cloud" (Hakuun Chawan; Pl. 27) and Unnamed Red Raku Tea Bowl (Fig. 43) Both these tea bowls were made by Rikkansai in

42. Box inscription by Rikkansai for his Red Raku tea bowl "White Cloud."

43. (upper right) Red Raku tea bowl by Rikkansai, unnamed.

44. Rikkansai's lacquered-paper natsume.

1726. The unnamed piece was later given to Ittō by Lord Matsudaira Sadataka of Iyo on the occasion of the one hundred fiftieth anniversary of Rikyū's death. The box inscription by Ittō indicates that this tea bowl was paired with another Sen family treasure, an Old Seto-ware broad-bottomed tea caddy known as "Rock Cleft Roots" (*iwane*).

"White Cloud" features a crescent-shaped area inside the bowl where the glaze is scraped away to reveal the clay body underneath. The piece exhibits a strong angularity; the lip in particular shows a keen awareness of crafting in its brisk trimming strokes. Both works embody Rikkansai's creative powers at their height.

Rikkansai's Lacquered-Paper Natsume (Urushibari Natsume; Fig. 44) Unlike *ikkanbari*, in which paper is glued over a base form before lacquer is applied, in this piece the lacquer itself served as a bond between the paper and the base form. Dark amber in color inside and out from the translucent lacquer known as *shunkei*, it is also called the *hosho*-covered natsume (*hōshobari natsume*) after the heavy paper, known as *hōsho*, with which it is covered. Nintokusai is recorded to have used it as a thick-tea con-

64 CHAPTER THREE

45. *Chikusō's "Cold Cloud"* natsume, *with his inscription inside the lid.*

tainer on the twenty-eighth day of the seventh month of 1825 at a tea function held in the Yūin tearoom to commemorate the centennial of Rikkansai's death and the twenty-fifth anniversary of Fukensai's death. The extant copy is by the seventh-generation Nakamura Sōtetsu.

Seventh-Generation Grand Master
Chikusō Sōken

For three consecutive generations—Jōsō, Rikkansai, and Chikusō—the Urasenke grand masters died extremely young. It was only through the cooperation of the other branches of the Sen family that Urasenke survived.

Chikusō's "Chinese Hat" Flower Basket (Tōjingasa Hanaire; Pl. 28)   Although *Tōjin* actually means "Chinese," the shape of this flower basket is reminiscent of traditional Korean hats—an understandable misnomer, since to most people of the insular Edo period everything from the continent was equally exotic. The basket is woven of wisteria vine with a light-colored bamboo tube set inside, on which Chikusō wrote the character *konomi*, "favored." The box is inscribed "Chikusō's basket flower container" by Ittō, the next Urasenke grand master. Gengensai later created a black-lacquered bentwood tube to set inside the basket, inscribing it:

> The thought of picking flowers
> And arranging them makes the heart
> A field in full blossom.
>
> Tube for Chikusō's "Chinese Basket"

Chikusō's "Cold Cloud" Natsume (Kan'un Natsume; Fig. 45)   A favorite cherry tree of Sōtan's used to stand outside the tearoom Kan'untei. This tree inspired the seventy-three-year-old Sensō to write:

> Time being what it is—
> The blossoms at their peak,
> This aged body of mine;
> Both yet have a moment
> Of spring before falling away.

Chikusō had the third-generation Nakamura Sōtetsu use a withered branch of this cherry tree to create a number of large *natsume* finished outside in dark brown *tamenuri* lacquer and inside in black lacquer. Inside the lid of each, Chikusō wrote "Cold Cloud," while the box bears the number thirty. This may have been the first instance of a grand master having a design produced many times over.

Eighth-Generation Grand Master
Yūgensai Ittō

The fifty-two years of Ittō's life probably represent the peak of popular chanoyu, to judge by the sheer number of practitioners who left records. Although they were not necessarily "tea adepts" *(chanoyusha)* or "tea aesthetes" *(sukisha)*, to borrow Yamanoue Sōji's classifications, or even critics in the true sense of the word, their records do provide a fairly full picture of the tea world of their time.

Ittō himself was apparently quite aware of the special nature of his times and consciously endeavored to shape an era, writing notes on everything from Urasenke manners and procedures to matters of greater cultural import. His career showed a marked shift away from the nonverbal "mind to mind" Zen reticence of previous Urasenke grand masters. But this, too, was a product of the times.

On the other hand, Ittō's collaboration with his brother Joshinsai, the seventh-generation Omotesenke grand master, and the three hundred forty-second and three hundred seventy-ninth Daitokuji abbots, Dairyū Sōjō and Mugaku Sōen, in creating the Seven Special Tea Exercises was a notable attempt to reawaken a sense of tea practice as spiritual training. Unlike former times, when it had gone without saying that Zen was central to tea, in the pleasure-seeking Genroku era the connection of Zen to tea had grown tenuous. An ingenious solution to this problem, the Seven Special Tea Exercises used the paradigm of interactive participation by host and guests to encourage the sense of immediacy, of acting "in the moment," that is at the heart of both Zen and chanoyu.

Ittō's "Rice-Cake Mortar" Fresh-Water Container (Usu Mizusashi; Pl. 29)   Cakes of steamed and pounded glutinous rice are traditionally served on festive occasions in Japan. Originally associated with harvest time, they were eaten in the tenth month as fortification against the rigors of the coming winter. In a court ceremony dating

46. Ittō's tsubotsubo natsume.

from the Heian period, rice cakes were pounded in small wooden mortars to the following chant:

> This Month of No Gods,
> True as the rains do fall,
> I would ask that my wishes
> Be granted, I would ask
> Again and again.

Playing on the last line of this chant, which puns on "pounding" *(tsuku)* and "again and again" *(tsukutsuku),* Ittō called this piece the *tsukutsuku* fresh-water container. According to his inscription on the bottom of the box, which is dated the twenty-seventh day of the ninth month, Meiwa 6 [1769], he received this fresh-water container from the court.

Ittō's "Salt Basket" Charcoal Basket (Shiokago Sumitori; Pl. 30) Ittō's eye for using things in unusual ways led him to make this ordinary basket for gathering sea salt into a charcoal basket. Covered with paper and stained with persimmon tannin to a chestnut hue, then lined with gold leaf, this small basket (19 cm in diameter at the top, 18 cm in diameter at the bottom), with its associations of the seashore, is perfect for the summer season.

Ittō's Tsubotsubo Natsume (Fig. 46) In Ittō's time the design called *tsubotsubo,* derived from auspicious, disk-shaped objects connected with Fushimi Inari Shrine, came to be used as an alternate to the standard "spinning top" crest of the Sen family. The lid of this large Rikyu-style *natsume* is decorated with the *tsubotsubo* pattern in gold.

THE MASTER'S TASTE: TEA UTENSILS   67

The seventh-generation Omotesenke grand master, Joshinsai, also created a *tsubotsubo natsume,* but with the three objects arranged according to the Omotesenke style.

Ninth-Generation Grand Master
Fukensai Sekiō

Fukensai played an active role in preserving the integrity of the Urasenke tradition at a time when the central influence on popular culture was shifting from Kyoto townspeople to Edo merchants. The high point of Fukensai's career was the 1790 commemoration of the bicentennial of Rikyū's death, only two years after a great fire had ravaged the capital. Fukensai represented all three branches of the Sen family, brought together by the hardships caused by the fire, when he paid a formal visit to Jukōin, where Rikyū was buried.

Fukensai's Octagonal Incense Container (Hakkaku Kōgō; Pl. 10) This Awa-ware press-molded incense container, coated inside and out with a transparent blue-green glaze, bears the incised character "affirmation" *(kore)* on the top. Fukensai's box inscription reads, "Noble is the no-mind," an allusion to the famous words of the ninth-century Chinese Zen master Linqi Yixuan: "Noble is the no-mind, but it cannot be fabricated, for it is of itself perfectly ordinary." Fukensai presented this incense container to his Zen master, Daitetsu Sōto, four hundred thirty-first abbot of Daitokuji, who wrote on the box, "Octagonal incense container, made from clay obtained from the garden of Konnichian, character *kore* written by Fukensai, box also signed by him."

Fukensai's "Coiled Thread" Lacquer Food-Service Set (Itome Kaigu; Pl. 31) The *chaji,* or complete tea function, is composed of three main elements: the preparation of the charcoal fire, the offering of a meal, and the sharing of a bowl of tea. For the second element, the *kaiseki* meal, the host needs a complete set of matching lacquerware. Modeled on the formal lacquerware services used in Zen monasteries, the sets are generally made in multiples of five to accommodate the usual five guests at a tea function. For each guest's place setting there is a rice bowl, soup bowl, boiled-food bowl, and broth cup—the stackable "four bowls" *(yotsuwan)*—and a meal tray. In addition to these utensils for each guest, a set includes one rice server with rice ladle and a hot-water pitcher with ladle. There is also the host's serving tray and a side tray.

Fukensai's set features a pattern of thin concentric circles in dark brown *tame nuri* lacquer on most pieces, accenting the black lacquer finish. His inscription on the box dates the wares to 1780.

Fukensai's "Spinning Top" Individual Small Trays (Koma Meimeibon; Fig. 47) On his way home to Kyoto from his post in Edo, Fukensai passed through the mountain town of Hakone, long renowned for its woodcraft. There he bought a round tray, which

47. Fukensai's "Spinning Top" individual small trays.

inspired him, it is said, to commission these from Nakamura Sōtetsu. This set of small trays, lathe-turned top and bottom and finished in dark brown *tame nuri* lacquer and decorative rings of green, red, and yellow, is a copy from the original and was made by the eighth-generation Nakamura Sōtetsu.

Tenth-Generation Grand Master
Nintokusai Hakusō

Nintokusai left fewer tea utensils than his grandfather, Ittō, or his successor, Gengensai, though the pieces that do survive are highly refined in taste.

Nintokusai's "Ivy" Natsume (Tsuta Natsume; Pl. 32) Fashioned of ivy wood, this medium-sized *natsume* by the sixth-generation Nakamura Sōtetsu is lavishly decorated with an ivy-leaf design in gold *maki-e* over black lacquer. The eighth-generation Sōtetsu's records reveal that the piece was extremely costly to make. The inside is finished in translucent brown lacquer, and Nintokusai's cipher appears on the underside of the lid.

Nintokusai's Lacquered Bentwood Fresh-Water Container (Nuri Mage Mizusashi; Fig. 48) Almost exactly the same size as Rikyū's unfinished bentwood fresh-water container, Nintokusai's fresh-water container has decorative groove marks under the dark brown *tame nuri* lacquer of its outer surface. The inside and base are finished in

48. Nintokusai's lacquered bentwood fresh-water container.

49. Nintokusai's "Matsuyama" charcoal basket.

black lacquer. The main structural characteristic of the piece is the attachment of the feet by a method usually associated with the old round trays found in Zen temples.

Nintokusai's "Matsuyama" Charcoal Basket (Matsuyama Kago Sumitori; Fig. 49)
Urasenke grand masters since Jōsō held posts with the Hisamatsu clan of Matsuyama on the island of Shikoku, which is where Nintokusai seems to have found this piece. A rectangular basket woven of light-colored bamboo, the inside is lined with paper and coated in black lacquer. Nintokusai's cipher appears in black lacquer on one outer face. This charcoal basket is more in line with the *wabi* Sen family tradition than is his ornate "Ivy" natsume.

Eleventh-Generation Grand Master
Gengensai Seichū

Generally acknowledged as one of the greatest figures in the history of chanoyu, Gengensai probably had the most markedly individual style of all the Urasenke grand masters, and his writings are distinguished by a unique command of the major issues facing tea in a transitional period. His original thinking and vigorous action to keep chanoyu abreast of the rapid modernization of the years spanning the end of the Edo period and the beginning of the Meiji era revealed him to be a kindred spirit to the tea master Matsudaira Fumai (1751–1818), who wrote, "Those who take no account of the changing times, who plant their feet in one place and never move forward, will remain unaccomplished all their lives."

A prime example of Gengensai's forward-looking approach to tea is his invention of the *ryūrei* table-top service, which raised chanoyu off tatami mats and brought it into Western-style rooms where people sat in chairs. At the time, Gengensai was severely criticized by other schools for "profaning" the Way of Tea. Yet he stood by his penetrating vision, and in time the other schools established table-top tea services of their own. More than a hundred years later, it is amazing to see just how accurately he was able to chart a viable path through difficult times.

Gengensai's "Feather Cloak" Natsume (Hagoromo Natsume; Pl. 33) As indicated by his box inscription, "One of five utensils made of the wood of a pine I saw at Mount Fuji on returning from Lord [Takatsukasa Sukenobu] Yūrin's in the eastern capital," this *natsume* was created in conjunction with four other items: the "Ascending Dragon" (*shōryū*) tea scoop (Fig. 73), the "Pearl Diver's Boat" incense container (*ama obune kōgō*), the "Reed-thatched Boat" censer (*tomaya fune kōro*), and the "Snowflake" censer (*yukiwagata kōro*). All five pieces were made by the eighth-generation Nakamura Sōtetsu. The "Feather Cloak" *natsume* is barrel shaped, with some bark left where the top and bottom halves meet. A particularly fine featherwork pattern in gold *maki-e* trails down over a reddish brown *benitame nuri* lacquer finish. The inside is lacquered black, and the underside of the top half bears Gengensai's cipher and mark of approval in vermilion.

Gengensai's "Brushtip Persimmon" Incense Container (Fudegaki Kōgō; Pl. 34) As indicated by Gengensai's inner-box inscription, "Made from Hitomaro's sacred tree," this is one of four incense containers he had the eighth-generation Nakamura Sōtetsu fashion from a branch of the "Brushtip Persimmon" tree at the Shintō shrine in Akashi, Hyōgo Prefecture, dedicated to the poet Kakinomoto Hitomaro (d. 710?), who became the patron deity of poets. The four incense containers were named "Orchid," "Flowering Plum," "Chrysanthemum," and "Bamboo"—the so-called Four Gentlemen of Chinese literati painting. There is a tasteful balance between the natural bark surface and such crafted features as the pewter rims where the top and bottom halves meet. Both halves of the "Brushtip Persimmon" incense container are finished in reddish brown *benitame nuri* lacquer, with a *maki-e* design of persimmon leaves and fruit on the top. The lid of the inner box bears a poem by Hitomaro in vermilion lacquer.

Gengensai's "Rabbit Lugs" Fresh-Water Container (Usagi-mimi Mizusashi; Fig. 50) Gengensai's box inscription for this unusual piece reads: "Empress Tōfukumon'in's favored Ninsei "Rabbit Lugs" fresh-water container with her hollyhock crest and an inscription by the tea connoisseur Kanamori Sōwa [1584–1656] was presented to Gempaku Sōtan and passed down for generations. The present copy by Raku Kichizaemon [Keinyū] replaces her seal with the *genjikō* seal corresponding to the "Hollyhock" chapter [of the *Tale of Genji*]."

50. Gengensai's "Rabbit Lugs" fresh-water container and the lid of its box, inscribed by Gengensai.

51. Gengensai's box inscription for his Red Raku tea bowl "Suspended Light Piebald."

This copy of the original work by the seventeenth-century potter Nonomura Ninsei was made in 1855, the year of the rabbit in the Chinese twelve-year cycle.

Gengensai's Red Raku Tea Bowl "Suspended Light Piebald" (Kenkōsō Chawan; Pl. 35) Gengensai was justly famous for his handmade tea bowls. This piece is one of sixty Black Raku and Red Raku bowls that he made for his disciples and acquaintances to commemorate his sixtieth birthday in 1870, the year of the horse. The three characters *kenkōsō*, "suspended light piebald," appear in white glaze on the side of the bowl, as does Gengensai's cipher. The box inscription reads (Fig. 51) "Bowl with horse name, made in the spring of my sixtieth year."

72 CHAPTER THREE

52. Yūmyōsai's "Sumiyoshi Shrine" kettle.

Twelfth-Generation Grand Master
Yūmyōsai Jikisō

The years immediately following the Meiji Restoration of 1868 were difficult for the tea world, especially after the government abolished the old fief system and established a new currency in 1871, destroying the tea masters' former economic base. Yūmyōsai found it hard to cope with the sudden changes and retired early, handing the position of Urasenke grand master to his son Ennōsai. For this reason he left relatively few tea utensils.

Yūmyōsai's "Sumiyoshi Shrine" Kettle (Sumiyoshigama; Fig. 52) Matched with a black-finished *mayugata* (eyebrow-shaped) earthenware brazier by Jūsanken Kikkō, this kettle by the first-generation Sasaki Hikobei bears a stylized relief design of Sumiyoshi Shrine in Osaka, two shrine halls depicted on one side and the torii gateway and Taiko Bridge in front of distant hills on the other. Yūmyōsai's cipher and mark of approval are also cast into the piece. The lugs are in the traditional "demon mask" style, and the lid is bronze. The box inscription reads, "Made for the Sumiyoshi Shrine tea presentation, November 1916."

Yūmyōsai's "Chinese Brush Basket" Charcoal Baskets (Tōhitsu Kago Sumitori; Pl. 36) These two charcoal baskets—a smaller one for the summer brazier season nested inside a larger one for the winter hearth season—are of loosely woven light-colored bamboo over a bamboo-husk liner. Yūmyōsai's box inscription reads, "Approved pieces made of Chinese bamboo in the shape of Chinese brush baskets."

53. Ennōsai's "Tortoise Constellation" natsume.

Thirteenth-Generation Grand Master
Ennōsai Tetchū

Ennōsai's career saw the Urasenke tradition reach out to a wider public, especially to women and schoolgirls. Systematization of instruction established a modern basis for the dissemination of tea, and mass production of tea utensils was initiated to meet the increased demand. There were stumbling blocks, of course: some people, for example, newly versed in the Western science of hygiene, objected to the practice of all guests drinking thick tea from the same tea bowl, which prompted Ennōsai to create a new "one bowl each" tea function. Nonetheless, on the whole the promotion of chanoyu proceeded smoothly.

Ennōsai's "Yoshino" Tea Utensil Stand (Yoshinodana; Pl. 37)   This small four-posted stand features a round portal inspired by the famous round "Yoshino window" of a two-mat tearoom in Kōdaiji once favored by the seventeenth-century courtesan Yoshino Tokuko. The slender posts of cedar from the Yoshinoyama mountains are roughly planed, and the side opposite the portal has two interchangeable panel insets—translucent shoji paper for winter and a reed screen for summer.

Ennōsai's "Tortoise Constellation" Natsume (Kizō Natsume; Fig. 53)   This medium-sized black *ikkanbari natsume* bears constellation-like groupings of *maki-e* dots in various colors. The iconography relates to the ancient Chinese geomantic practice of telling fortunes from the patterns on tortoise shells, specifically to the legend of King Yu of Xia, who read a pattern of nine stars on the shell of a magic tortoise that emerged from the Yellow River. Ennōsai's use of ancient lore as a motif results in a highly refined aesthetic expression. This *natsume* was produced in connection with

54. Tantansai's "Autumn Stream" tea utensil stand.

the one-hundred fiftieth anniversary of Ittō's death and is provided with a white silk wrap stamped in black with one of Ittō's names, Yūgen.

Fourteenth-Generation Grand Master
Tantansai Sekisō

Of all the generations of Urasenke grand masters, Ittō, Gengensai, and Tantansai were the most prolific in terms of the tea utensils they left. According to the *Mugen no Fu* (Curriculum of Mugensai [Tantansai]), a catalogue of Tantansai's works, he was responsible for one hundred seventy-three pieces. Tea containers accounted for the greatest number, followed by utensil stands. His first piece was the "Chitose" utensil stand (*Chitosedana*), made to commemorate his own wedding. Most of his pieces are rather understated, yet have a subtle touch of color.

Tantansai's "Autumn Stream" Tea Utensil Stand (Shūsendana; Fig. 54) The empress Teimei was very fond of chanoyu and had the four-and-a-half-mat tearoom Shūsen (Autumn Stream) built in the grounds of the Ōmiya Palace in Kyoto, asking the heads of the various schools to provide tea utensils. This piece was one of several Urasenke contributions. Made by the eleventh-generation Nakamura Sōtetsu, this

55. Tantansai's "Plum-Blossom Moon" natsume.

stand, finished in dark brown *tame nuri* lacquer, has three maple leaf-shaped cutouts in each upright panel and a middle shelf in the shape of a flowing stream. Tantansai's box inscription reads, "Made of lumber left over from the construction of the Shūsen tearoom in the Ōmiya Palace; approved at the beginning of 1931."

Tantansai's "Plum-Blossom Moon" Natsume (Baigetsu Natsume; Pl. 38, Fig. 55) This superlative tea container was inspired by a verse by the Song-period Chinese poet Lin Bu, quoted in the inscription on the lid of the box:

> Brief shadows slant across the shallow stream,
> A dark fragrance drifts past the twilight moon.

The outside of this large *ikkanbari tame nuri natsume* was decorated by the eleventh-generation Nakamura Sōtetsu in black lacquer with the silhouette of an old flowering plum tree, the single branch over the silver *maki-e* moon on the lid rendered in gold *maki-e*.

CHAPTER FOUR

The Master's Touch: Tea Scoops and Scrolls

by Hiroichi Tsutsui

First-Generation Grand Master
Rikyū Sōeki

The making of the figure the world has come to know as Rikyū closely parallels the crystallization of his *wabi* aesthetic. Around the time he was taken on as an adviser in chanoyu by Hideyoshi, he took a major step in the *wabi* direction with the building of the tearoom Taian on the grounds of Myōkian. He exchanged many letters with the temple's head priest, Kōshuku (d. 1594), and in these—especially in the *Yuki no Utairi no Fumi* (Letter with Verses on Snow; Pl. 40), dated the eighteenth day of the twelfth month of 1583—Rikyū revealed a warm and lighthearted side. The verses in the letter read:

> Out viewing the snow
> In ordinary clothes
> I forgot all about the cold
> It looked so wonderfully
> Much like cotton.
>
> It stands to reason:
> Seeing how the snow
> Piles up just like cotton
> Who wouldn't forget the cold
> In ordinary clothes?

For six years, Rikyū basked in Hideyoshi's favor. This came to an abrupt end in 1591, ostensibly over Rikyū's compliance with a request to fund the building of a second story for the Daitokuji temple gate in which his own statue

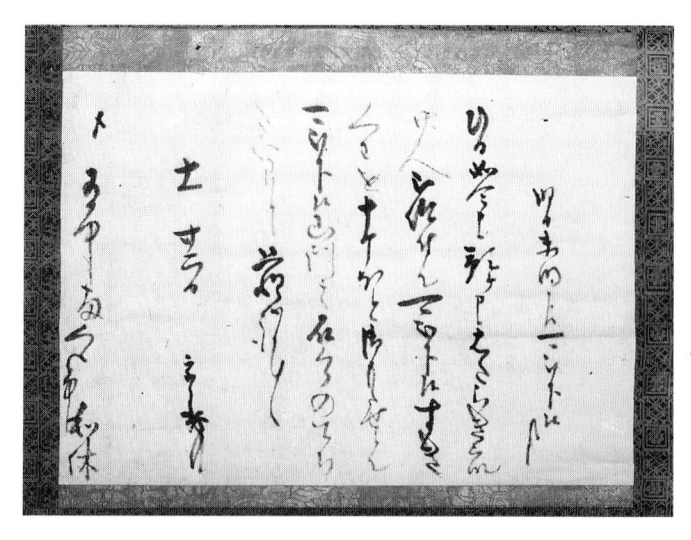

56. Letter from Rikyū to Arima Noriyori concerning the Daitokuji gate. The letter reads in part: "For the time being I would like to request the services of twenty laborers with perhaps ten spades and shovels to help out at the temple gate stoneworks."

was to be installed. Judging from letters, Rikyū's power and connections enabled him to enlist the services of everyone around him for the project (Figs. 56, 143). He was eager to see it finished by the fiftieth anniversary of his father's death. When the gate was completed in 1589, Rikyū's Zen master, Daitokuji abbot Kokei Sōchin, conducted a memorial service for Rikyū's father. It was Kokei, together with the priest Shun'oku Sōen, who "rewarded" Rikyū with the statue that led to his downfall. But despite Rikyū's suicide at Hideyoshi's command, his aesthetic lived on to shape an entire tradition.

The modern scholars Sutemi Horiguchi and Matsunosuke Nishiyama have suggested that just as writings bear the "signature" of the writer's character, tea scoops personally carved by a tea master most concisely embody the master's aesthetic sensibility. This is certainly true in the case of Rikyū, whose tea scoops, along with his bamboo flower containers, are considered to be among his strongest and most revealing pieces.

The standard Rikyū tea scoop is of light-colored bamboo with a thin *fuki urushi*, or "wiped-on lacquer," finish. It is slender overall, with a rounded tip and a deep bowl, and is undercut in an inverted-*V* "pheasant's crotch" *(kijimata)* to form a highly raised "ant's waist" *(arigoshi)*. The node is centrally positioned. The standard length for his tea scoops is twelve and a half woven rows of a tatami mat, or a little less than nineteen centimeters, although the *Nampō Roku* remarks that "overall, Rikyū's [tea scoops] were variously carved so as to match different tea bowls and tea caddies." Rikyū's tea scoops exhibit a freedom of expression that fully takes into consideration the interplay of utensils and the nature of the individual piece of bamboo.

Besides these standard scoops, there are some characterized by flaws in the wood *(mushikui;* literally, "worm-eaten") or by "warping" *(yugami)*, such as the famous asymmetrical tea scoop "Teardrop" *(namida)*. The two scoops illustrated here are

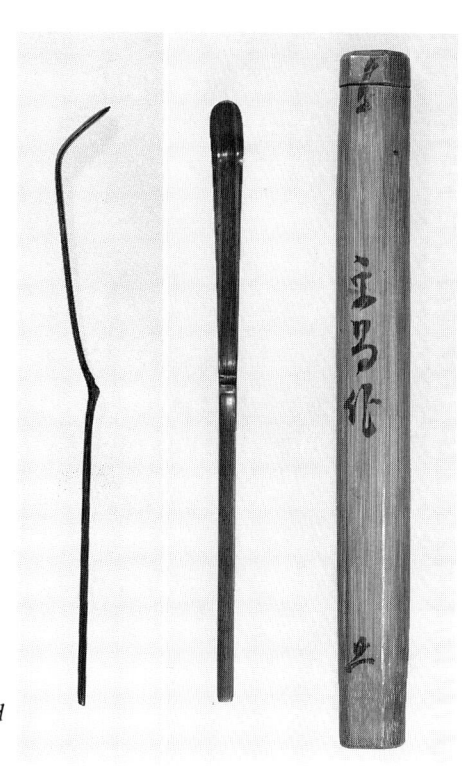

57. *Tea scoop by Rikyū; case inscribed by Sōtan and box inscribed by Ittō.*

of Rikyū's standard type: one with a case inscribed by Sōtan and an alternate case inscribed by Sensō (Pl. 39), the other with a case inscribed by Sōtan and a box inscribed by Ittō (Fig. 57).

Second-Generation Grand Master
Shōan Sōjun

Rikyū once placed two green bamboo kettle-lid rests in front of his sons Dōan and Shōan and asked which of them each preferred. Dōan chose the thicker one with a joint in the middle, Shōan the more slender one with no joint. This anecdote is recorded in the *Kōshin Gegaki* by Sōtan's third son, Sōsa, the fourth grand master of Omotesenke. The anecdote concludes with the words "In Sōeki's [Rikyū's] view, the one without the joint was superior." As symbolized by their selections, Dōan's character was perhaps a little too brusque or direct; Shōan's was quieter and more introspective.

The same was true of the tea scoops of their making. Both patterned their tea scoops after Rikyū's, but Dōan's invariably showed a rugged individuality, while Shōan's were gentler in feeling. The Shōan tea scoop in Plate 42 has a deep bowl and an undercut and raised node but exhibits an overall harmony. Deeply attached to the ways of Rikyū, Shōan worked with his son Sōtan to keep Rikyū's vision alive, as indicated by his transcription of one of Rikyū's farewell verses (Pl. 41) and his letter on a memorial service for Rikyū (Fig. 146).

Third-Generation Grand Master
Gempaku Sōtan

With Sōtan, the Urasenke tradition took a decisive step forward. He created his own brand of *wabi,* one that appealed to many people of culture and influence. The scroll *Eggplants* (Pl. 43) with its clever inscription, painted when Sōtan was nearly seventy, exemplifies the mature taste of his later years. While his close friendship with the multitalented Hon'ami Kōetsu no doubt contributed to his art, Sōtan's *wabi* aesthetic owed most to his deep understanding of Zen. No less than Rikyū himself, Sōtan saw chanoyu as a spiritual path. The scroll bearing the words "A single stream cuts through the dust of this world" (Fig. 58), a verse from the Chinese Zen classic *Pudeng Lu* (Transmission of the Lamp; 1201), bespeaks the earnestness of Sōtan's tea practice.

Sōtan preferred to leave the natural bamboo surface of his tea scoops untouched, unlike Rikyū, who wiped on a light coating of lacquer. The joint is placed midway on the shaft, and on most scoops the skin of the bamboo is left intact below the joint, resulting in a plain, unaffected appearance. Sōtan pared away the left shoulder of the tip because powdered tea is released from that part of the scoop when the host taps the shaft on the lip of the tea bowl. This slight departure from symmetry adds a *wabi* appeal to Sōtan's tea scoops.

Both Sōtan tea scoops illustrated—"Opening the Tea Leaf Jar" (*kuchikiri;* Pl. 44) and "Higaki," the latter named after a Noh play (Fig. 59)—are highly representative of this style. In Sōtan's time it became the accepted practice for grand masters to provide each scoop with a bamboo case signed and inscribed with a poetic name, the tube and its wooden plug "sealed" with an *x*-like mark in ink. The names of many of Sōtan's tea scoops are inspired by Noh plays or famous Zen aphorisms; this reflected his erudition, brought a literary air into the tearoom, and encouraged later tea masters to express freely their personal background through the poetic names they chose for the tea scoops they carved.

Fourth-Generation Grand Master
Sensō Sōshitsu

Sensō's tea scoop "Homecoming" (*satogaeri;* Pl. 46) was made from bamboo he found on his way back to Kyoto from an extended stay at his post in Kaga. Believed to have been carved from start to finish in one sitting—unlike some tea scoops, which were roughly carved by other hands before the master finished them—the silhouette

Pl. 39. *Tea scoop by Rikyū; case inscribed by Sōtan; alternate case inscribed by Sensō.*

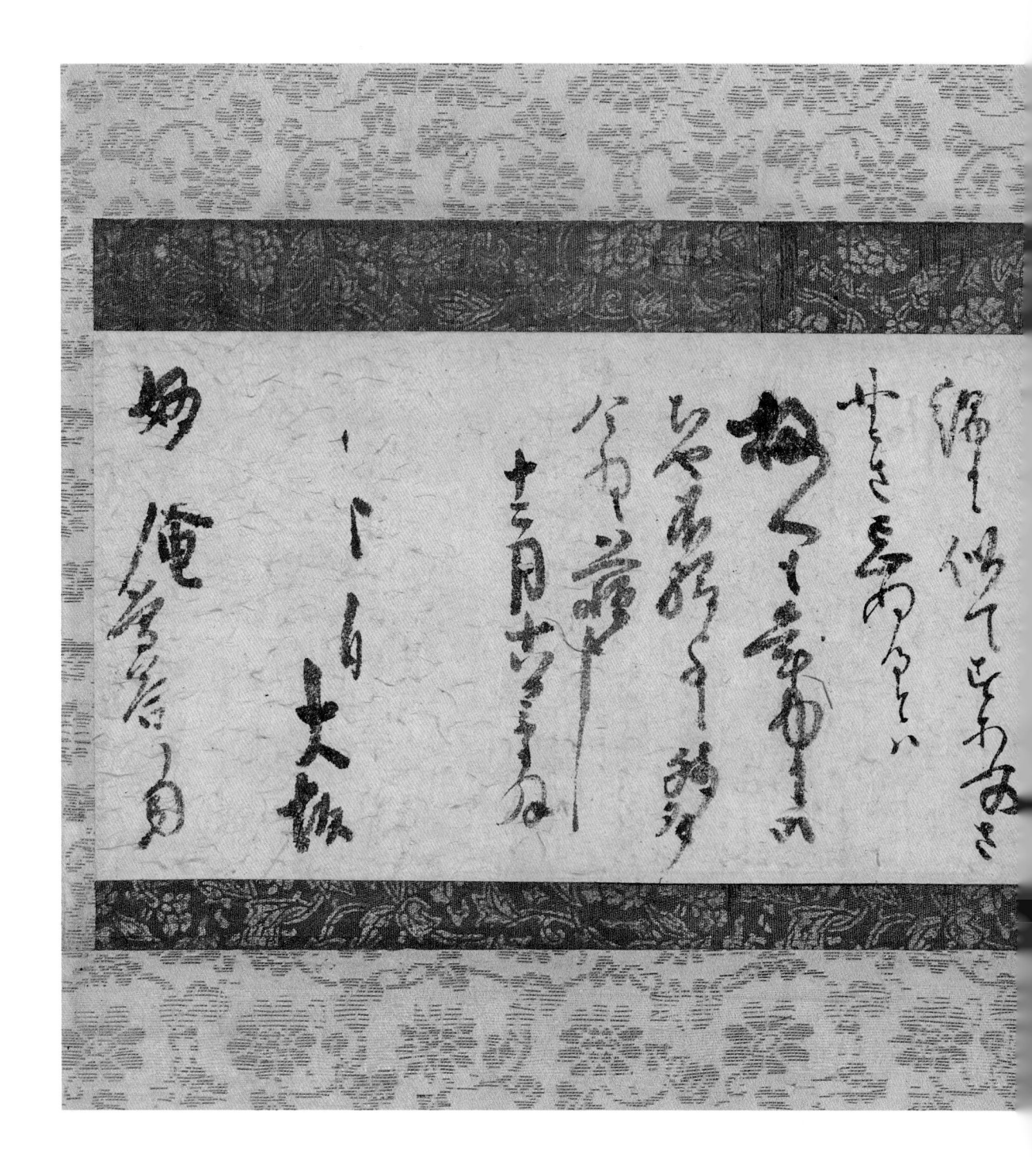

源氏供御うちあき
せきをあけられては
おくり参らせ申
候也かしく
十月廿三日
とり大切
女房参る

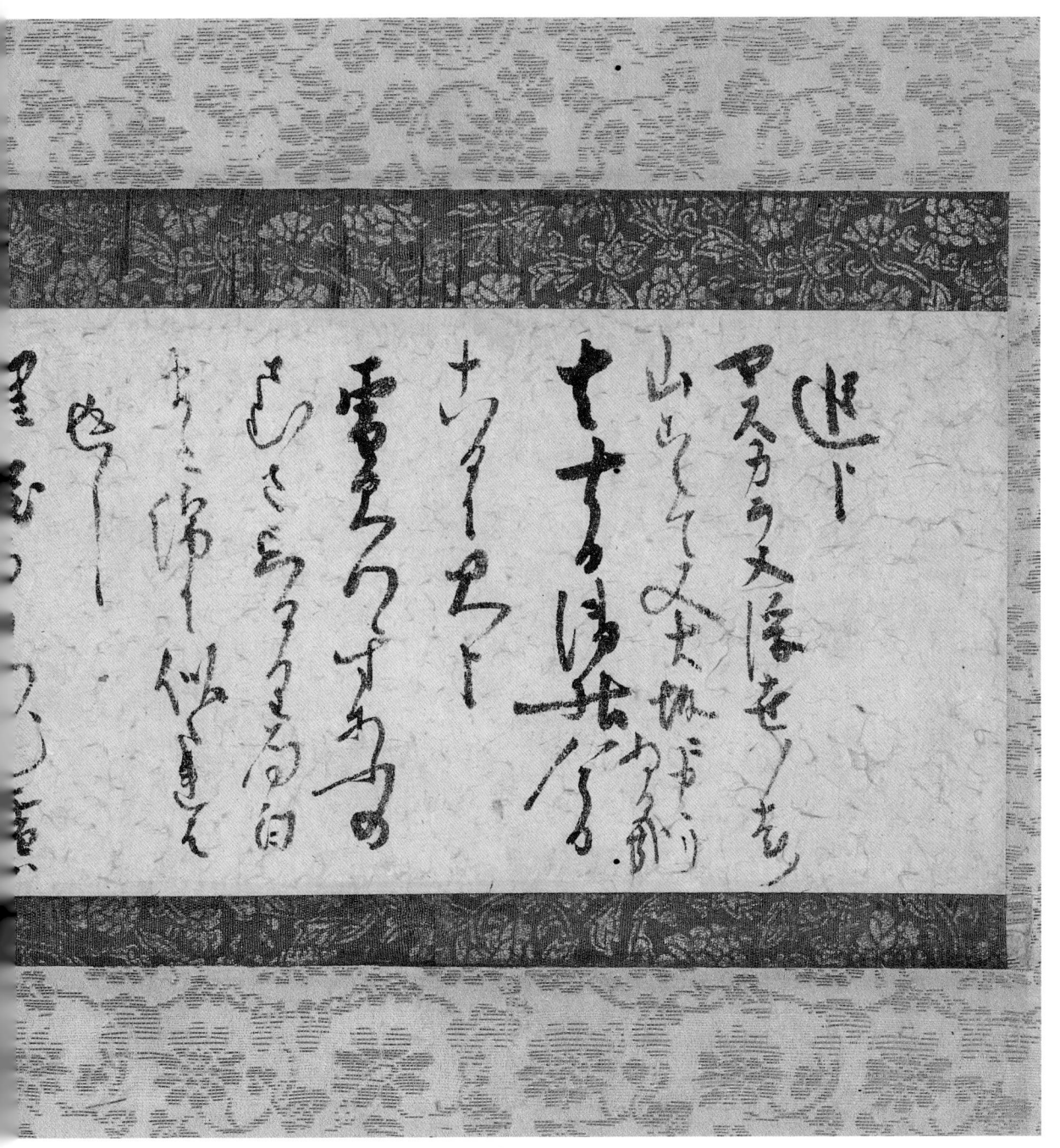

Pl. 40. Rikyū's Yuki no Utairi no Fumi.

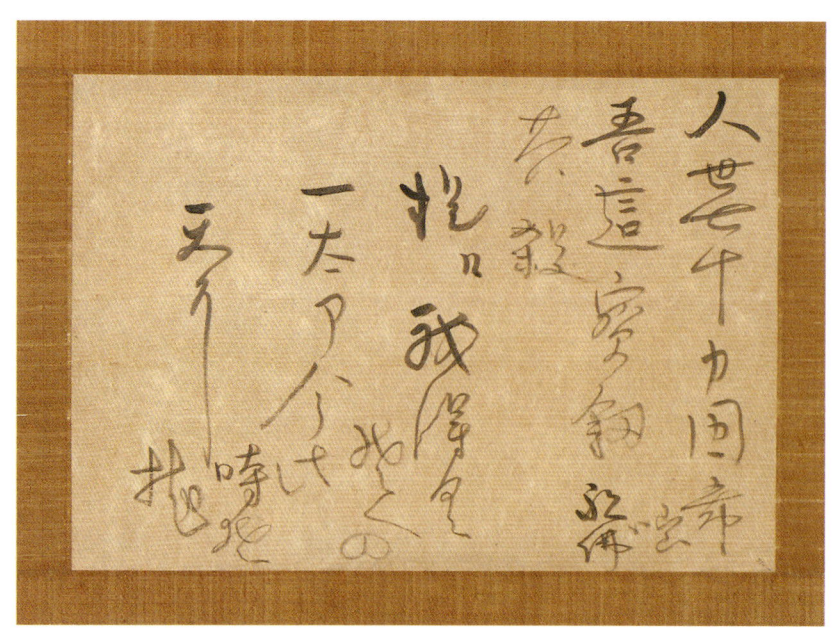

Pl. 41. One of Rikyū's farewell verses, transcribed by Shōan.

Pl. 42. Tea scoop by Shōan; case inscribed by sixth-generation Omotesenke grand master Kakukakusai; box inscribed by Rikkansai.

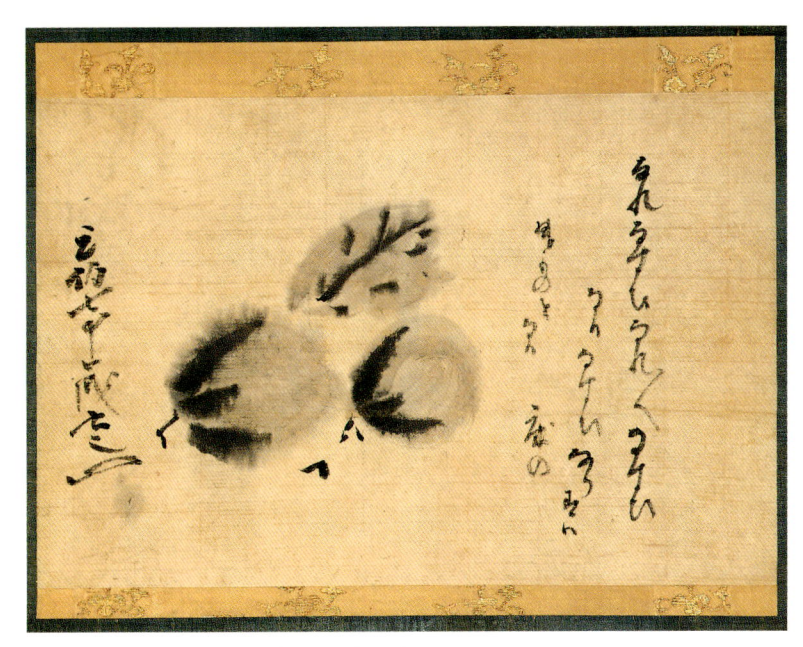

Pl. 43. Eggplants by Sōtan.

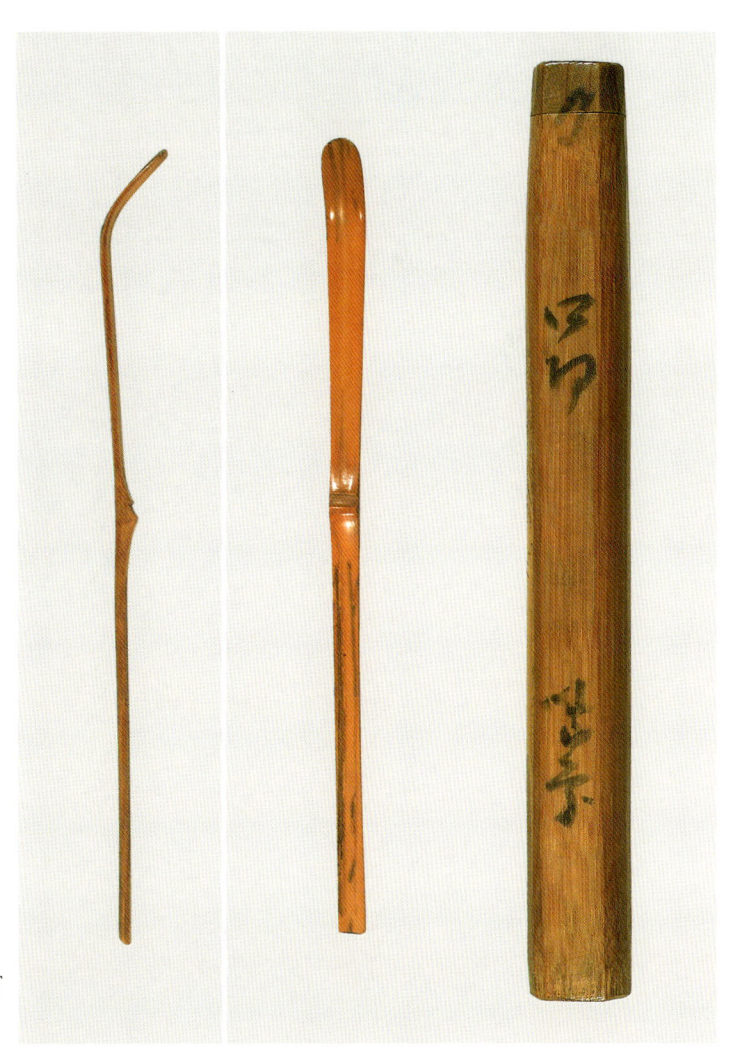

Pl. 44. Tea scoop "Opening the Tea Leaf Jar" by Sōtan; case inscribed by Sōtan.

Pl. 45. Camellia *by Sensō.*

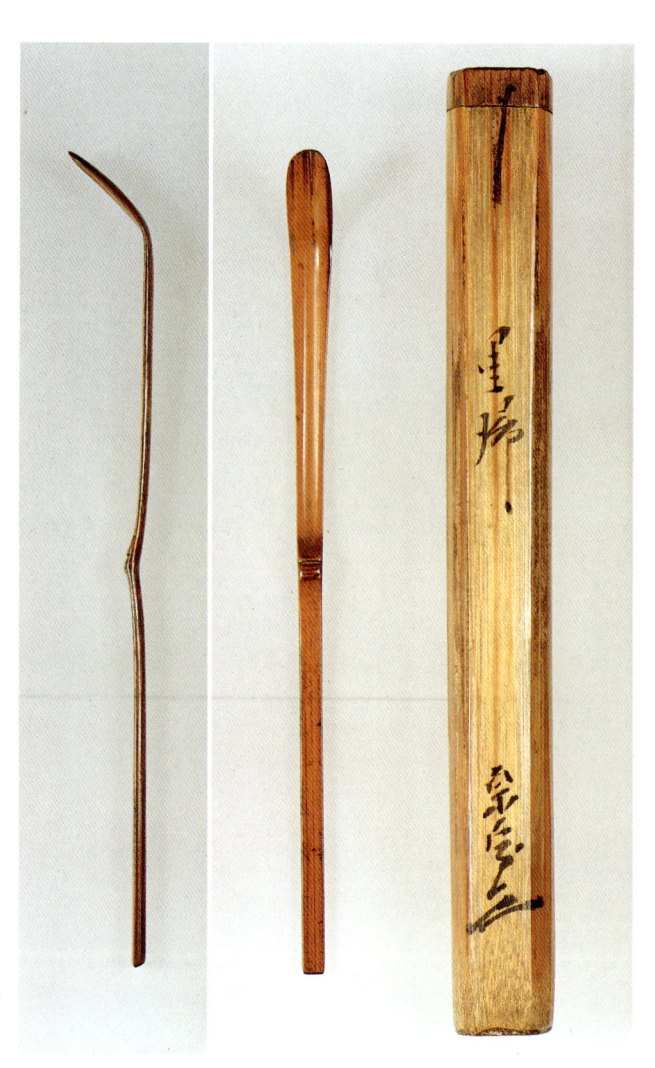

Pl. 46. Tea scoop "Homecoming" *by Sensō; case inscribed by Sensō.*

Pl. 47. Raven in the Cold by Jōsō.

Pl. 48. Tea scoop "Spreading Fortune" by Jōsō; case inscribed by Jōsō.

Pl. 49. Girls' Day Dolls by Rikkansai.

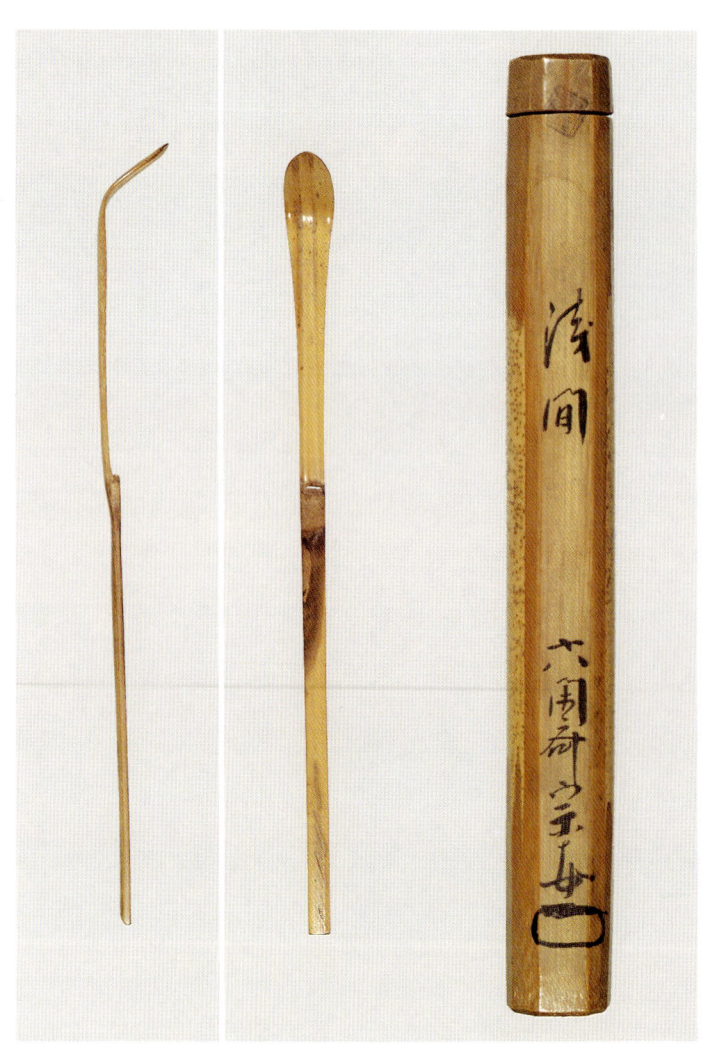

Pl. 50. Tea scoop "Mount Asama" by Rikkansai; case inscribed by Rikkansai.

Pl. 51. Calligraphy by Chikusō, reading "Scooping up water, the moon in your hands"; box inscribed by Gengensai.

Pl. 52. Tea scoop "Crane in Rice Field" by Chikusō; case inscribed by Chikusō.

Pl. 53. Calligraphy by Ittō, reading "Crane at dawn."

Pl. 54. Ittō's chrysanthemum and paulownia maki-e tea scoop; case inscribed by Nintokusai.

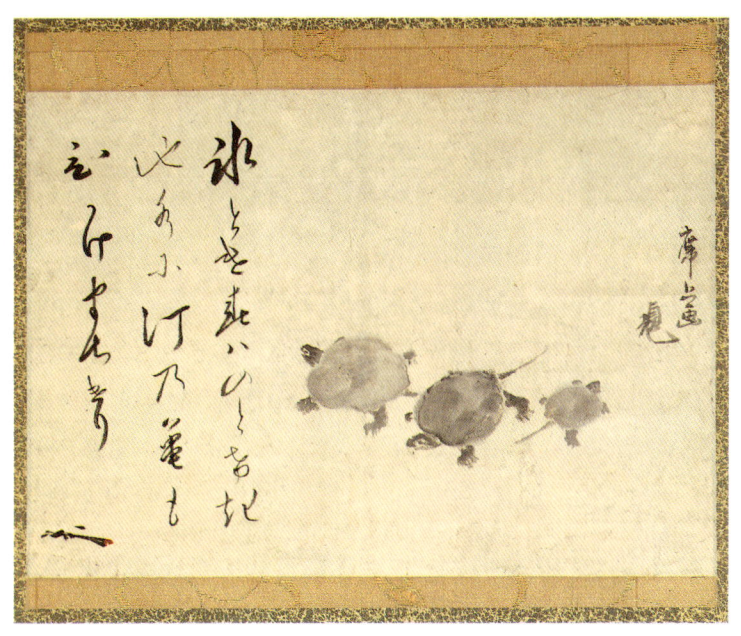

Pl. 55. Turtles by Tosa Mitsusada; inscription by Fukensai.

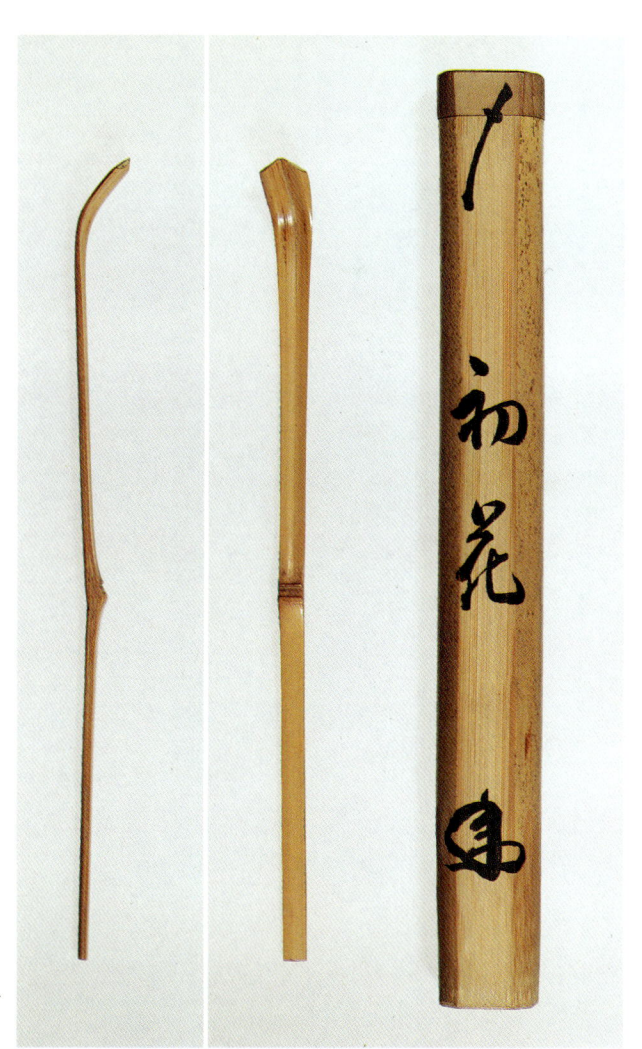

Pl. 56. Tea scoop "First Blossom" by Fukensai; case inscribed by Fukensai.

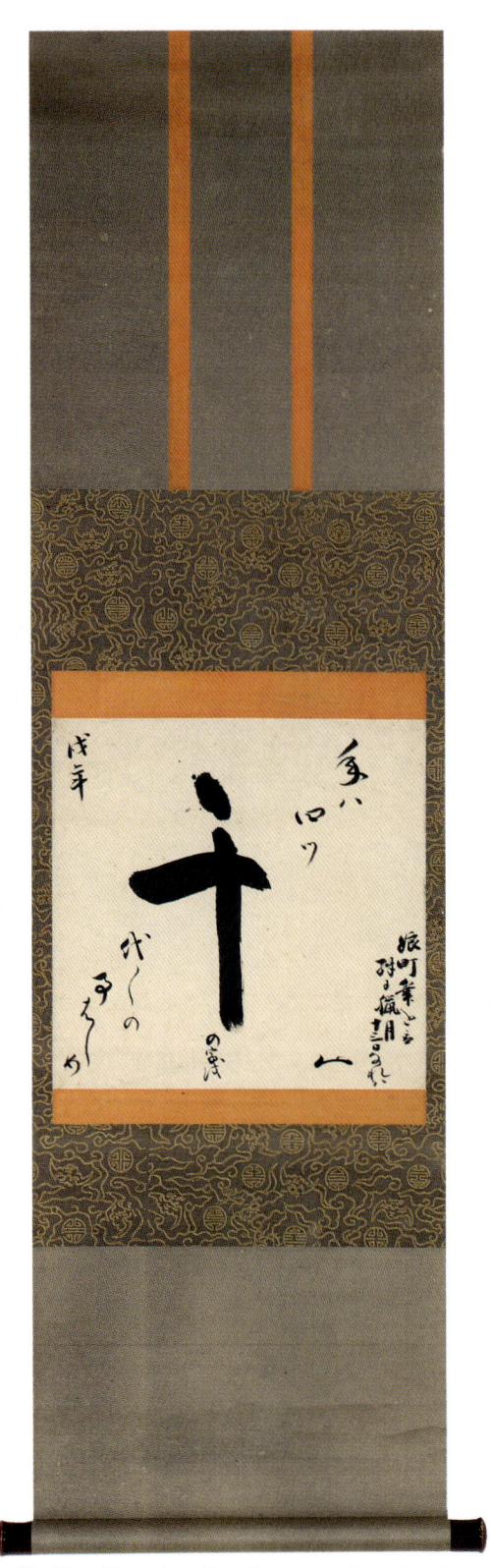

Pl. 57. Verse by Nintokusai on his daughter Machiko's writing of the character *sen*.

Pl. 58. Tea scoop "Fukurokuju" by Nintokusai; case inscribed by Nintokusai.

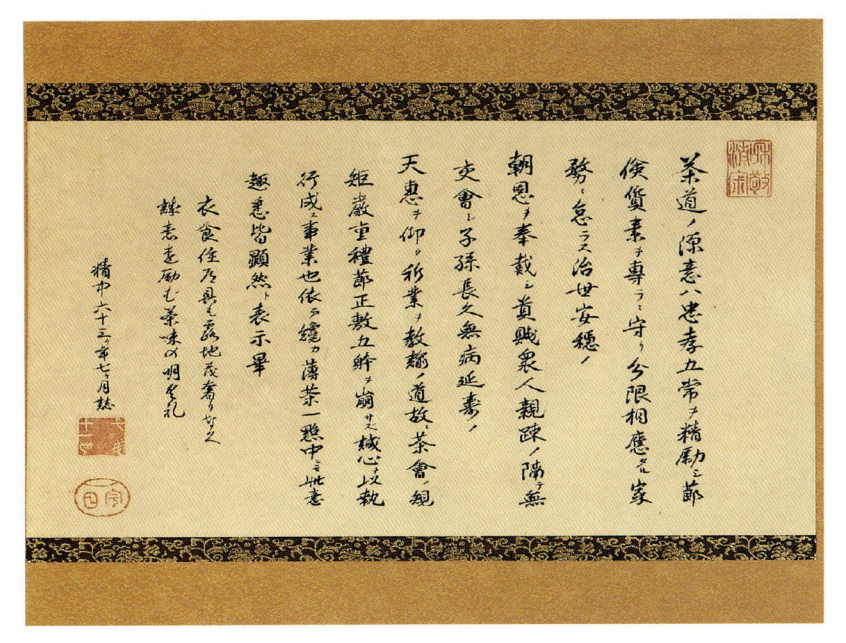

Pl. 59. Chadō no Gen'i *by Gengensai.*

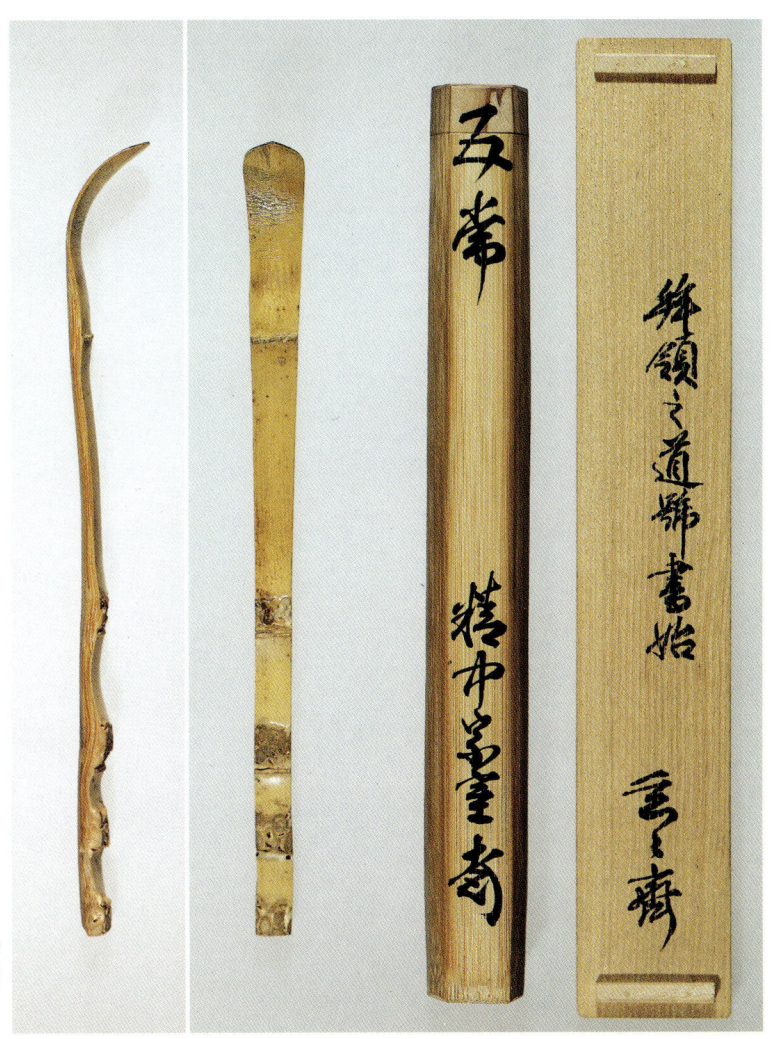

Pl. 60. Tea scoop "Five Constant Virtues" *by Gengensai; case inscribed by Gengensai.*

Pl. 61. Calligraphy by Yūmyōsai, reading "A crane alights on a thousand-year-old tree."

Pl. 62. Tea scoop "Ant Hole" by Yūmyōsai; case inscribed by Yūmyōsai.

Pl. 63. Calligraphy by Ennōsai, reading "Sitting 'neath the blossoms, rapt in the moon."

Pl. 64. Tea scoop "Great Rectitude" by Ennōsai; case inscribed by Ennōsai.

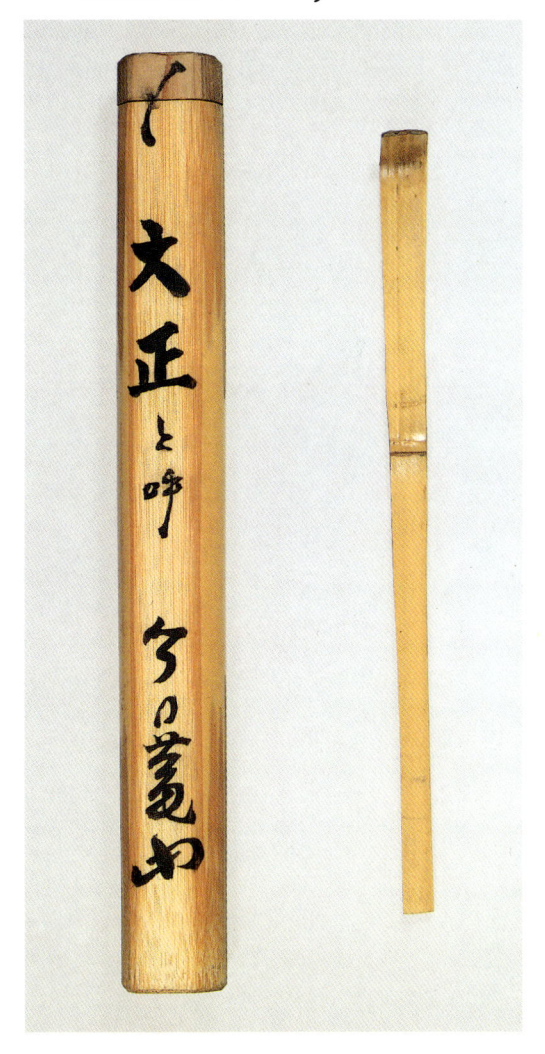

Pl. 65. Calligraphy by Tantansai, reading "Give thanks for tea."

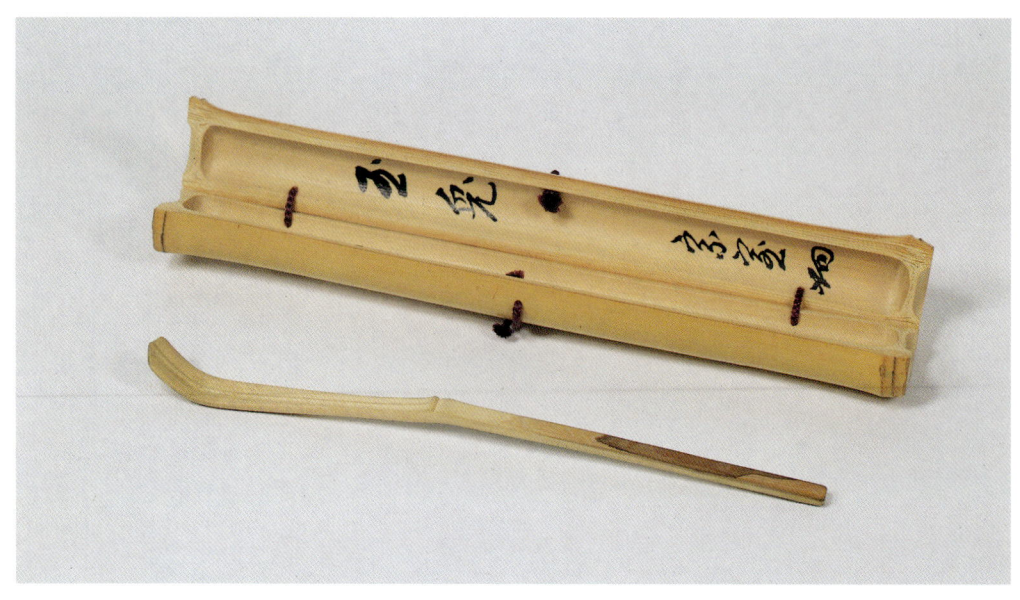

Pl. 66. Tea scoop "Jeweled Hare" by Tantansai; case inscribed by Tantansai.

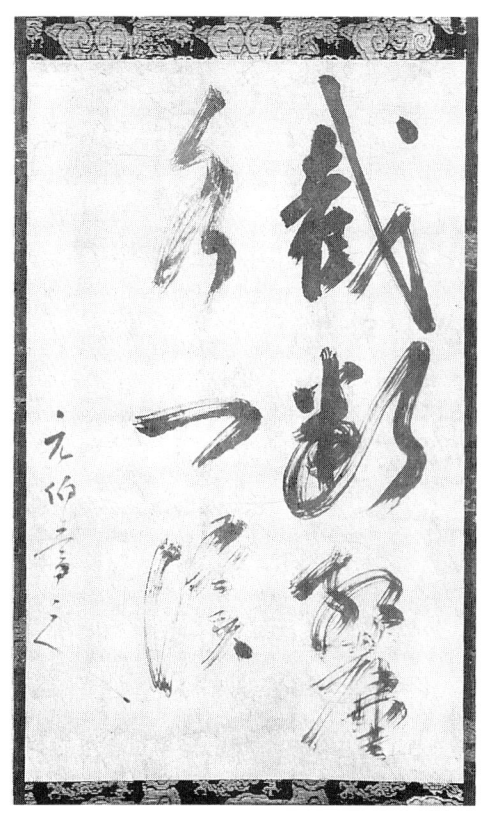

58. Calligraphy by Sōtan, reading "A single stream cuts through the dust of this world."

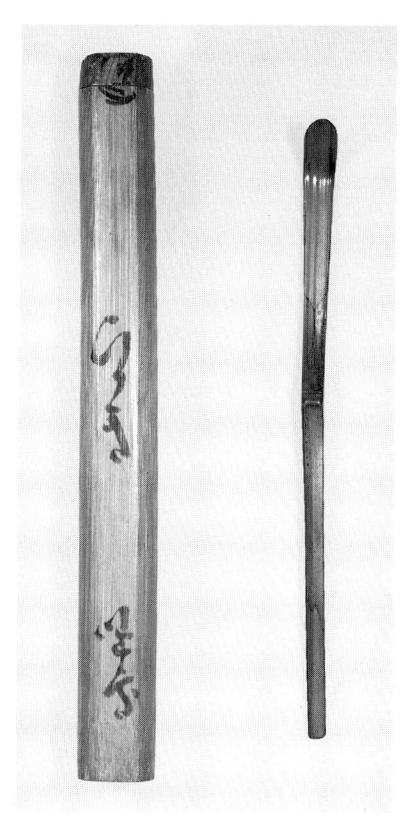

59. Tea scoop "Higaki" by Sōtan.

tapers to a straight, narrow shaft below the joint, the tip is bent sharply upward, and the raised joint is undercarved, with Sensō's customary knife marks in evidence. The shaft gradually increases in thickness toward the base, imbuing the piece with a distinctive charm and propriety.

The same sensibility informs Sensō's tea scoop "Nestled Rice Fields" (taori; Fig. 60), though the piece itself is somewhat smaller. As with almost all Sensō's bamboo cases for his tea scoops, the style of the case approaches that of the formal *shin* type, with most of the outer bamboo skin pared away, while the inscription is in light ink. Other tea scoops by Sensō include "Bedtime Story" (nemonogatari), "One Laugh" (isshō), and "Fishing Pole" (tsurizao); indeed, most of his tea scoops have names. Most were made from bamboo he found on his frequent travels and bear two or three knife notches under the joint.

Sensō's scrolls also embody a keen and sensitive artistry, such as his masterful monochrome ink-wash painting *Gourds* (Fig. 61) and his *Camellia* (Pl. 45), painted in light colors and bearing a witty inscription:

THE MASTER'S TOUCH: TEA SCOOPS AND SCROLLS

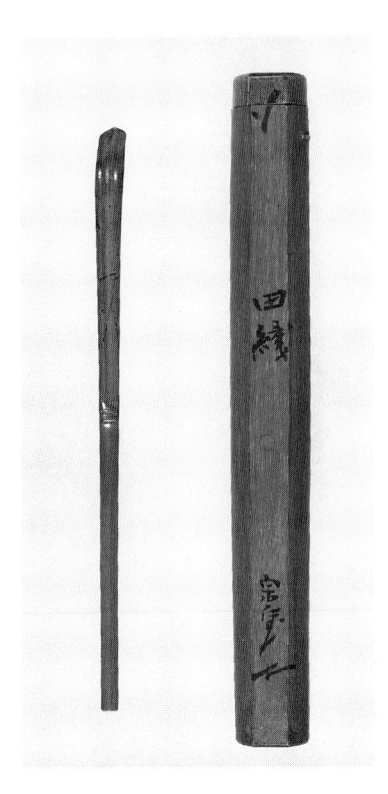

60. Tea scoop "Nestled Rice Fields" by Sensō; case inscribed by Sensō.

61. Gourds by Sensō.

> Commanded, "Paint!"
> I would hardly think this
> Resembles a flower:
> The camellia blushes red,
> But so surely does my face!

On a more serious note, Sensō wrote a brief summation of his understanding of Rikyū's tea, titled *Rikyū Chanoyu Hon'i* (The Basic Idea of Rikyū's Tea), addressed to a certain Nishio Tōkurō. The document is dated the twentieth day of the sixth month of 1694. Here Sensō revealed his awareness of the need to preserve the authentic heritage of Rikyū at a time when the more elaborate warrior-class tea practice was greatly popular. Sensō's text reads:

> The basic idea behind Rikyū's style of chanoyu is that it is best to view chanoyu on the level of daily life. Even in matters of tea utensils and procedures, it comes down to a matter of simply preferring what is fitting and shunning what is ill suited. Then it is understood that [chanoyu] is to be conducted wholly without sound and without special fragrances. When chanoyu is done from the heart, the preparation of tea and the use of all the utensils becomes a lifelong pleasure. Thus, to abide in chanoyu conforms to the Five Constant Virtues, occasionally

62. Calligraphy by Jōsō, reading "Zen in one taste."

with some additional reasoning in the background. It is these thought-out elements that allow room for improvement with training, so that there is no one in all of society who would not benefit from the study [of tea]. The pleasure it brings is inexpressible.

Fifth-Generation Grand Master
Fukyūsai Jōsō

Calling himself by the Buddhist name Sōan during his brief seven years as Urasenke grand master, Jōsō is remembered for the remarkable maturity of his taste, exemplified in the sure hand of his calligraphic scroll reading "Zen in one taste" (Fig. 62) and his scroll *Raven in the Cold* (Pl. 47). The latter evokes *haiga* painting, a combination of painting and poetry popular among haiku poets of the mid-Edo period, in its spontaneous brushwork of a lone crow in flight and its verse:

> Face turned skyward,
> Gazing at the clouds,
> Cold to the tail end.

To judge from the accompanying letter to an unnamed Buddhist priest of high rank (Fig. 63), Jōsō's tea scoop "One Thousand Autumns, Ten Thousand Years" (*senshū banzai*; Fig. 64) was made as a token of thanks for an introduction to Lord Hisamatsu Sadanao of Matsuyama, who then employed Jōsō as a tea instructor: "I cannot deliver this in person, since I have been summoned by Lord Matsudaira [Hisamatsu] of Sanuki, . . . but I wanted to send you something as a token of my happiness. Hence I am giving you this tea scoop, inscribed in celebration of the improvement in my fortunes. I owe this joy to you."

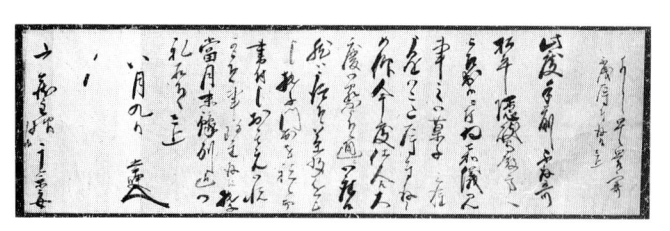

63. Letter by Jōsō accompanying the tea scoop "One Thousand Autumns, Ten Thousand Years."

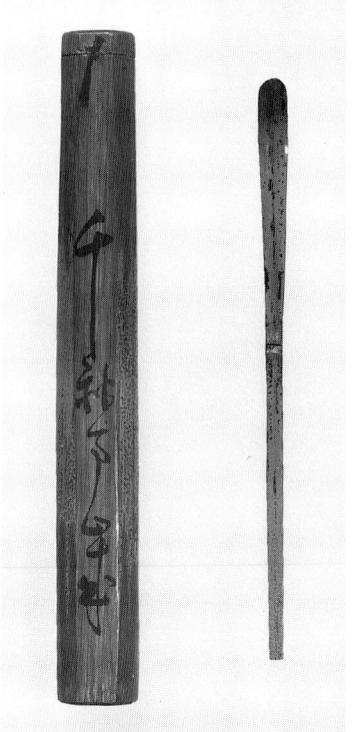

64. Tea scoop "One Thousand Autumns, Ten Thousand Years" by Jōsō.

In an inscription on the box containing this letter, eleventh-generation Urasenke grand master Gengensai identified the priest as the one hundred ninety-first abbot of Daitokuji, Tenshitsu Sōjiku, although this priest actually died in 1667, before Jōsō was even born. The tea scoop itself is made of spotted "sesame bamboo" (*goma take*) and displays only minimal shaping.

Another tea scoop, "Spreading Fortune" (*suehiro*; Pl. 48), is made of plain light-colored bamboo. The tip is bent slightly to the left, there is the barest hint of curvature under the joint, and there is a decisive cutoff at the base of the shaft. The smooth bamboo skin is sharply scraped away from the joint to about midway down the lower part of the shaft, providing a textural accent, while the tip bends up in a very gentle curve. The spareness of both tea scoops attests to Jōsō's *wabi* sensibility.

Sixth-Generation Grand Master
Rikkansai Taisō

Although Rikkansai left a large number of distinctive tea utensils during his twenty-two years as Urasenke grand master, little is known about the man. His works display a sense of self-fulfillment, however, as if his life, though a brief thirty-two years,

65. Calligraphy by Rikkansai, reading "Old Zen abbot, snow-roofed abbot's quarters."

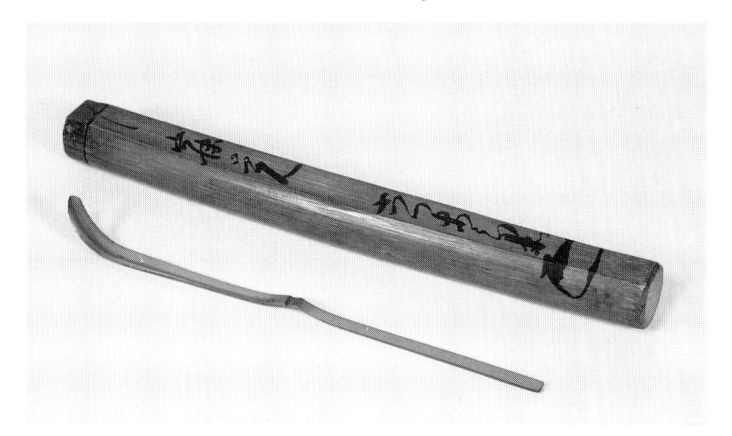

66. Tea scoop "Awakened from Sleep" by Rikkansai; case inscribed by Rikkansai.

was a full one. In his calligraphy scroll reading "Old Zen abbot, snow-roofed abbot's quarters" (Fig. 65), dated the winter of 1725, the year before his death, and signed "From the dreamer Rikkansai," one can almost see the deeply enlightened aged Zen priest as a vision of Rikkansai himself, so commanding is the brushwork.

Other works reveal a lighter side. Behind the delightful scroll *Girls' Day Dolls* (Pl. 49) is the smiling face of Rikkansai, father of two daughters. Another scroll, *Pine Tree,* celebrates the sixtieth birthday of his patron, Lord Hisamatsu of Matsuyama, with a clever verse playing on the word *matsu,* "pine," a component of the names Hisamatsu and Matsuyama:

> A thousand years on
> Awaiting *(matsu)* the spring
> Pines *(matsu)* the world over.

Rikkansai traveled frequently to Edo. His tea scoops "Mount Asama" (Asama; Pl. 50) and "Awakened from Sleep" *(nezame;* Fig. 66) reflect his experiences on

THE MASTER'S TOUCH: TEA SCOOPS AND SCROLLS

the road. The former, named after a famous volcano along the Nakasendō, a highway through the mountains linking Edo and Kyoto, is a particularly pleasing piece: dark markings marble the surface from the joint partway down the left side of the shaft, while the scoop end flares out in a lotus-petal shape, with a clean bend up to a pointed tip. A highly sophisticated eye for counterpoint and balance is manifest in the combination of straight lines and curves, in the positioning of the joint, and in the interplay between the right-slanted knife marks near the base of the shaft and the cutoff at the base. The other scoop illustrated is closer to the classic style of Rikyū; it has a deep crease running the length of the scoop, a slender body, and a deeply undercut, raised joint, although the tip is pointed. This pointed tip is generally acknowledged to have set the precedent for what was to become the standard Urasenke style of pointed tea scoops.

Seventh-Generation Grand Master
Chikusō Sōken

Chikusō's calligraphy scroll reading "Scooping up water, the moon in your hands" (Pl. 51) represents a bit of Urasenke history in itself. Gengensai's box inscription tells the story of how this scroll figured in Sen family tradition:

> When the younger brother of Hakusō [Nintokusai] was adopted into Kankyūan [Mushanokōjisenke] and became Kōkōsai [the sixth grand master of Mushanokōjisenke], he asked Nintokusai whether, since Kankyūan did not have the Seven Special Tea Exercises, Nintokusai could make a present of the procedures for the *kagetsu* [flower moon] tea exercise. Nintokusai agreed immediately and presented Kōkōsai with this piece, a one-line calligraphy scroll by Chikusō. This inspired Nintokusai to carve a tea scoop. Naming it "Playing with Flowers, the Scent Fills Our Robes" [*hana o rōshi kaori koromo ni mitsu*], Nintokusai sent him on his way with it as a sign of the entrusting of the *kagetsu* exercise—or so it has come down to me.*

Chikusō's tea scoop "Crane in Rice Field" *(tazuru;* Pl. 52), made of light-colored sesame bamboo, features a joint somewhat closer to the tip than usual and shifted slightly to the right, and a dramatic scrape through the spotted skin from the left side of the shaft just below the joint all the way to the base. The slightly pointed tip shows Rikkansai's influence. The entire piece evokes the image of a standing crane, hence the name. For a young man like Chikusō, who died at the age of only twenty-four, the piece is exceedingly well conceived and executed.

---

* In the *kagetsu* ("flower and moon") tea exercise, the host and four guests exchange roles by drawing lots from a set bearing various nature motifs.

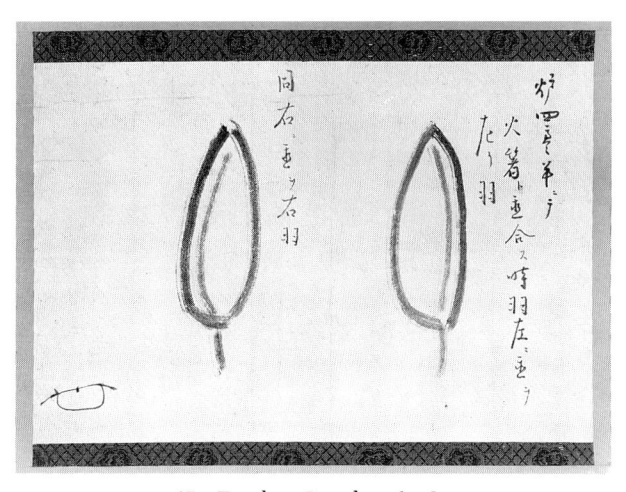

67. Feather Brushes *by Ittō*.

Eighth-Generation Grand Master
Yūgensai Ittō

Ittō is remembered as the Urasenke grand master who codified the various procedures passed down since Rikyū's time for preparing tea and handling tea utensils, in order to meet the demands of the rapidly growing number of tea devotees. These procedures were compiled in the invaluable texts *Chadō Hama no Masago* and *Yūgen Yawa* (Night Talks of Yūgensai [Ittō]).

Among the pages not includes in these books is *Feather Brushes* (Fig. 67), which may have been painted with the intention of mounting it as a scroll. On the painting is a commentary on the feather brush's proper use: "When set down together with fire chopsticks in a four-and-a-half-mat room with a hearth, [a feather brush] that faces left is to be placed to the left; one that faces right is placed to the right." As with Jōsō, Rikkansai, and Chikusō before him, Ittō's calligraphy conveys a striking sense of control. Another fine example of his hand is the calligraphy scroll reading "Crane at dawn" (Pl. 53).

Ittō's taste also reveals a certain aspiration toward the aristocratic, perhaps due to the lingering influence of Genroku splendor. This is clearly visible in his tea scoops. One tea scoop, named after Ariwara Narihira (825–80), one of the so-called Six Immortal Poets, is thick overall and has a deep trough running up to a broad triangular scoop (Fig. 68). A singularly impressive piece, it was made as one of a set of six and comes with an extra tea scoop in a case inscribed with this famous verse by Narihira:

> Is this not the moon?
> Is this spring not the spring

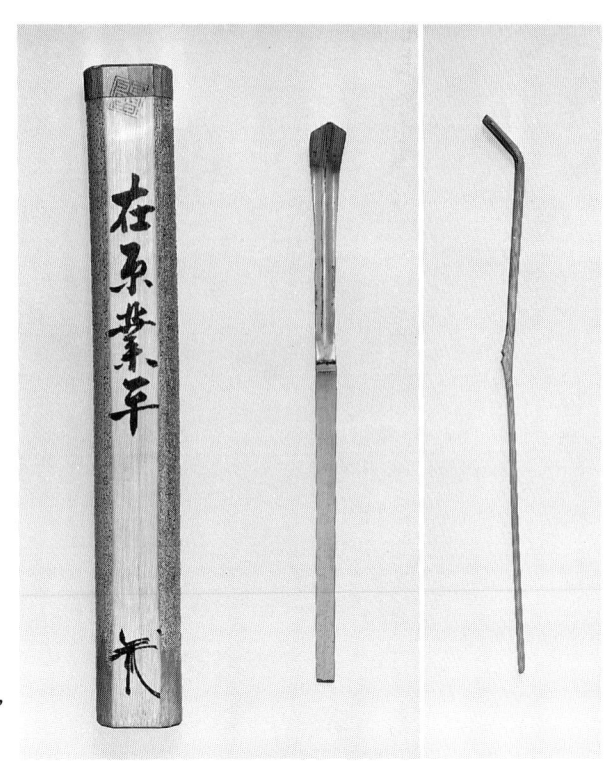

68. Tea scoop "Ariwara Narihira" by Ittō; case inscribed by Itto.

> Of years past?
> Would only that I myself
> Were the same self I was.

An even more formal tea scoop, attesting to Ittō's association with warrior-class families and feudal lords, is the chrysanthemum and paulownia *maki-e* tea scoop he favored (Pl. 54), a slim, unjointed, black-lacquered piece bearing two aristocratic crests—a gold paulownia crest inside the scoop and a gold chrysanthemum crest on its back. Nintokusai inscribed the case "Chrysanthemum and paulownia *maki-e* tea scoop favored by Grandfather."

Ninth-Generation Grand Master
Fukensai Sekiō

In 1758, at a memorial tea function observed by both Urasenke and Omotesenke on the centennial of Sōtan's death, the scroll in the tokonoma was Sōtan's farewell verse, the tea bowl a Raku Chōjirō piece called "Taken by Force" *(muritori)*, the tea scoop one by Sōtan, and the flower container a bamboo piece named "Master

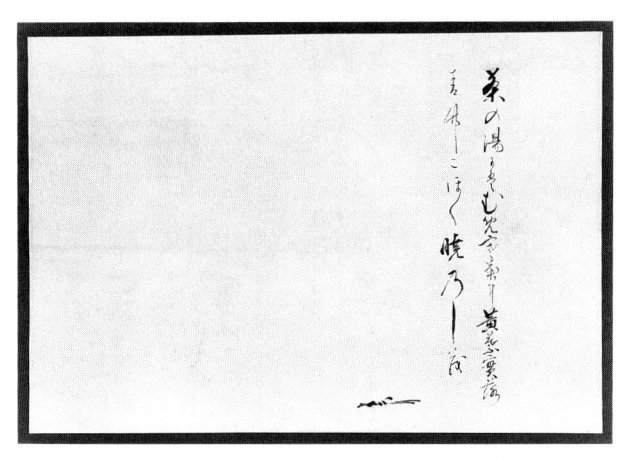

69. Fukensai's transcription of one of the verses in the Rikyū Hyakushu.

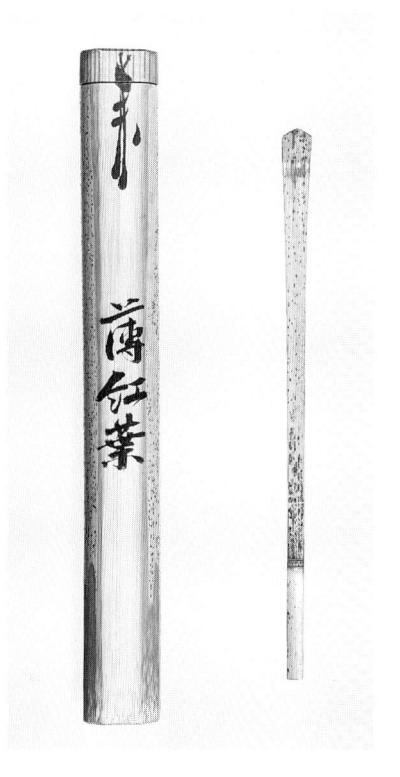

70. Tea scoop "Light Autumn Leaves" by Fukensai; case inscribed by Fukensai.

Genshitsu" (Genshitsubō), in which Ittō's twelve-year-old son Genshitsu himself arranged flowers. In fact, Genshitsu arranged the flowers for more than a hundred tea gatherings before assuming the name Fukensai. After becoming the ninth-generation Urasenke tea master, he in turn let his oldest son, who later became Nintokusai, arrange flowers and his second son, Yosaburō, prepare thin tea at tea functions.

A man of great learning and poetic talent, Fukensai inscribed a favorite painting, *Turtles,* by the Tosa-school artist Tosa Mitsusada (1738–1806; Pl. 55), with this verse:

> As the ice melts
> Tranquilly in spring
> To pond water,
> So too the turtles at the water's edge
> Await the rays of the sun.

Fukensai's tea scoops "First Blossom" (*hatsuhana*; Pl. 56) and "Light Autumn Leaves" (*usumomiji*; Fig. 70) feature joints low on the shaft and a very short bend of the triangular scoop. Both are named for traditional themes in Japanese verse. The former is of light-colored bamboo and the latter of sesame bamboo.

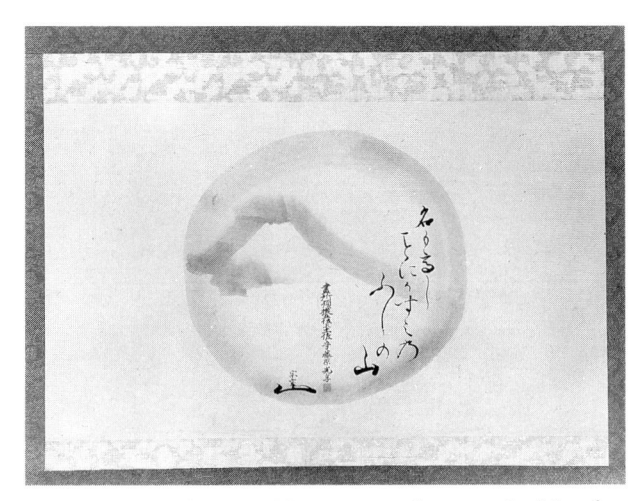

71. Mount Fuji by Tosa Mitsuzane, with a verse by Nintokusai.

Tenth-Generation Grand Master
Nintokusai Hakusō

Nintokusai left a number of memorable scrolls. Among them is one that bears an impromptu verse written to accompany his daughter Machiko's childish rendering of the family name, Sen (Pl. 57), on her third birthday (her fourth birthday according to the traditional Japanese method of reckoning, by which a baby is one year old at birth):

> At four years
> The character Sen of generations
> To start things off.

Another fine scroll has a monochrome ink-wash sketch of a misty Mount Fuji by the Tosa-school artist Tosa Mitsuzane (1780–1852) and a verse by Nintokusai (Fig. 71):

> Its name all the more exalted
> For being cloaked in mist,
> The venerable Mount Fuji.

Nintokusai's tea scoop "Fukurokuju" (Pl. 58), named after the a god of good fortune, is made of soot-darkened bamboo *(susu take)* from an old rafter, handsomely varied in shade above and below the joint. This piece has a single deep trough to the triangular scoop and minimal bending and carving underneath the joint. His tea scoop "Long Abalone Strip" *(naganoshi;* Fig. 72) has its joint at the base of the shaft, a formal style rarely seen in sesame bamboo pieces, although the scoop has the standard Urasenke triangular shape.

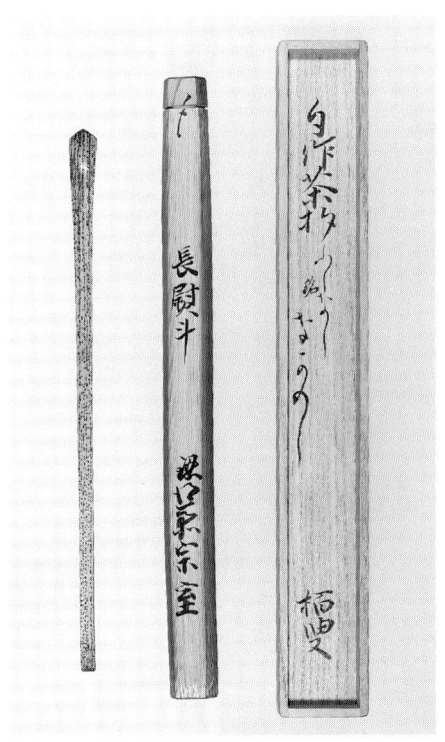

72. Tea scoop "Long Abalone Strip" by Nintokusai; case inscribed by Nintokusai.

Eleventh-Generation Grand Master
Gengensai Seichū

A student of the Chinese classics in his youth, Gengensai gave many of his tea utensils Chinese-style literary names. His five-jointed tea scoop "Five Constant Virtues" (*gojō*; Pl. 60), for example, refers to the five Confucian virtues cited in his famous statement *Chadō no Gen'i* (Pl. 59). The inscription on the case states that the piece was "carved in the spring of my fiftieth year of Ming Chinese bamboo received from Lord [Shimazu Narinobu] Keizan of Satsuma [Kagoshima]." Since Narinobu had died in 1841, nearly twenty years earlier, Gengensai must have received the bamboo long before he actually carved it. Gengensai signed the case for this tea scoop with the art name Seichū, which he had just received from the nobleman Kujō Hisatada.

Another Gengensai tea scoop bears the name "Ascending Dragon" (*shōryū*; Fig. 73). His inscription inside the box lid reads, "One of five pieces made of pine brought from Mount Fuji on my return from Lord [Takatsukasa Sukenobu] Yūrin's in the eastern capital." The piece was lacquered and decorated with *maki-e* by the eighth-generation Nakamura Sōtetsu. On the case Gengensai brushed the verse:

> An immortal visitant is borne on a cloud beyond the peaks,
> An enchanted dragon dwells ages in the cavernous abyss.

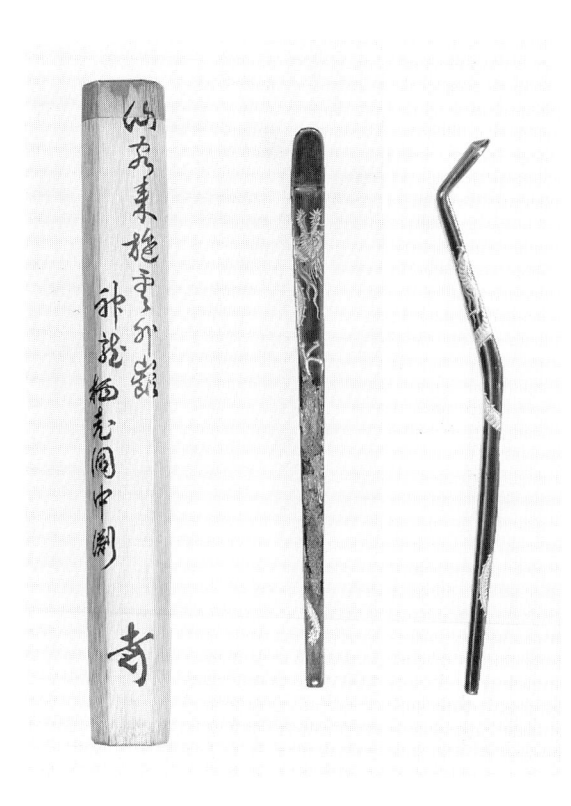

73. Tea scoop "Ascending Dragon" by Gengensai; case inscribed by Gengensai.

74. Calligraphy by Gengensai, reading "One iron bar, ten thousand leagues long."

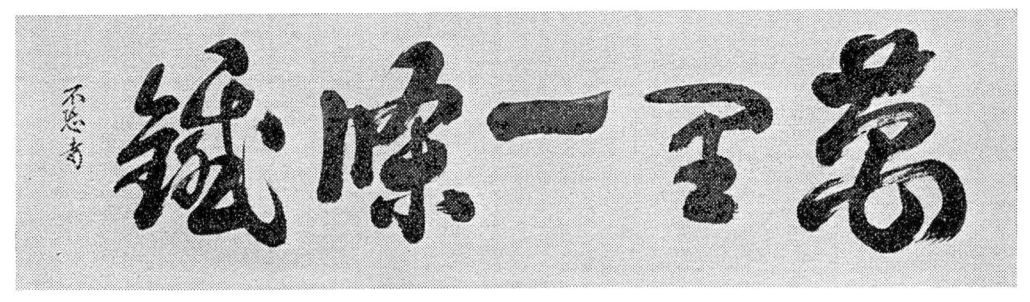

Other expressions of Gengensai's forceful character include calligraphy scrolls, such as the one reading "One iron bar, ten thousand leagues long" (Fig. 74).

Twelfth-Generation Grand Master
Yūmyōsai Jikisō

Yūmyōsai lived in a period when the importance of chanoyu was reevaluated and recognized anew. Hand in hand with this revitalization came a renewed interest in tradition, which provided both strength and inspiration. Yūmyōsai's respect for tra-

75. Calligraphy by three grand masters, reading "Fukurokuju" (fuku by Yūmyōsai, ro and ku by Ennōsai, ju by Tantansai).

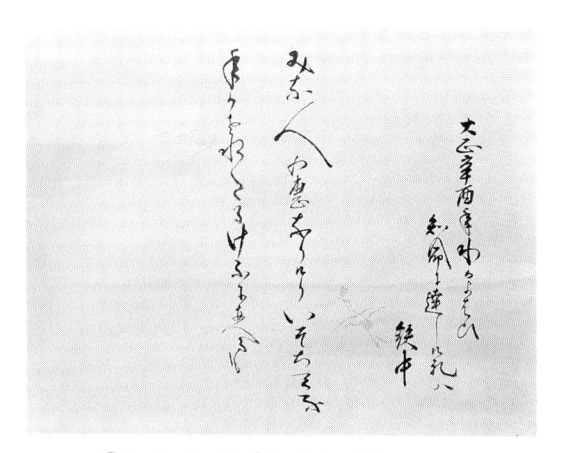

76. Ennōsai's fiftieth-birthday verse.

dition is succinctly displayed in his calligraphy scroll reading "A crane alights on a thousand-year-old tree" (Pl. 61).

His tea scoop "Ant Hole" (*ari tōshi;* Pl. 62) likewise looks back to tradition, taking its name from a famous tea scoop by the sixth-generation Omotesenke grand master, Kakukakusai.

Thirteenth-Generation Grand Master
Ennōsai Tetchū

A few years after Ennōsai, with the help of his father, Yūmyōsai, and his son Tantansai, organized the 1907 memorial tea service commemorating the two hundred fiftieth anniversary of Sōtan's death, a young emperor ushered in a new era in Japanese history. Ennōsai carved the tea scoop "Great Rectitude" (*taishō;* Pl. 64) in commemoration of the new Taishō era (1912–26). It was rare for three generations of the Urasenke family to be active contemporaries in tea, and this too was celebrated in a scroll bearing the name of the god of good fortune Fukurokuju (Fig. 75): Yūmyōsai wrote the character *fuku,* Ennōsai the characters *ro* and *ku,* and Tantansai the character *ju.*

THE MASTER'S TOUCH: TEA SCOOPS AND SCROLLS   93

77. Xiang Xiao Landscape *by Tantansai, in the manner of Yujian.*

In his later years Ennōsai dedicated himself fully to tea and spiritual training, having the utmost confidence in his successor, Tantansai. He held a great many tea gatherings for those dear to him and always maintained an optimistic outlook, as evinced in his fiftieth-birthday verse (Fig. 76):

> May there be
> A blessing for all
> Whom at this fiftieth path
> In this summing of years
> I chance to meet today!

Fourteenth-Generation Grand Master
Tantansai Sekisō

Tantansai showed an early aptitude for many forms of creative expression. He excelled in painting and calligraphy and was accomplished in the performance of Noh chant and *nagauta* singing. At the age of seventeen he began studying under the painter Shūseki Okutani, receiving the art name Genseki. Married at twenty-four to the similarly talented Kayoko Itō of Sendai, he and his wife often collaborated in composing verses and writing colophons for paintings. For several decades Tantansai also kept an illustrated diary, portions of which were eventually published as the *Urasenke Tantansai Ihō Shū* (Posthumous Writings of Tantansai).

A superlative example of Tantansai's brushwork is his *Xiang Xiao Landscape* (Fig. 77), inspired by the painting *Autumn Moon over Dongting Lake* by the Southern Song painter Yujian. Here Tantansai has sketched a quick circle for the moon over a tranquil autumn scene. To the left is the first line of a famous Chinese verse, "Moonlight

78. Tea scoop "First Carving" by Tantansai; case inscribed by Tantansai.

bathes the hills on all four sides of the placid lake," to which Tantansai has added a humorous verse of his own:

> Though Yujian's
> Brushwork seems rusty,
> Lo! The autumn moon.

The scroll bearing the calligraphy "Give thanks for tea" (Pl. 65) expresses Tantansai's profound gratitude that, contrary to the Meiji government's initial policy of disregarding chanoyu, popular support for the tea tradition had grown steadily, especially after World War II. This work also bears a verse by the four hundred ninety-second abbot of Daitokuji, Sessō Oda, comparing Uji to the Chinese tea-growing region of Jianqi.

The signatures Genku on the case and Eisei on the box of Tantansai's tea scoop "First Carving" (*hatsu kezuri*; Fig. 78) date this piece to the period between 1909 and 1915 when the young Tantansai went by the name Nagayo Genkuken. Representative of later pieces is a pair of tea scoops made of laurel—"Drops of Moonlight" (*tsuki no shizuku*) and "Jeweled Hare" (*tama usagi*; Pl. 66), names that allude to the lunar associations of laurel and of the "rabbit in the moon" of Oriental folklore, respectively.

CHAPTER FIVE

Urasenke Tearooms and Their Settings

Masao Nakamura

The main entrance to the Urasenke compound, on Ogawa Street in Kyoto's Kamigyō Ward, opens onto a veritable treasure trove of tea history and architecture. In March 1976 the Japanese government designated the entire compound an important cultural property.

The Helmet Gate (*kabuto mon*; Pl. 67), the main entrance to the compound, was built by Gengensai as part of the expansion of the compound undertaken just before the great tea gathering of 1840 commemorating the two hundred fiftieth anniversary of Rikyū's death. The gate (whether it is the original gate is not known) incorporates a large hipped roof over the two gate posts and adjoining sleeve walls, whose symmetry is broken by a slatted window on one side and a low portal on the other. The roof, thatched in cedar bark, covers part of the walls to left and right. The main posts are of cedar.

Offset by a chest-high hedge instead of the low *komayose* (horseguard) slatted screen more common to Kyoto houses, the gate has an overall effect of stately poise. The actual construction, however, is pleasantly light in feeling: the undereaves are surfaced in bamboo shafts between slender radial rafter beams. The sides of the roof curve slightly, giving the roof the appearance of a helmet, hence the name. A similar gate can be found at the Ryōkōin, a subtemple of Daitokuji, and it has been suggested that both may have antecedents in the so-called Korean gates (Kōrai *mon*) often seen at Japanese castles.

Just why Gengensai chose this gate design is unknown, but he may have seen an old drawing of the similar gate to Rikyū's quarters on the grounds of Hideyoshi's Jurakudai villa; moreover, given his own warrior-class origins, he would have been accustomed to such gates. The Helmet Gate may thus represent an attempt by Gengensai to bridge his two heritages by adapting the warrior-class architectural vocabulary to tea architecture.

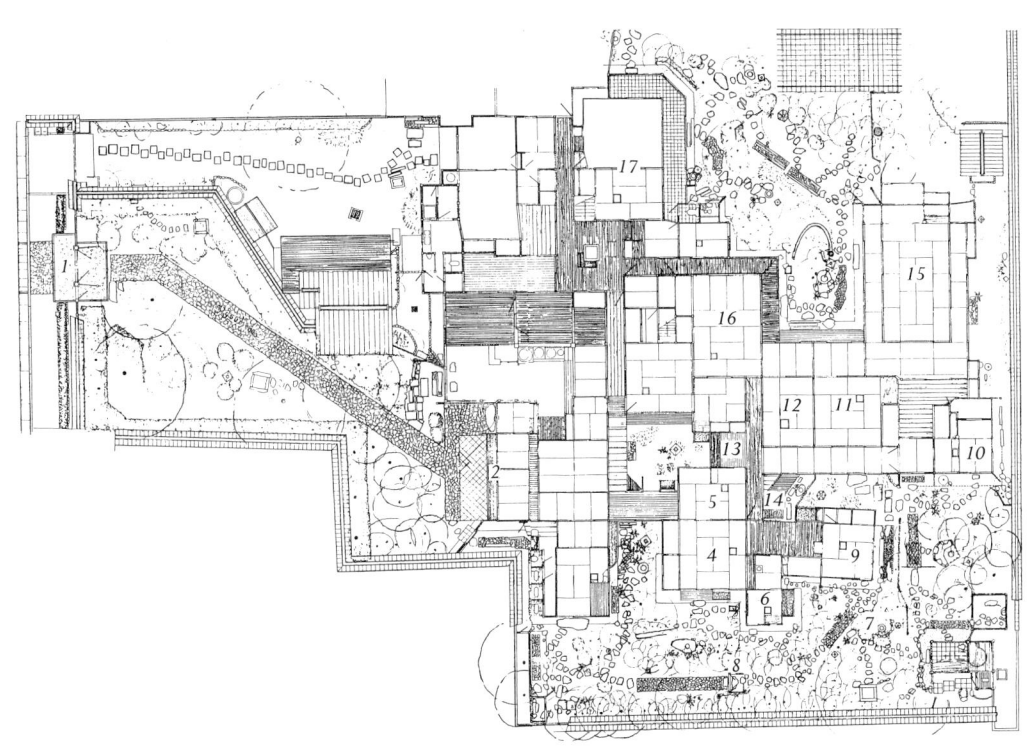

79. *Ground plan of the Urasenke compound in Kyoto. Major features: 1. Helmet Gate. 2. Entrance area. 3. Mushikiken. 4. Kan'untei. 5. Ryūseiken. 6. Konnichian. 7. "Buddha Tetrad" basin. 8. Middle Gate. 9. Yūin. 10. Rikyūdō. 11. Totsutotsusai. 12. Dairo no Ma. 13. Ōmizuya. 14. Plum Well. 15. Tairyūken. 16. Hōsensai. 17. Yūshin.*

Inside the gate, a narrow path, or *roji,* paved with irregular "chestnut stones" (*kuri ishi*) bends once, then leads straight to the entrance to the house (Pl. 68). On both sides a tall hedge screens off the rest of the *roji* garden, creating an atmosphere of mystery.

The entrance to the house faces west. A paved area is covered by deep overhanging eaves roofed in shingles and attached beneath the front edge of the large hipped and gabled tiled main roof. The eaves of the main roof are slightly raised over the extended entrance roof; the gable inset is a wall without any special features. To the left of the entrance is a sleeve wall. A bamboo-slat floor raised about thirty centimeters above the ground runs parallel to the entrance and, at its left end, is attached to the sleeve wall (Fig 80). The entrance area itself is divided into two parts: the southern half, to the right, being the more formal entrance, has a *shoin*-style lath-paneled sliding door (*mairado*) on each side, and between these, meeting at the center, two sliding doors papered with translucent white shoji from about knee-level up; the northern half, to the left, has plain sliding doors with shoji from waist level up. These differences in style reveal the differences in purpose and status of the two

80. Entrance to the house, showing the deep eaves, sleeve wall, and bamboo-slat raised floor.

81. Southern facade of Konnichian, ▶ showing the crawl-in entrance.

82. Western facade of Konnichian.

entranceways, yet when viewed as a whole, the entire entrance area presents a harmonious picture.

The Konnichian Tearoom, "Hut of This Day"

In 1646 Sōtan announced his retirement in a written statement giving charge of the family quarters on Ogawa Street to his third son, Sōsa, with the provision that he himself be allowed to establish a small villa of about sixteen *ken,* or bays, square (about 84.1 sq. m) at the northern end of the family property. Sōtan immediately began planning the construction. In a letter to Sōsa dated the eighteenth day of the fifth month of 1646, he wrote, "I can begin work out back now that I have put things in order, having seen Shōsai the other day and received twenty *ryō* with which I hope to build." A letter dated the twelfth day of the sixth month states:

> The construction out back is going to require a great deal of work, and I have had to make quarters for the carpenters, but it should be finished before Bon [the late-summer Buddhist ancestral festival]. The main house will be four *ken* by three *ken* [about 7.3 m by 5.5 m], and the small tearoom [will be] two mats in size. I will be able to hold tea gatherings here next spring, and I am already looking forward to opening the first tea-leaf jars of the year. It is most satisfying.

The final phase of construction began at the end of the following month, and the house was ready for Sōtan to move into by the beginning of the ninth month. In a letter dated the twenty-third day of the eighth month he wrote, "The house out back [*ura no ie*] is finished at last. Yesterday they cleaned up around the site. I feel worn out, its having taken sixty days now."

Through the generations, and especially due to the fire of 1788 which greatly damaged the Urasenke property, many of the original, old structures have undergone changes, yet an extant sketch that Sōtan is thought to have drawn for the carpenters makes it possible to visualize his new house and tearoom. Indeed, just as he had mentioned in his earlier letter, the sketch shows a house of four *ken* by three *ken*, with a two-mat tearoom on the south side. It also shows a southern *roji* garden enclosed by a high fence opening to the west. Apparently, the two-mat tearoom was almost identical to Konnichian as it is today (Pl. 69, Figs. 81–85).

At the edges of the sketch are written such instructions as:

Doors and shoji as in the old house.
Ceiling height and trim as in the old house.
  Unplaned log posts the size of those in the *shoin* [of the old house], while those of the four-and-a-half-mat room and small tearoom are to be made thinner.
[As to these two rooms], I will express my preferences.

Clearly, Sōtan devoted the greater part of his attention to the two smaller rooms. In the *Matsuya Kaiki,* the tea connoisseur Matsuya Hisashige (1566–1652) gives details of the tearoom in an entry describing a tea gathering hosted by Sōtan on the fifth day of the fourth month of 1649:

[The gathering was held in] the two-mat tearoom of the retreat, albeit only a one-and-a-half-mat area is in tatami, the rest being wood-floored. There is a central post but no recessed alcove [*nuki*], hence the two-level bamboo [flower container] was hung by the wood-floored area.

Earlier, when Hōrin (1592–1668), head priest of Kinkakuji, was invited to a tea gathering of Sōtan's held on the twenty-eighth day of the first month of 1648, he too recorded the occasion in some detail:

> Tearoom of one and a half mats. Hanging scroll, a painting of Rikyū with colophon by Shun'oku [Sōen] of Daitokuji. Flower container present from the start, with one sprig of *kakitsubata* [a kind of iris] and two lotus leaves. Rikyū's small *natsume* in silk pouch used in place of a thick-tea container.

This would be an unnoteworthy passage, were it not for two things: in small *wabi* tearooms without tokonoma, as a rule flowers and hanging scrolls were never displayed at the same time; and, unlike the *Matsuya Kaiki* account written nearly a year earlier, there is no mention of a board floor area. The central post and inverted placement of the hearth indicated in Sōtan's construction sketch would have allowed for a wood-floored area, though—as with Hōrin's account—no such area is actually cited. Was the board inset added to the room the following year? Kawakami Fuhaku comments in his *Fuhaku Hikki* that "insetting a board beyond the host's mat accorded with Sōtan's taste, and he preferred to use it in small *wabi* tearooms in place of the tokonoma."

In Sōtan's earlier years, at the quarters where he resided before his retirement, he had built a one-and-a-half-mat tearoom, later adding an adjoining formal *shoin* room; in his retirement retreat there was no such formal room, so when he invited Hōrin to his retreat, after serving tea to him in the small tearoom, he conducted the priest to the six-mat room of his living quarters. Here, too, there was neither a tokonoma nor a *tsukeshoin* window-desk. Sōtan's retreat was the ultimate embodiment of his minimalist *wabi* sensibility, the end of a long process of paring his chanoyu to its barest essentials, eschewing even the tokonoma. As Sōtan's disciple Yamada Sōhen states in the *Chadō Bemmō Shō*: "According to his own preference Sōtan had a board put in beyond the hearth, and he set the flower container in the center of the board, placing it directly [on the board] without any thin platform [*usuita*; normally placed under flower containers when set in tokonoma with tatami flooring]."

Another disciple, Sugiki Fusai, added a further note to Sōhen's observation:

> [Sōtan] would even set the brazier on this board, placing the fresh-water jar alongside to serve tea as with the lacquered semiformal utensil board [*nagaita*]. Of course, the brazier would be placed directly on the board inset. Such board insets are sometimes found in small tearooms of, say, three mats or in an extended four-mat layout where the tatami mats are laid two crosswise and two lengthwise, not just in [small tearooms of] two mats. Of course, when laying the hearth before the *kaiseki* meal, he would also place the charcoal basket there and remove it to the preparation room afterward.

The remarkable versatility of the board inset seems to have been a major factor in Sōtan's planning, as were a number of other clever schemes of presentation, such as leaving the preparation-room door open, with a flower container beyond in view of the guests. The inclusion of the half-mat board inset served as a simple way to compensate for the constraints of the one-and-a-half-mat room without having to

83. Interior of Konnichian, showing the crawl-in entrance and the host's mat.

84. Interior of Konnichian, showing the built-in utensil cabinet.

resort to a tokonoma. Though Sōtan had designed a one-and-a-half-mat tearoom with a tokonoma for the Hōshun'in, a subtemple of Daitokuji, he obviously did not consider that combination—a tearoom of minimal size, yet having a tokonoma—*wabi* enough. Thus, instead of a tokonoma he expanded the space accessible to the host's mat by interposing a central post and sleeve wall in front of the guests' mat by the crawl-in entrance so as to enclose the board inset (Fig. 83).

The second distinctive feature of Konnichian is the built-in utensil cabinet (Fig. 84), which is essentially a scaled-down preparation-room shelf brought within reach of the host's mat. In the *Matsuya Kaiki* entry of the fifth day of the fourth month, 1649, there is, in addition to the information regarding the wood-floored area, some mention of this cabinet:

> The built-in cabinet [*dōko*] has two sliding doors. One side [of the cabinet] has a shelf for the tea containers and tea bowls, while farther back on the other side there is space for the rice server and water jar, not to mention the wastewater receptacle and just about anything else.

According to the *Nampō Roku*, Rikyū had installed such a utensil cabinet in designing a two-mat tearoom for an elderly tea connoisseur. Sōtan corroborated this: "This again accords with Rikyū, who held [the built-in utensil cabinet] to be a device proper to the elderly."

Sōtan thus emerges as a true advocate of the tradition of Rikyū, who had found that practicing tea within "the confines of one and a half mats can be most interesting." Though Konnichian is only slightly larger than one and a half mats, its special features allowed for an intensive use of space.

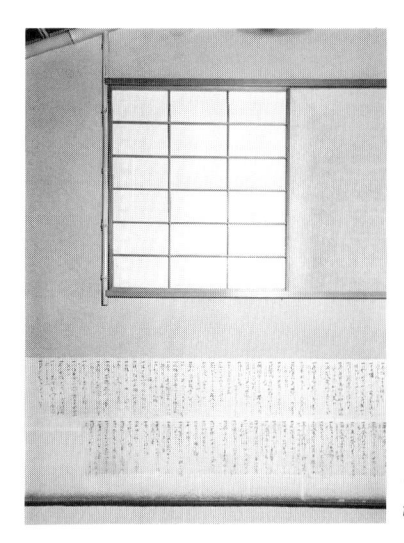

86. Interior of Yūin, looking from the host's mat toward the crawl-in entrance.

87. Interior of Yūin, showing the tokonoma and partially concealed post.

85. Interior of Konnichian, showing the wall behind the guests' mat.

The Yūin Tearoom, "Further Retreat"

In 1653 Sōtan announced his second retirement, writing, "Going on seventy-six [seventy-five by Western reckoning], I now take further retreat from Konnichian." Since the previous year, when his fourth son, Sensō, attained an official post, he had been considering "the possibility of sooner or later moving into a three *ken* by two *ken* [5.5 m by 3.6 m] thatched dwelling out back." It is not clear whether Sōtan had already formed an image of the tearoom Yūin, "Further Retreat," for his second-retirement quarters, but by the eighteenth day of the twelfth month of 1653 he had invited Hōrin to an inaugural tea gathering at his new four-and-a-half-mat tearoom.

Earlier, Sōtan had built a four-and-a-half-mat tearoom, which according to the *Chadō Mochizuki Shū* (Mochizuki Collected Tea Anecdotes), compiled in 1723, was an "orthodox four-and-a-half-mat room . . . following the preferences of the old master Sōeki [Rikyū]," that is, a thoroughly *wabi* four-and-a-half-mat tearoom, probably similar to the one Rikyū had built for his quarters at Jurakudai. As Yamada Sōhen noted in his *Rikyū Chadōgu Zue*, Rikyū-style four-and-a-half-mat tearooms were popular well into the Edo period.

The oldest historical sources make little distinction between Yūin and Konnichian. A plan in *Sōzen Sashizu Chō* (Sōzen's Notes and Diagrams) by the tea connoisseur Hisada Sōen, of the "Konnichian four-and-a-half-mat room" reveals the Yūin to have been modeled quite closely on the Rikyū-style tearoom. The room faces south, with two "unfinished" bamboo-lattice windows (*shitaji mado,* created by leaving a small portion of the wall unplastered, thereby exposing the bamboo-lattice understructure), one placed diagonally above the crawl-in entrance, just as in Rikyū's Jurakudai tearoom, and one in the wall behind the guests' mat. There is also a skylight cut through the eaves (Pl. 70, Fig. 86). The ceiling is rather low, only 1.8 meters high, and when the preparation-room door is shut, the room has a singularly hermetic feeling. The post by the built-in utensil cabinet of Rikyū's four-and-a-half-mat tearoom is missing here, and the corner post by the host's mat is partially plastered over, while a new post has been added midway along the entrance wall. Otherwise, the layout is almost identical. The omission of two vertical members, leaving a broad unbroken expanse of wall, was probably intended to create an illusion of space.

The half-hidden corner post that snakes into the plastered wall—the so-called partially hidden post (*yōjibashira;* Fig. 87)—is another feature that can be traced back to Rikyū. At the Grand Kitano Tea Gathering of 1587, Rikyū built a four-and-a-half-mat tearoom with "a post left exposed from some two *shaku* five *sun* [about 75 cm] above the floor and completely plastered over below that," according to the *Yukimasō* (Grasses through the Snow), a collection of tea anecdotes by Sakamoto Shūnsai (1666–1749). This work also mentions "a post warped in such a way that it naturally curved in and was plastered over, bark and all"—a happy accident that gave rise to an architectural expression of *wabi*. Sōtan, a *wabi* purist, incorporated this feature into Yūin, although his concealed corner post emerges higher up the wall—at one meter—and bears a hook for hanging a flower container 1.4 meters above the floor.

The *Sōzen Sashizu Chō* indicates that Yūin originally had a thatched hipped and gabled roof, either in imitation of some Rikyū tearoom or simply in keeping with the rustic *wabi* image. The present roof still retains thatched eaves, through one of which the skylight is cut. Other *wabi* touches that date from Sōtan's time include the ceiling of seven-centimeter-wide wood strips, the 24.5-centimeter-high wainscoting of white paper on the wall behind the host's mat, and the wainscoting of gray paper behind the guests' mat from the floor to the bottom of the window (Fig. 88).

88. Interior of Yūin, looking toward the tokonoma and the guests' mat from the preparation-room door.

A plan in the *Konnichian Yūintei Shiyō Chō* (Record of Functions at the Konnichian Yūin Arbor), compiled in the Kyōhō era (1716–36), shows certain differences from the tearoom of the Sōzen plan. For instance, Sōtan's "unfinished" window diagonally above the crawl-in entrance has now become a framed window *(renji mado)*, edged on its interior right-hand side with a slender bamboo post. This and other changes were probably undertaken by Sensō. Comparison of the Sōzen plan of Yūin, which is thought to represent the Yūin of Sōtan's time, with plans from Sensō's time indicates no change in the dimensions of the crawl-in entrance or in the height of the eaves. In the middle of the facade, however, there suddenly appears an unplaned cedar log post six centimeters thick, and a bamboo post about four centimeters in diameter edges the now-framed window (5.9 cm by 160 cm) in the wall behind the guests' mat. The height of the tokonoma ceiling—about 1.9 meters in the Sōzen plan—has been raised by about two centimeters, while a hook for hanging a flower container has been attached to the right-hand post of the tokonoma, a change that the *Fuhaku Hikki* suggests was carried out to afford a better view of the flowers from the host's mat.

It is conceivable that these improvements were part of a program of general repairs that Sensō undertook before the 1690 centennial of Rikyū's death. Certainly the change from "unfinished" bamboo-lattice windows to framed windows was calculated to let more light into the interior and thus open up the room, for although Yūin manifested the authentic Rikyū style as transmitted through Sōtan, the austerity of their *wabi* chanoyu was rapidly becoming a thing of the past; their austere taste for religious discipline required updating to accommodate the trend toward lighter and more spacious tearooms. Even the bamboo posts now added to the windows were meant as nothing more profound than a note of visual relief, though this went directly against Rikyū's caution in *Hosokawa Sansai Godenjusho* (Hosokawa Sansai's Transmitted Instructions) to "place bamboo posts where they will not attract attention." It is

Pl. 67. Helmet Gate, the main entrance to the Urasenke compound.

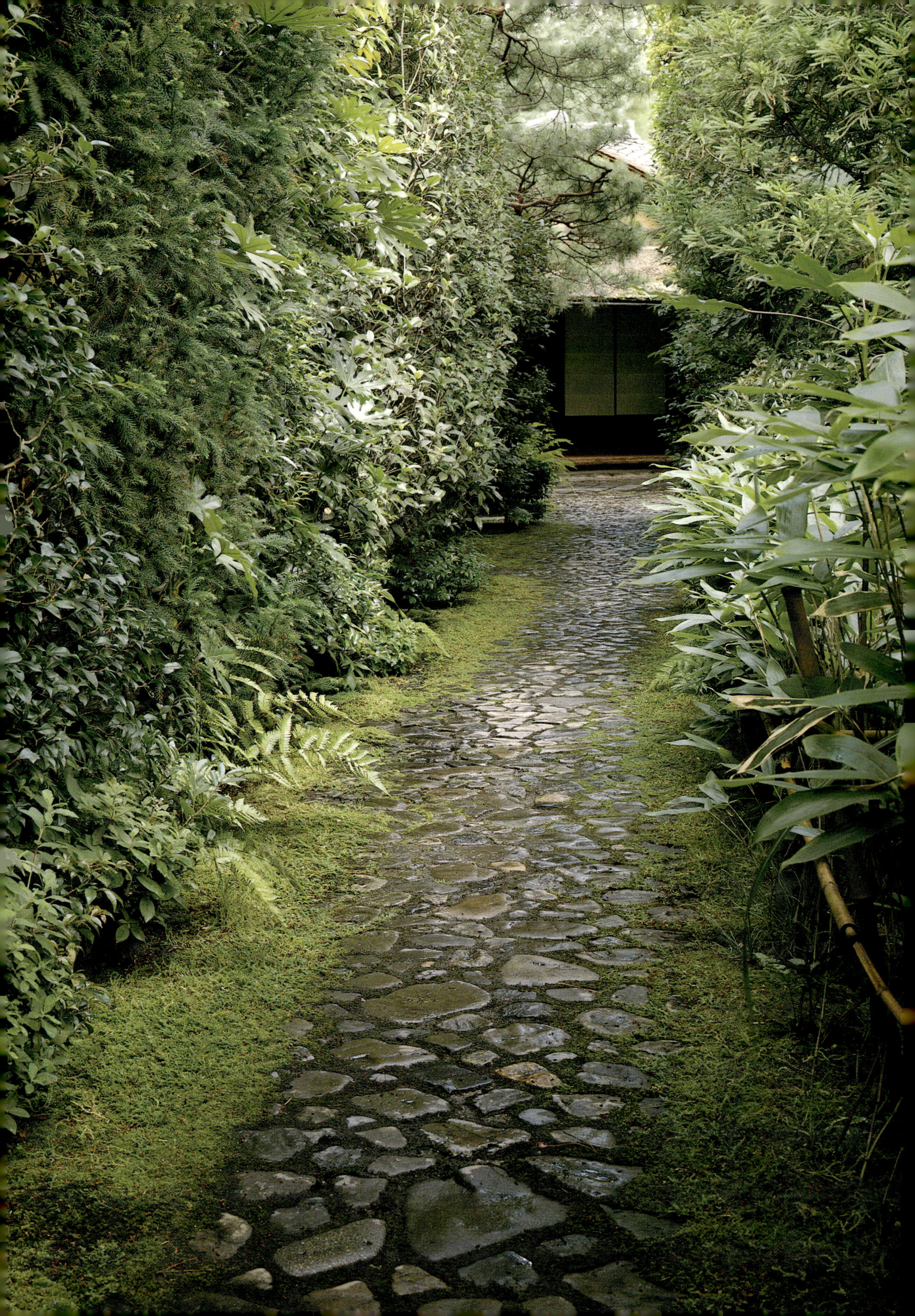

Pl. 69. Interior of Konnichian, looking from the crawl-in entrance toward the plain-wall scroll display and the preparation-room door.

◀ *Pl. 68. Outer roji garden, looking from Helmet Gate toward the entrance to the house.*

又隠

Pl. 71. *Interior of Kan'untei, showing the tokonoma as seen from the host's mat.*

◀ Pl. 70. *Southern facade of Yūin, showing the crawl-in entrance.*

Pl. 72. Interior of the Rikyūdō, showing the host's mat and Sensō's "Clamshell" shelf.

Pl. 73. Interior of the Rikyūdō, showing the family shrine.

Pl. 74. Interior of Mushikiken; the plain-wall scroll display is on the left, the host's mat on the right.

instructive to note that not long thereafter a bamboo post also appeared in Saan (Straw Rain Cape Hut), a tearoom built at Gyokurin'in, a subtemple of Daitokuji.

Sensō's Yūin was destroyed in the great fire that devastated Kyoto in 1788, but Fukensai reconstructed it the following year in time for the bicentennial of Rikyū's death.

This four-and-a-half-mat tearoom occupies a place of unique importance in the world of tea, linking the *shoin* and *sōan* styles. It was Rikyū who fully transformed the four-and-a-half-mat format into the setting proper to *wabi* chanoyu, and Yūin represents one of the best embodiments of that ideal. There are only two entrances to the tearoom, the crawl-in entrance for the guests and the preparation-room door for the host. Except for two bamboo-lattice windows, the walls offer no openings. The ceiling, too, is quite plain, consisting only of a flat expanse of wood strips and a smaller slanted area revealing the understructure of the roof. The austere effect hardly differs from that of a two-mat *wabi* tearoom. Yūin affords little in the way of creature comforts or recognition of worldly status, stringencies that latter tearooms modeled on Yūin sought to alleviate by such additions as two-panel sliding doors and extra guest entrances. It remains perhaps the single best model of Rikyū's classic four-and-a-half-mat tearoom.

The Kan'untei Tearoom, "Cold Cloud Arbor"

This eight-mat tearoom, the oldest *shoin*-style room in the Urasenke compound, is said to have been built to Sōtan's specifications, although the exact order of events leading to its construction have long been forgotten. A plan of the grounds from the time of Sōtan's initial retirement in 1646 shows a six-mat room, but nothing that would correspond to Kan'untei (Cold Cloud Arbor). Nor could the house "three *ken* by two *ken*" that he moved to at the time of his second retirement have practically accommodated an eight-mat room. It thus becomes difficult to ascertain just when Sōtan would have built this tearoom.

Konnichian ni Kore Aru Niwa no Zu (Plan of the Grounds of Konnichian; Fig. 89), drawn in 1727 by Nakai Mondo, shows the existence of rooms that most probably correspond to Kan'untei and Mushikiken (Shelter of No Colors) in the *roji* garden to the west of Yūin. It is also known from records of the bicentennial observances of Rikyū's death than Kan'untei underwent repairs in 1789 and was the site of tea functions beginning the twenty-seventh day of the ninth month of that year.

The following year, at the dedicatory tea function for the restored statue of Rikyū installed in the Rikyūdō, thin tea was served in Kan'untei. A record of the gathering states that a box belonging to Rikyū was displayed on the *tsukeshoin* window-desk, which indicates that Kan'untei looked much the same as today's *shoin*-style room (Pl. 71, Fig. 90). A diagram accompanying the record of the Rikyū bicentennial shows a small one-mat area—the so-called Yanagi no Ma (Willow Room)—next to the Kan'untei tokonoma, connecting to the wood-floored area of Mushikiken; the

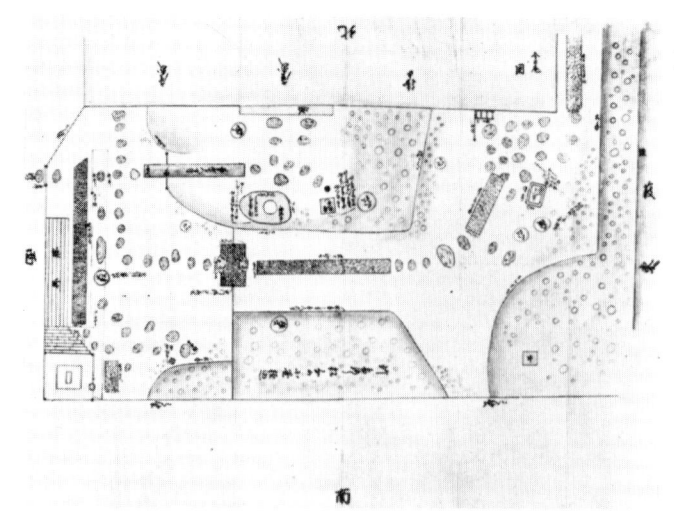

89. Konnichian ni Kore Aru Niwa no Zu by Nakai Mondo. 1727. Tadashige Nakai collection.

90. Interior of Kan'untei, looking from the tokonoma toward the tsukeshoin *and the host's mat in front of it.*

two rooms were then adjacent, not separated by a courtyard as they are now. It was only much later, at the time of Gengensai's massive expansion of the Urasenke compound, that they were moved apart.

Kan'untei appears again in an untitled collection of tearoom plans dating from the late Edo period, looking largely as it does today. The ceiling comprises three parts: a flat ceiling in front of the tokonoma drops one level over the host's mat—a note of humility—while a more decorative "boat-hull ceiling" (*funazoko tenjō*) covers the remaining area in front of the *tsukeshoin*. The partition beside the tokonoma features an intricate random-pattern bamboo inlay, and there is a comb-shaped transom, said to have been designed by Sōtan to acknowledge the gift of a comb from the empress

Tōfukumon'in. All these details agree with the present appearance of Kan'untei. The only discrepancy is the hearth, which another late-Edo sketch locates in the mat in front of the *tsukeshoin*, a placement that seems closer to that seen in four-and-a-half-mat rooms.

The most striking aspect of Kan'untei is the ceiling. It is very rare to find a *shoin*-style room with a three-part ceiling; even Rikyū's nine-mat *shoin*-style room at Jurakudai only had a slanted ceiling in addition to the usual flat ceiling. The "patchwork" effect of the Kan'untei ceiling seems more appropriate to a smaller *sōan*-style tearoom, suggesting a conscious effort to create a certain tension through the counterpoint of styles. Such an innovative design concept, though, seems hardly in keeping with Sōtan's *wabi* taste; thus it may be that Kan'untei represents some later generation's alteration of his second-retirement quarters. Either way, this tearoom is one of the most distinctive in the Urasenke compound.

The Rikyūdō Family Shrine, "Hall of the Honorable Ancestor"

The centennial of Rikyū's death was a mere two years away in 1688, when the fourth-generation grand master, Sensō, returned from his appointment to the Maeda clan of Kaga. He decided to prepare a family shrine in time for the occasion. Sensō brought out the head of the wooden statue of Rikyū, which—ostensibly, at least—had begun all the trouble when it was installed in the Daitokuji temple gate, and which had been decapitated on Hideyoshi's order. The torso of the statue had been thrown into Kyoto's Kamo River, but the head had been saved by Rikyū's friend Kokei Sōchin, head priest of Daitokuji, and later secretly passed into Sōtan's hands. It was now time to have the statue restored and enshrined.

According to Gengensai, Sensō's inspiration for the somewhat rustic appearance of the Rikyūdō—more properly called the Onsōdō, or "Hall of the Honorable Ancestor"—was the farmhouses he had seen on the way to Kaga. Even today, there is no true ceiling beneath the thatched roof.

Nakai Mondo's plan of the Rikyūdō shows it to have been much the same as today, facing south in the part of the house farthest from the street entrance, at the far eastern edge of the Urasenke complex. A narrow passage at the west connecting the Rikyūdō to the rest of the compound opens first into a two-mat anteroom *(tsugi no ma)* and then into the main room (Fig. 91). This is divided in half. On the north side is a raised wooden-floor area and, against the north wall, a board-floored enclosure that houses Rikyū's image. On the south side of the room are tatami and a board inset. This side is for the preparation, offering, and partaking of tea.

The south wall of the room consists of five sliding doors. The three to the east are papered from waist level up, and the two to the west are papered from knee level up. Above the two sliding doors on the west is an "unfinished" bamboo lattice window. On the east wall, opposite the entrance to the room from the anteroom, is another papered window.

91. The entrance to the Rikyūdō from the rest of the compound.

The southern section of the room is also divided into two parts. Immediately upon entering, one steps onto the *tencha za,* or the mat for the preparation of tea (also called the "host's mat," but in the Rikyūdō there is no host-guest relationship, since all tea prepared there is regarded as an offering to Rikyū's spirit). A 36-centimeter-wide board insert is adjacent to and runs the full length of the *tencha za*. Beyond these to the east are two tatami mats. In the center of the room's north-south axis but rather far to the west side is an unplaned chestnut-log post. It stands at the meeting place of the northwest corner of the two-mat area and the southwest corner of the raised, wooden-floored area that forms the room's northern side.

All the tatami mats are now trimmed with decorative brocade borders. However, since such borders are not shown in the Nakai plan, the *tencha za* may have been without borders at that time. The board inset, between the *tencha za* and the two-mat area, is fitted with a hearth, above which runs, north to south, a cedar-log crossbeam and a partially plastered lintel with a bamboo-lattice portal. Midway along the inner wall on the north of the *tencha za* is Sensō's "Clamshell" shelf (Pl. 72), fashioned of a rounded cedar board suspended from a slender bamboo rod.

The board inset continues up into the northern side of the room, forming a tokonoma area that effectively merges with the raised board floor, and is partitioned by means of a partial sleeve wall beginning 76 centimeters above the floor and fitted with an "unfinished" bamboo-lattice portal. Another cedar-log crossbeam spans the room, beyond which lies the board-floored enclosure housing the statue. This "altar" is viewed through a large rounded window raised about 12.4 centimeters above the floor and surmounted by an elongated bamboo-lattice portal (Pl. 73). Whereas the rest of the shrine has exposed underroofing, the "altar" area has a suspended ceiling.

Since Sensō's time the Rikyūdō has functioned as the household sanctuary, the

92. Southern facade of Mushiki-ken, with the waiting arbor on the left.

place for carrying out official transmissions of the tea lineage and for offering tea to the founder of the Urasenke tradition. Built at a time when Furuta Oribe's more colorful tea style commanded the attention of the tea world, the Rikyūdō's subdued architecture represents a continuation of Sōtan's return to the *wabi* chanoyu of Rikyū, albeit imbued with a certain "folk art" flavor.

The Mushikiken Vestibule, "Shelter of No Colors"

Situated close to the entrance to the house, Mushikiken (Shelter of No Colors) is suitably located to serve as a *yoritsuki*, a place where guests may deposit their belongings and prepare themselves for tea functions (Pl. 74, Fig. 92). The Nakai plan of the Urasenke grounds also shows a room in the same location with stepping stones leading from it to an outdoor waiting arbor. In the time of the ninth-generation grand master, Fukensai, the entrance led to Kan'untei through Mushikiken, which, just as today, was six mats in size, including a board-floored one-mat area. In Gengensai's time, however, Mushikiken was moved three meters away from Kan'untei, opening up a small courtyard between the two, and about 3.6 meters south of the entrance, necessitating the creation of a three-mat anteroom with mats in the three-quarter size called *daime,* a hallway, and two new rooms to fill the gap: a six-mat "disciples' quarters" and a four-*daime*-sized-mat auxiliary room.

After Mushikiken was separated from Kan'untei, a passageway communicated across the courtyard from the board-floored area through three sliding doors, half-papered in shoji, to the one-mat area next to Kan'untei's tokonoma for the convenience of important guests in inclement weather. More significantly, Mushikiken

93. Interior of Mushikiken, showing Sensō's "Carpenter's Workbox" shelf by the host's mat.

itself was also conceived as a tearoom. In place of a tokonoma, a white-papered scroll-display wall *(kabedoko)* diagonally opposite the board-floored area is set off on one side by a log post, and is bordered with a black lacquer frame. This scroll-display wall is visually recessed by a 53-centimeter-wide wooden sleeve wall that adjoins it on the north. Next to the sleeve wall on this north wall are two sliding doors leading to the three-*daime*-sized-mat anteroom. A slightly arched chestnut timber spans the sleeve wall and the sliding doors—the entire north wall of the room—its arc providing an opening between the door tops and the transom, for ventilation. The host's mat, beside the east wall, is separated from the board-floored area by a raised sleeve wall, a hearth-screening device common in the tearooms of the Sen family. The sleeve wall ends in a thick cedar-log post and features a large "unfinished" bamboo-lattice portal. The host's mat is illuminated by two waist-height shoji windows, and in the corner is affixed a small set of shelves known as Sensō's "Carpenter's Workbox," upon which to place tea utensils (Fig. 93). Over the main four-mat area of the room is a ceiling, whose narrow panels and thick molding give it a rustic look, while the host's mat and board-floored area have a slanted ceiling revealing the understructure of the roof. At the south end of the room are two sliding doors papered with shoji from waist height up. These open onto the *roji* garden near the waiting arbor (Fig. 94).

In Gengensai's record of a tea gathering commemorating the two hundred fiftieth anniversary of Rikyū's death, the room is listed as "a five-mat room for changing into *hakama* [the formal split skirt worn by men over kimono] and resting." Another document from Gengensai's time, the *Higashi Honganji Daigomonshu Otachiyori no Ki* (Memorandum of a Visit by the Head Priest of Higashi Honganji Temple), mentions "Fukensai's five-mat room, with central post and calligraphic plaque by Chikusō reading 'Pines show no colors old or new.'" Apparently Mushikiken as it exists today

94. Waiting arbor.

was rebuilt according to the taste of the ninth-generation Urasenke master, Fukensai. Whatever the case, a previous form of Mushikiken does appear in the Nakai plan and does bear a close relationship to the outdoor waiting arbor, supposedly of Sensō's design, so that Sensō may well have constructed the original vestibule.

The Evolution of the *Roji* Gardens

To judge from the Nakai plan, the present-day *roji* gardens do not differ significantly from those of the Kyōhō era, when the plan was drawn, although the Middle Gate has been moved a little to the east at the end of a straight section of stone-paved walkway. Today's bamboo-thatched Middle Gate with split-bamboo paneled doors was built by Gengensai; previously the gate had had a rush-thatched roof and cedar-paneled double doors. The straight walkway was paved, then as now, with small stones in a "spilled hailstone" pattern. The *Chafu* (Tea Curriculum), a late-Edo-period collection of tea anecdotes, describes the walkway thus: "The way from the Rikyū-style waiting arbor to the small tearoom has, besides stepping stones, an area of stone-paved walkway. The stones of this walkway are small, and the spaces between are packed with a mixture of topsoil and subsoil."

On the other side of the Middle Gate, the stepping-stone path branches; taking the branch that leads to the left (north), one reaches Konnichian. Then, continuing along this same branch of the path, one reaches Kan'untei. To the side of the stepping stones leading to Kan'untei is a rather large stone water basin known as the "Small Sleeve." This water basin serves both Kan'untei and Konnichian. The Nakai plan does not show Konnichian, let alone the portion of the path which leads to Konnichian. All that it shows are tearooms corresponding to Yūin and Kan'untei and the notation

95. Sōtan's "Scattered Bean" stepping stones, Yūin roji.

96. "Buddha Tetrad" stone water basin, Yūin roji.

"cooking area" *(katte)* between the two. Since the plantings of the *roji* garden outside Kan'untei are drawn in some detail, the question remains whether the artist merely neglected to draw in Konnichian or whether it was located elsewhere at the time. The plan of the Yūin *roji* closely matches the present layout, with a stone water basin to the right of the point at which another straight block of "spilled hailstone" walkway ends, followed by a grouping of apparently randomly scattered stepping stones—Sōtan's famous "Scattered Bean" stepping stones (*mamemaki ishi*; Fig. 95). The squarish stone water basin in the plan can be identified as the rectangular one known as the "Buddha Tetrad" (*shihōbutsu*; Fig. 96).

The inner *roji* of *sōan*-style tearooms typically have small stepping stones, and in Yūin's *roji* the stones are smaller than usual—the raised stone outside the tiny *nijiriguchi* entranceway is just barely large enough to accommodate one pair of straw sandals. Sōtan's placement of stones was by no means random, however; it skillfully integrates the diverse parts of this small area. Guests proceeding along the walkway would first encounter the stone water basin, then go to the sword rack to lay aside their weapons, and next head for the crawl-in entrance; the host would follow other stepping stones back to the preparation room; still other stones led to the *roji* garden area east of Yūin.

The Nakai plan shows a well to the south of Yūin that still exists today. Next to it towers the famous ginko tree planted by Sōtan. A straight walkway extends along the east side of Yūin toward the present site of the Rikyūdō, though there is no indication where it led at the time. The rest of the area east of Yūin is marked "undergrowth." The *Kyoto Chaen Teishitsu Zu* (Plans of Tea Gardens and Arbors in Kyoto;

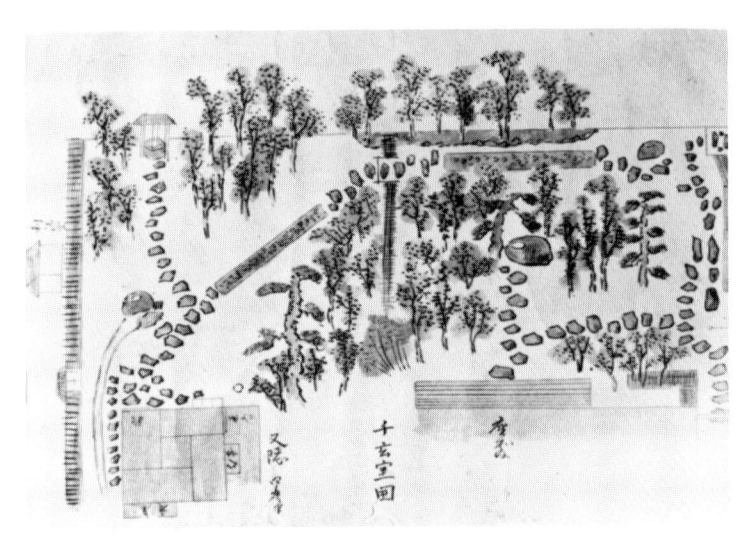

97. Plan of the Urasenke roji *garden, from the* Kyoto Chaen Teishitsu Zu. *Eighteenth century.*

Fig. 97), probably contemporaneous with the Nakai plan, shows a fence on the eastern side; beyond, to the east, is the notation "Rikyūdō." "Yūin four-and-a-half-mat room" and another, nameless tearoom are clearly marked on the plan. In place of Konnichian the plan shows "Sen Genshitsu's quarters"—"Genshitsu" probably referring to the ninth-generation Urasenke grand master, Fukensai. It was he who held the Rikyū bicentennial observances and rebuilt the Rikyūdō after the 1788 fire, meanwhile setting up a temporary shrine in a waiting room at the rear of the Urasenke property. Probably it is this temporary Rikyūdō that appears on the plan. In fact, the present waiting room at the rear of the property, called the Oku no Machiai, has a large round window in front of the tokonoma, like the round window in the Rikyūdō, bespeaking the room's former days as the temporary Rikyūdō.

The last change in the *roji* gardens came during Gengensai's time, when, as previously mentioned, Mushikiken was moved away from Kan'untei, creating a small courtyard. This necessitated several minor adjustments in the area around the two rooms and the waiting arbor. Close to the waiting arbor, a path leading from a small garden gate to the first stone-paved walkway was now made to branch off toward the courtyard, conducting guests first to a large stone step outside the three shoji doors of Mushikiken's board-floored area, then to the hallway between the main entrance to the Urasenke compound and a six-mat room, Ryūseiken (Arbor of Restful Spirit). In the center of the courtyard are a stone water basin and a stone lantern, and a narrow bamboo garden-viewing veranda runs along part of the eastern side of Mushikiken. The courtyard itself, planted with Japanese cypress and wild foliage, is a splendid example of garden design in a compact area.

Gengensai's Additions to the Compound

In 1839 Gengensai carried out a program of massive construction and expansion in the Urasenke compound in preparation for a series of tea functions commemorating the two hundred fiftieth anniversary of Rikyū's death. He added the tearooms Hōsensai (Sanctuary of the Cast Fishtrap), Totsutotsusai (Sanctuary of Pleasant Surprise), and Dairo no Ma (Great Hearth Room) and constructed the small free-standing tearoom Baishian (Plum Thread Hut) just inside the Helmet Gate, which he also built at this time.

Gengensai's record of one of the commemorative tea functions includes the following entry, dated the twelfth day of the ninth month of 1839:

Room adjacent to the Rikyūdō
    Scroll: Biographical scenes of Rikyū by Sensō
    Ashiya "Hundred Gatherings" kettle by Dōya
Tokonoma of practice room
    [Calligraphy of] Rikyū's art name by Sengaku [Sōtō]
    Xiang Xiao landscape by Kokei [Sōchin]
    Calligraphic transmission of Rikyū's lay name, also by [Kokei]
    In front of these a censer on a plain *nagaita* board
    Gong, an heirloom
    Plain board ceiling
Adjacent room
    Clothes rack hung with priest's robe

Judging from a plan of the Urasenke compound as it was in Gengensai's time, the "room adjacent to the Rikyūdō" was probably the two-mat area leading to the main chamber, with a hearth set in the host's mat. The "practice room" with its its tokonoma, "plain board ceiling," and "gong" would then be Totsutotsusai, and the "adjacent room," the Dairo no Ma. Moreover, in *Urasenke Sōezu* (An Overall View of Urasenke), Totsutotsusai is clearly marked "eight-mat practice room," and so we know that Totsutotsusai was generally referred to as "the practice room." A folding paper model made by a tearoom carpenter, Kimura Seibei, shows Totsutotsusai and the Dairo no Ma, together with the Ōmizuya (the main preparation room) and Hōsensai. The notations on the model indicate that the carpenter consulted Gengensai on details of the construction and give us a clear picture of Gengensai's preferences.

Totsutotsusai is an eight-mat room (Fig. 98), adjoined on its western side by the six-mat Dairo no Ma; both rooms are flanked north and south by two long passages that can be made directly accessible by removing the sliding doors that separate the passages from the rooms. The south passage, which also leads to the Rikyūdō, has sliding doors with papered shoji windows from hip height up along its south side. They open onto a strip of lush greenery; beyond lies the Yūin tearoom. At the west end of this open space is the famous "Plum Well" (*ume no i*; Fig. 99). The passage itself has exposed underroofing of wickerwork and lashed logs with the bark still

98. Interior of Totsutotsusai, looking from Dairo no Ma toward the tokonoma and host's mat.

99. Plum Well (ume no i).

100. Interior of the Dairo no Ma, showing the transom, with its openwork pattern of paulownia leaves, and the sliding doors leading to Totsutotsusai.

intact; the north passage has a panel-and-molding ceiling. The boundary between Totsutotsusai and the Dairo no Ma is spanned by a log crossbeam tooled on its undersurface with tracks for sliding doors. The transom above is a single large cedar board carved with an elegant openwork pattern of paulownia leaves (Fig. 100).

The tokonoma of Totsutotsusai is more than 2.3 meters wide, and next to it is a recessed pine board inset; both are special features of this room. The tokonoma post is the eighteen-centimeter-thick trunk of a pine planted by the eighth-generation grand master, Ittō. The timbers of the lintels were provided by Lord Hisamatsu of Matsuyama. On Seibei's model the tokonoma post is labeled "Big pine from in front

101. Ōmizuya, the main preparation room, with Gengensai's plaque listing the proper "practice setup" (keiko no sekijō).

102. Interior of Hōsensai, showing the tokonoma and the adjacent display shelf.

of Konnichian," while the ceiling materials are labeled "Old pine boards from Daitokuji." Indeed, the tokonoma ceiling is made of narrow pine boards, perhaps to counterbalance the heaviness of the thick tokonoma post and lintels. The recessed board inset next to the tokonoma has a lower ceiling, also surfaced in narrow boards, and a large bamboo-lattice window in the back wall. The panel-and-molding ceiling of the main eight-mat area of the room has *nagaita*-size pine boards alternately set lengthwise and crosswise. The room is illuminated by four shoji doors along the south passageway, papered from 23 centimeters above the floor to the lintel, and one shoji door along the north passageway, papered from about 53 centimeters above the floor to the lintel.

The recess next to the Totsutotsusai tokonoma has neither display shelves, as might have been seen in *shoin*-style rooms, nor a built-in floor-level cabinet *(jibukuro)*. There is only a simple yet bold bamboo-lattice window. Undoubtedly this was Gengensai's way of counterbalancing the unprecedented inclusion of such a large *soan*-style tokonoma post in the room. Yet the combination of stylistic elements on such a large scale seems perfectly natural, even stately—a powerful testimony to Gengensai's innovative genius.

Gengensai built Totsutotsusai as a practice room in which he could teach a relatively large number of people at once and could hold the Seven Special Tea Exercises, where host and guests exchange roles. The usable space could be further expanded by removing the sliding doors to the side passages and the Dairo no Ma. This layout, together with the large preparation room (Fig. 101), was exactly what Urasenke required for teaching.

Diagonally tangent to the northwest corner of the Dairo no Ma is Hōsensai (Fig. 102), which Gengensai's record mentioned above refers to as the "new room, Hōsensai," indicating that it was probably completed just before the tea function. Its inclusion in Seibei's model, however, proves that it was not built as an afterthought. Twelve mats in size, this formal room is bordered on two sides by sliding doors half-papered with shoji, beyond which is an enclosed veranda. A tokonoma 2.1 meters wide, with a 13.8-centimeter-diameter tokonoma post and black-lacquered crosspieces, occupies the northwest corner of the room. Next to it is a 1.4-meter-wide display recess with a built-in shelf and a floor-level cabinet. The two tatami mats directly in front of the tokonoma are trimmed with decorative brocade borders, an indication that these mats are reserved for nobility or honored guests. The ceiling is rather low (2.06 meters). Even with such *shoin*-style touches as the special display-shelf recess, the overall accent is on simplicity.

Finally, it should be mentioned that Gengensai's program of expansion also encompassed the kitchen and the entryway. A plaque commemorating the completion of the roof, dated the twenty-fourth day of the fourth month of 1856, mentions the carpenters Kimura Seibei and Kimura Kōjirō and lists "rooms from the practice room to the kitchen" among the labors accomplished.

Twentieth-Century Additions to the Compound

Ennōsai, the thirteenth-generation Urasenke grand master, held a formal tea service at Heian Shrine in Kyoto in 1923, the same year that his grandson Hōunsai, the present grand master, was born. His good fortune that year inspired him not only to carry out repairs to Yūin but to build a new room, the fourteen-mat Tairyūken (Shelter Facing the Stream; Fig. 103).

Located in the northeastern corner of the Urasenke property, at the end of the passageway along the north side of Totsutotsusai and north of the storehouse attached to the Rikyūdō, where a small Buddhist hall had once stood, Tairyūken was laid out on a grand scale. The central fourteen-mat area is surrounded on three sides—south, east, and west—by passages totaling an additional fourteen mats. The mat count of the Tairyūken wing as a whole is greater than that of Hōsensai and is equaled only by that of Totsutotsusai, the Dairo no Ma, and the north and south passageways opening onto these two rooms combined.

Tairyūken, conceived in basically the same mixture of styles as Totsutotsusai, has a 2.1-meter-wide tokonoma with a massive tokonoma post of red pine with the bark still attached. Next to it is a display recess with a built-in floor-level cabinet. The crosspieces extending from the tokonoma post are equally sturdy logs, but their heaviness is alleviated by the delicate shoji-papered sliding doors to either side. A further point of attention is the *tsukeshoin* window-desk in the eastern side passage.

The courtyard bordered by Tairyūken, Hōsensai, and the passageway north of Totsutotsusai was landscaped at the same time, and a stone water basin was set in the

103. Interior of Tairyūken.

104. Interior of Yūshin, showing the ryūrei *room on the right and the traditional six-mat room on the left.*

shade of a huge pine named "Reclining Dragon." In 1954, across this courtyard to the northwest of Hōsensai, the fourteenth-generation Urasenke grand master, Tantansai, constructed Yūshin (New Again), a tearoom that includes a semi-Western-style room for the *ryūrei* table-top tea service and a traditional six-mat room (Fig. 104). In 1956, when the Chadō Kaikan, a building housing a tea study center, was constructed south of Hompōji, across Ogawa Street from the Urasenke compound, it, too, was given a *ryūrei* tearoom. In a sense, Yūshin served as a prototype.

The *ryūrei* tea service can be traced back to Gengensai, who invented the special lacquered brazier-table for presenting tea to foreign guests at the First Kyoto Exposition of 1872. In the century that followed, however, no grand master designed a tea room especially for the *ryūrei* service. Two temporary *ryūrei* rooms were set up by an architect in 1950 at the Japanese Way of Tea Exhibition at Matsuzakaya Department Store in Tokyo, but they were coolly received by the tea world.

It was only with the construction of the Yushin *ryūrei* room by Tantansai that the *ryūrei* service finally received the approval of the grand masters of tea. The Yūshin *ryūrei* room, bordered on two sides by a traditional covered veranda, is an approximately ten-mat tile-floored area incorporating old post and ceiling timbers that give it a certain "folk art" effect. Here are arranged the lacquered brazier-table, named the "Honorable Garden" *(misonodana),* for the host, and long benches for the guests. The adjoining six-mat tatami room is designed to allow the use of both rooms for special combined tea services—the perfect reflection of contemporary Japan, poised between East and West.

CHAPTER SIX

Midday Tea in the Urasenke Manner

by Sōbin Kawashima

The *chaji,* or "tea function," is the ever-present goal of practice in chanoyu; the various guidelines and procedures one learns orchestrate all aspects of this "one meeting" between host and guests. The ultimate aim of the tea function is the realization of harmony *(wa),* respect *(kei),* purity *(sei),* and tranquillity *(jaku).*

The midday tea function, or *shōgo no chaji,* embodying as it does the fundamentals of chanoyu, is considered the standard tea function. Yet even this orthodox framework allows virtually limitless variations. The function described in this chapter took place in autumn; the setting was a four-and-a-half-mat tearoom in Tokyo modeled on Urasenke's Yūin. The host was fifteenth-generation grand master Hōunsai (Sōshitsu Sen); the guests were among the most eminent tea practitioners in Tokyo. Following is a summary of the function, parts of which will be explained in detail later in this chapter.

Once the guests have been met by the host, they purify themselves at the stone water basin and enter the tearoom. They view the calligraphy scroll by fourth-generation grand master Sensō displayed in the tokonoma, then go to their seats. At this point the host greets his guests and the guests return his greeting; then the host lays the hearth. Next the guests retire to a larger room modeled on Totsutotsusai for the *kaiseki* meal. In the tokonoma here the host has hung a painting by Tawaraya Sōtatsu (d. 1643?) above a simple arrangement of wild chrysanthemums in a vermilion lacquer saké saucer, beside which is displayed an antique red-on-black *negoro*-lacquer bottle. Little by little the guests are beginning to "read" their host's message—but before they can satisfy their curiosity, they step outside to the *roji* garden for an intermission.

The sound of a gong is the signal to reenter the tearoom. Now a white camellia bud and a branch of autumn leaves in a bamboo flower container made by third-generation grand master Sōtan are the focus of the tokonoma. Utensils for the thick-

Pl. 75. The hearth utensils and charcoal basket.

Pl. 76. The mukōzuke *appetizer, rice, and* miso *soup on an individual meal tray.*

Pl. 77. The rice server and paddle.

Pl. 78. Nimono, *morsels in seasoned broth.*

Pl. 79. Yakimono, *broiled tidbits.*

Pl. 80. Hassun, *dishes from land and sea or river, served on a square tray.*

Pl. 81. *Hot water pitcher (yutō), ladle, and pickles.*

Pl. 82. *Moist sweets, served in stacked lacquer boxes, with cake picks.*

Pl. 83. The tokonoma contains a camellia and a branch of autumn leaves in Sōtan's "Priest Genshitsu" bamboo flower container.

Pl. 84. The tea caddy in its brocade pouch and the fresh-water container used in the thick-tea service.

Pl. 85. Dry sweets served with thin tea, on Gengensai's "Mountain Path" tray.

Pl. 86. Sōshitsu Sen preparing thick tea.

tea *(koicha)* presentation include a prized Old Seto tea caddy and a tea scoop by Sensō. There is silence in the tearoom as the host prepares the tea; all that can be heard is the light patter of raindrops on the leaves outside, mingled with the murmur of the water boiling in the kettle. The guests share a single bowl of tea, communing without speech.

After another brief intermission, thin tea *(usucha)* is served. Now the scroll in the tokonoma is a letter by Rikyū containing a poem that sums up the spiritual theme of the entire "one meeting." After partaking of thin tea, the guests take leave of their host, knowing that together they have created a living, if fleeting, work of art. In a small way, they have experienced the perfection that is possible when hearts and minds truly share in the profound beauty and mystery of the world.

Kaiki, "Tea-Gathering Records"

Guests at tea functions often keep diaries called *kaiki,* or "tea-gathering records," by which to recall these all-too-brief events. Such a record lists all the items displayed or used, in order of importance and appearance, with brief descriptions where necessary. The record not only serves as a memento but may in time become a valuable historical document as well; many past tea functions have been reconstructed on the basis of *kaiki.* The knowledgeable reader of a tea-gathering record can often catch intimations of the host's circumstances and thinking at the time of a particular gathering.

Following is a record of the midday tea function discussed in this chapter. Note that the *kaiseki* meal, an aesthetic statement in itself, is recorded in careful detail. From the *mukōzuke* (main appetizer), *nimono* (morsels in seasoned broth), and *yakimono* (broiled foods) to the *sakana* (tidbits to complement sakè), *kosuimono* (light broth), and *hassun* (tray of delicacies from land and sea), the painstaking selection of flavors and artistry of presentation convey the unspoken sentiments of the host as much as the actual tea service does.

First Sitting
  Tokonoma: one-line calligraphy scroll by Sensō reading "In fine rain arrives the October sky"
  Kettle: Old Ashiya ironware with cast pattern of rabbit over waves on one side and pine beach in mist on the other
  Hearth frame: antique striped persimmon wood
  Incense container: blue-and-white porcelain, with water buffalo motif
  Charcoal basket: Sensō's bamboo sheath charcoal basket, with Chikusō's cipher
  Feather brush: argus pheasant
  Charcoal chopsticks: antique, with mulberry-wood handles
  Ash scoop: antique, with mulberry-wood handle
  Kettle rings: iron, by Jōmi
  Kettle rest: paper

Ash dish: copy of Raku Nonkō bisque-ware ash dish, by Tsujii Harima

Kaiseki Meal
- Tokonoma: painting by Tawaraya Sōtatsu from the *Saigyō Monogatari Emaki* (Tale of Saigyō Picture Scroll)
- Flower: wild chrysanthemum
- Flower container: vermilion lacquer sakè saucer
  - Red-on-black lacquer bottle also displayed
- *Mukōzuke*: sea bream with seaweed and wild *bōfū* greens, seasoned with Japanese horseradish and soy sauce
  - Ware: assorted dishes
- Soup: *miso* broth with small potatoes cut into octagons, *azuki* beans, and mustard
- *Nimono*: millet gluten puff, finely chopped quail-meat balls, and chrysanthemum greens, scented with citron peel
  - Ware: black lacquer scooped-corner meal trays; "thread mark" turned black lacquer bowls for the rice, soup, and *nimono*; black lacquer rice server and serving tray
- *Yakimono*: pompano broiled with *miso*
  - Ware: Oribe-ware handled bowl
- Sakè server: loop-handled metal sakè warmer
- Sakè saucers: vermilion lacquer
- Saucer stand: black lacquer
- *Sakana*: soy-milk crisps and lobster, topped with citron peel
  - Ware: celadon bowl
- *Sakana*: arkshell, cockleshell, troughshell, *udo,* and lettuce stalks, with ginger vinegar
  - Ware: Old Hagi-ware bowl
- Sakè decanter: red overglaze enameled ceramic
- *Kosuimono*: sweet acorn in salted-plum broth
  - Ware: "thread mark" turned black lacquer lidded cups
- *Hassun*: *iwatake* fungus with Japanese horseradish dressing; grilled smoked salmon
  - Ware: unfinished-wood tray
- Pitcher: Hot water with crisp browned rice
  - Ware: black lacquer hot-water pitcher and ladle
- Pickles: radish, potherb mustard rolled in turnip slices, and *hinona* greens
  - Ware: Bizen-ware gong-shaped bowl
- Moist sweets: mashed sweetened bean balls
  - Ware: stacked lacquer boxes with openwork decoration

Second Sitting: Thick Tea
- Flower container: Sōtan's "Priest Genshitsu" bamboo flower container; inner boxes inscribed by Ittō and Fukensai; outer boxes inscribed by Gengensai
- Flower: "white jewel" camellia, with branch of autumn leaves
- Fresh-water container: Southeast Asian rope-pattern jar, with lacquered lid inscribed by Gengensai

Tea caddy: "Rock Cleft Roots," a Sen family treasure; Old Seto ware, broad bottom, with written appraisal by Kobori Enshū; outer boxes signed by Ittō and Tantansai
Silk pouches: Daikokuya gold brocade, Mochizuki *kantō* [fine-striped fabric]
Tea scoop: "Mountain Temple" by Sensō; case inscribed by Sensō; inner box inscribed by seventh-generation Omotesenke grand master Joshinsai; outer box inscribed by Tantansai
Tea bowl: "Thousand Pine Isles," Korean Yi-dynasty rain-spotted Katade ware
Kettle lid rest: bamboo, with Sōtan's cipher
Waste-water receptacle: white bronze with design of interlocking rings

Second Sitting: Thin Tea
Tokonoma: Letter from Rikyū to Jumyōin, containing the poem "How pathetic! / This brushwood hut, / So lonely / That only mountain gales / Blow people this way."
Flower: autumn varieties
Flower container: Iga ware
Kettle: Oribe's banded kettle, by Onishi Jōsei [1594–1682]
Hearth frame: grass-and-flower *maki-e* design
Fresh-water container: White Dutch tobacco-leaf jar, slender shape
Thin-tea container: large *natsume* favored by Rikyū, with Jōsō's cipher
Tea scoop: "Plover" by Ittō; case inscribed by Ittō; box inscribed by Fukensai
Tea bowl: "Hermit's Hut" by Hon'ami Kōetsu, Red Raku ware
   Additional tea bowl: "Sauna Hut," Shino-kiln Oribe ware
   Additional tea bowl: "Serenity" by Gen'etsu
Kettle lid rest: freshly cut green bamboo
Waste-water receptacle: arabesque relief, by Jōeki; box inscribed by Tantansai
Dry sweets: "Windblown leaves," pressed-sugar confections
Sweet dish: Gengensai's "Mountain Path" tray by [eighth-generation] Nakamura Sōtetsu

The Tea Function in Detail

Those invited to a tea function customarily arrive fifteen minutes early. The guests enter the vestibule *(yoritsuki)*, where they may leave their belongings and change clothes if necessary. Those wearing kimono generally bring a change of *tabi,* the split-toed socks worn with kimono, while those in Western dress usually bring a pair of white socks. The guests then move into the waiting room *(machiai),* where they await the arrival of all those invited and collect their thoughts (Fig. 105). The host, realizing that the right atmosphere here will help put the guests in the proper mood for tea, has carefully prepared the waiting room. Its decoration is subdued, so as not to detract from that of the tearoom; if a scroll is displayed, it will be of a light nature.

105. The guests sit quietly in the waiting room till all have arrived.

When the last guest announces that all have arrived, the host's assistant *(hantō)* brings in small cups of hot water on a tray and tells the guests that they may move to the outdoor waiting arbor as soon as they are ready. Proceeding in order from the main guest to the last, they step outside into the straw sandals the host has provided (Fig. 106), the last guest being sure to tidy the cups before leaving the room.

In the waiting arbor, the guests find a stack of round straw cushions—one for each person—with the top cushion turned upside down and a smoking set on top. The main guest arranges the cushions along the arbor bench for all the guests (Fig. 107), then sits down, followed by the others (Fig. 108). This is a pause in which to enjoy the beauty of the *roji* garden.

The host now presents himself to the guests to signal that all is in readiness. Having made sure that the tearoom is spotlessly clean and added incense to the hearth, he exits through the room's crawl-in entrance *(nijiriguchi)*, walks over to the stone water basin *(tsukubai)*, and purifies himself by rinsing his hands and mouth. The guests, seeing the host at the basin, know that he will soon call them into the tearoom. When the host steps up to the middle gate, the guests take a few steps forward, and all silently bow their heads in unison (Fig. 109). The host then turns and walks back to the crawl-in entrance, and when he has disappeared from view, the guests return to their seats.

The host reenters the tearoom through the crawl-in entrance, neatly placing his straw sandals sole-to-sole beside the stepping stone below the entrance and leaving the door panel slightly open. While the host is working in the preparation room *(mizuya)*, each guest in turn takes leave of the others to purify mouth and hands at the basin before going to the crawl-in entrance (Fig. 110).

106. The guests move to the outdoor waiting arbor, beginning with the main guest.

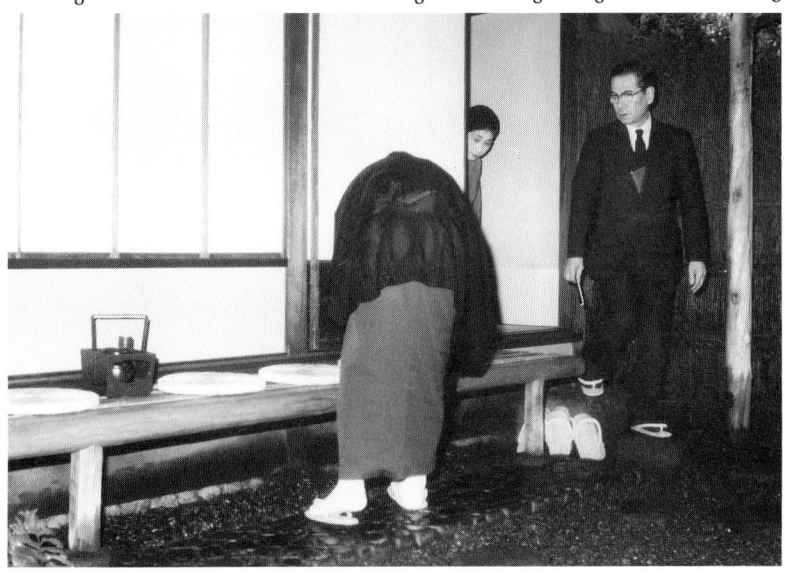

107. The main guest arranges the cushions in the waiting arbor.

At the crawl-in entrance, each guest in turn crouches on the stepping stone and, placing his or her folding fan on the threshold as a sign of respect, briefly views the interior. Then, ducking through the entrance, he or she places the straw sandals next to those of the host, out of the way of the next guest (Fig. 112). Once in the tearoom, each guest proceeds first to the tokonoma to admire the scroll, then to the hearth, each time sitting with fan placed in front of him or her. Each guest takes

MIDDAY TEA IN THE URASENKE MANNER   *125*

108. The guests relax in the waiting arbor until the host appears.

109. The host greets the guests.

110. The guests rinse mouth and hands at the stone water basin.

111. The tearoom waits in readiness. The calligraphy scroll in the tokonoma is by Sensō.

112. The guests enter the tearoom through the crawl-in entrance.

a temporary seat until all have finished, at which point bows are exchanged with the next in line, and all assume their places, the main guest taking the place of honor nearest the tokonoma.

Meanwhile, knowing by the sound of the last guest closing the door to the crawl-in entrance that all have entered the tearoom, the host steps outside through another door and replenishes the water in the stone basin. Returning to the preparation room, he ascertains when the guests have settled themselves in their places, then slides open the door between the tearoom and the preparation room to offer the guests his first spoken greeting of the day. Each guest in turn voices a brief greeting, then the main guest, as spokesman for the group, compliments the host on the thoughtful preparation of the waiting room and *roji* garden and inquires about the scroll in the tokonoma. These preliminaries over, the host goes back to the preparation room to get the charcoal basket. Sitting at the threshold, basket to one side, he bows and announces that he will now lay the charcoal in the hearth. The host takes up the charcoal basket and places it by the hearth (Pl. 75), then brings in the ash dish from the preparation room and, before bringing it up to the hearth, shuts the door.

113. The guests watch the host prepare the hearth.

The host removes the feather brush, kettle rings, metal charcoal chopsticks, and incense container from the charcoal basket, and places a thick pad of folded white paper near the hearth. Slipping the kettle rings into the lugs on the kettle, he lifts the kettle from the hearth, rests it on the pad of paper, moves it away from the hearth, and detaches the rings (Fig. 114). Next he uses the feather brush to dust off the hearth frame and the charcoal chopsticks to rearrange the pilot coals in the hearth (Fig. 115). He then takes up the ash scoop from the ash dish and lays a ring of moist ash inside the hearth as a boundary for the fire (Fig. 116). As soon as the host begins to dust off the hearth frame, each guest exchanges bows with the next in line and moves up to watch him prepare the hearth (Fig. 113). The host brushes off the hearth once again, then adds pieces of fresh charcoal in a prescribed order (Figs. 117, 118). With the positioning of the last small piece of charcoal, the guests return to their places.

Once all the charcoal has been added, the host touches up the hearth one last time with the feather brush, places a ball of slow-burning kneaded incense in the hearth, and sets the incense container out for the guests to inspect. The host returns the kettle to the fire and carries first the ash dish, then the charcoal basket back to the preparation room. In small tearooms like this one, the host will now also sweep the tatami mats in front of the hearth with a bird's-wing duster before exiting and sliding the door shut behind him.

114. The charcoal basket and hearth utensils.

115. The arrangement of the hearth and hearth utensils.

116. The ash dish and scoop.

117 and 118. Laying the charcoal.

119. The main guest takes a sakè saucer from the stack presented by the host.

The incense container, having been passed down the line for all the guests to inspect, is returned to the host's place by the head guest, whereupon the host returns to the room. He sits at the hearth, folds his silk wiping cloth *(fukusa),* and places the kettle lid slightly askew. The main guest may then inquire about the incense container. Finally, the host gathers up the incense container and bows at the preparation-room door, saying that he will now serve a light meal, then shuts the door. The guests now repair to a larger room for the *kaiseki* meal.

In the preparation room the host arranges three dishes on each guest's individual meal tray—two lidded lacquer bowls, one for rice and one for *miso* soup, and a "dish on the far side" *(mukōzuke)* of the tray as the main appetizer (Pl. 76, Fig. 120). He serves the guests one at a time, beginning with the main guest, first bowing at the door to the room with a tray set in front of him. On leaving the room after serving the last guest, the host again pauses at the door and says, "The food is nothing to speak of, but please partake." When the host shuts the preparation-room door, the other guests thank the main guest for this opportunity to share a meal with him.

The host reenters with a stack of sakè saucers and a sakè warmer and offers them to the main guest. After bowing to the next guest, the main guest receives the stack of saucers and raises it appreciatively while bowing slightly. He then lifts the saucers off the stand with both hands, leaves the bottom saucer on the tatami mat before him, returns the rest to the stand, and passes the stack on to the next guest (Fig. 119). The

130 CHAPTER SIX

120. The mukōzuke *appetizer, rice, and miso soup on an individual meal tray.*

host pours sakè for each guest in turn (Figs. 121, 122), then returns to the preparation room. Once the guests have sipped the sakè, they may taste the *mukōzuke* appetizer, which is meant to accompany the sakè.

The host brings out the rice server, on top of which has been placed a serving tray and rice paddle (Pl. 77), and sits in front of the main guest. Setting the serving tray to one side, he picks up the rice paddle with his right hand, opening the lid to the rice server with his left hand just enough to insert the paddle. He then holds out the serving tray for the main guest's rice bowl, offering to serve him. Usually the main guest declines, saying that he and the other guests can serve themselves, at which point the host turns the rice server so that the paddle faces the main guest, then holds out the tray for the main guest's soup bowl, asking if he would like more soup (Fig. 123). The host takes the soup bowl into the preparation room to refill it. When all the guests have been served in this manner, he brings out the bowls of *nimono*, morsels in seasoned broth (Pl. 78), followed by more sakè in the sakè warmer. The *yakimono*, or broiled food, appears next (Pl. 79), followed by another helping of rice, after which the host takes leave of the guests. He announces, "I will eat in the preparation room; please clap your hands if you require me," then closes the door behind him. The host waits until he ascertains that the guests have finished eating, whereupon he brings out small cups of *kosuimono*, or light broth.

The next course the host serves is the *hassun*, or "eight inch," square unfinished-

121 and *122*. The host pours sakè for each guest, beginning with the main guest.

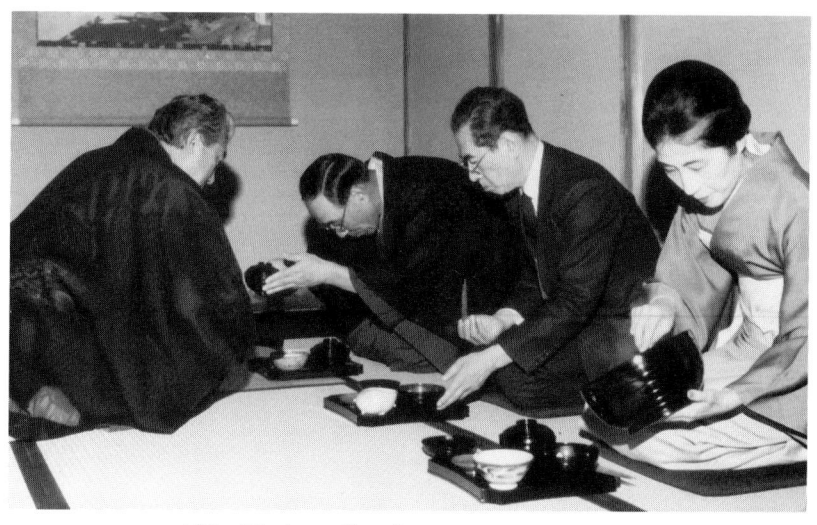

123. The host offers the main guest more soup.

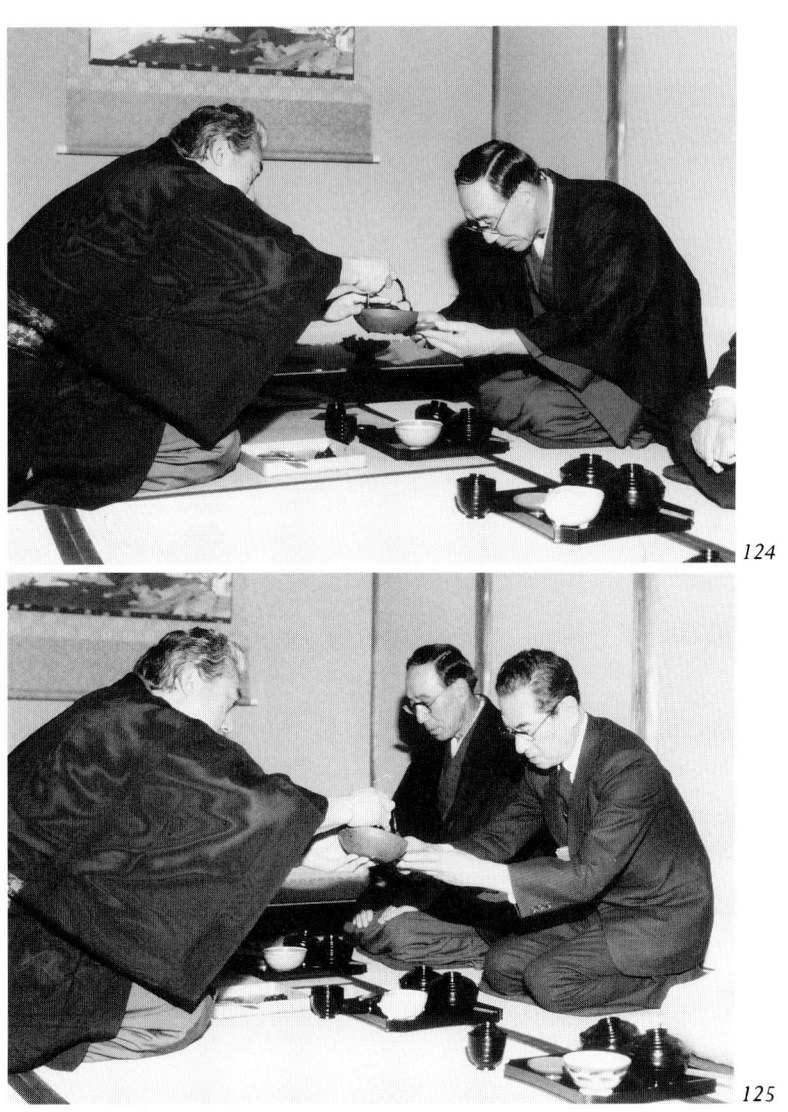

124 and *125. The host serves each guest in turn with* hassun *dishes and sakè.*

wood tray, bearing two types of delicacies: one from mountain or field, the other from ocean or river. They are arranged diagonally on the tray in two mounds of bite-size portions, along with serving chopsticks of green bamboo (Pl. 80). The host carries the tray in his left hand and the sakè warmer in his right. He sits in front of the main guest, serves sakè, then, taking the lid of the main guest's broth cup, places some of the sea delicacies in it. This procedure is repeated with the other guests, after which the host returns to the head of the line (Figs. 124, 125).

126. The host offers the hot-water pitcher and pickles to the main guest.

Here begins the so-called migrating-plover sakè service *(chidori no sakazuki),* in which the sakè is passed back and forth between the guests and the host. The host hands the sakè warmer to the second guest and turns the *hassun* tray to face the first guest, who wipes his sakè saucer with a sheet from the pad of paper tucked in the front of his kimono and hands the saucer to the host. The second guest pours for the host, then places the warmer on the tatami mat, facing the host. Meanwhile, the main guest takes a sheet or two from his pad of paper on which to serve the host both land and sea delicacies from the *hassun* tray. When the second guest requests sakè from the saucer which the host is holding, the host obliges, turns the sakè warmer to face the third guest, and serves the main and second guests land delicacies in the lids of their broth cups. This is repeated down the line, and when the host returns to the main guest, they exchange another round of sakè. The main guest then asks the host to collect the sakè saucers, which the host takes back to the preparation room.

Next the host brings out the hot-water pitcher *(yutō)* and ladle on a rectangular lacquer tray, along with a dish of pickles (Pl. 81). The host offers the pickles to the main guest, then places the ladle in the pitcher, setting it to the right of the main guest, and places the now-empty broth cups on the tray (Fig. 126). Withdrawing to the preparation room with the cups, he bows and closes the door behind him. In the host's absence, the main guest takes some pickles and passes on the pickle dish; similarly, he removes the lid from the pitcher, ladles some hot water and browned rice into both his rice and soup bowls, and passes on the pitcher. It is the last guest's task to return the pitcher and pickle dish to the preparation-room door. After

127. The guests prepare to reenter the tearoom.

drinking the liquid, all the guests wipe their bowls clean with paper and drop their chopsticks on their trays in unison as a signal that they have finished. When the host hears this, he opens the door, withdraws the pitcher and pickle dish, and removes the individual trays, bowing to each guest. This concludes the kaiseki meal.

Moist sweets are now served in stacked lacquer boxes *(fuchidaka),* with wooden cake picks partially stripped of bark *(kuromoji)* placed on the lid (Pl. 82). The stack is set in front of the main guest, at which point the host retreats to the preparation-room door. He tells the guests he would like to rearrange the other room for the tea service and allow them to stretch their legs before beginning the second sitting. The main guest replies that they will await the sound of a gong as a signal to return to the tearoom. After the host closes the preparation-room door, the main guest exchanges bows with the next guest, lifts the stack of sweet boxes with both hands, inserts a cake pick in the bottom tier, which he takes for himself, and passes the stack down the line. When all have finished the sweets, the last guest restacks the boxes and returns them to the preparation-room door. Starting with the main guest, each guest again admires the tokonoma and the hearth, then retires to the *roji* garden for a brief interlude *(nakadachi).*

The host sounds the gong five times (seven times if there are more than five guests)—loud, soft, medium, medium, loud—as a signal for the guests to return to the tearoom. Rising from their seats at the waiting arbor, the guests crouch down in respectful attention (Fig. 127).

Having purified themselves again at the stone water basin, the guests enter the

128. The guests admire the hearth and the flowers in the tokonoma.

129. The guests await the host.

130. The host prepares thick tea.

131. The tea bowl and a small brocade cloth on which to place it are set out for the main guest.

tearoom and admire the flowers in the tokonoma, the area where the fresh-water container has been placed, and the hearth before taking their places (Pls. 83, 84, Figs. 128, 129). The host proceeds to serve thick tea, then—after another interlude to allow him to rearrange the tearoom—thin tea, as shown in the illustrations (Pl. 86, Figs. 130–38).

132. *The main guest edges forward to receive the tea bowl.*

133. *The main guest partakes.*

134. The main guest inquires about the tea and about the sweets served before the intermission, having passed the tea bowl to the second guest.

135. The guests examine the tea bowl and brocade cloth.

MIDDAY TEA IN THE URASENKE MANNER

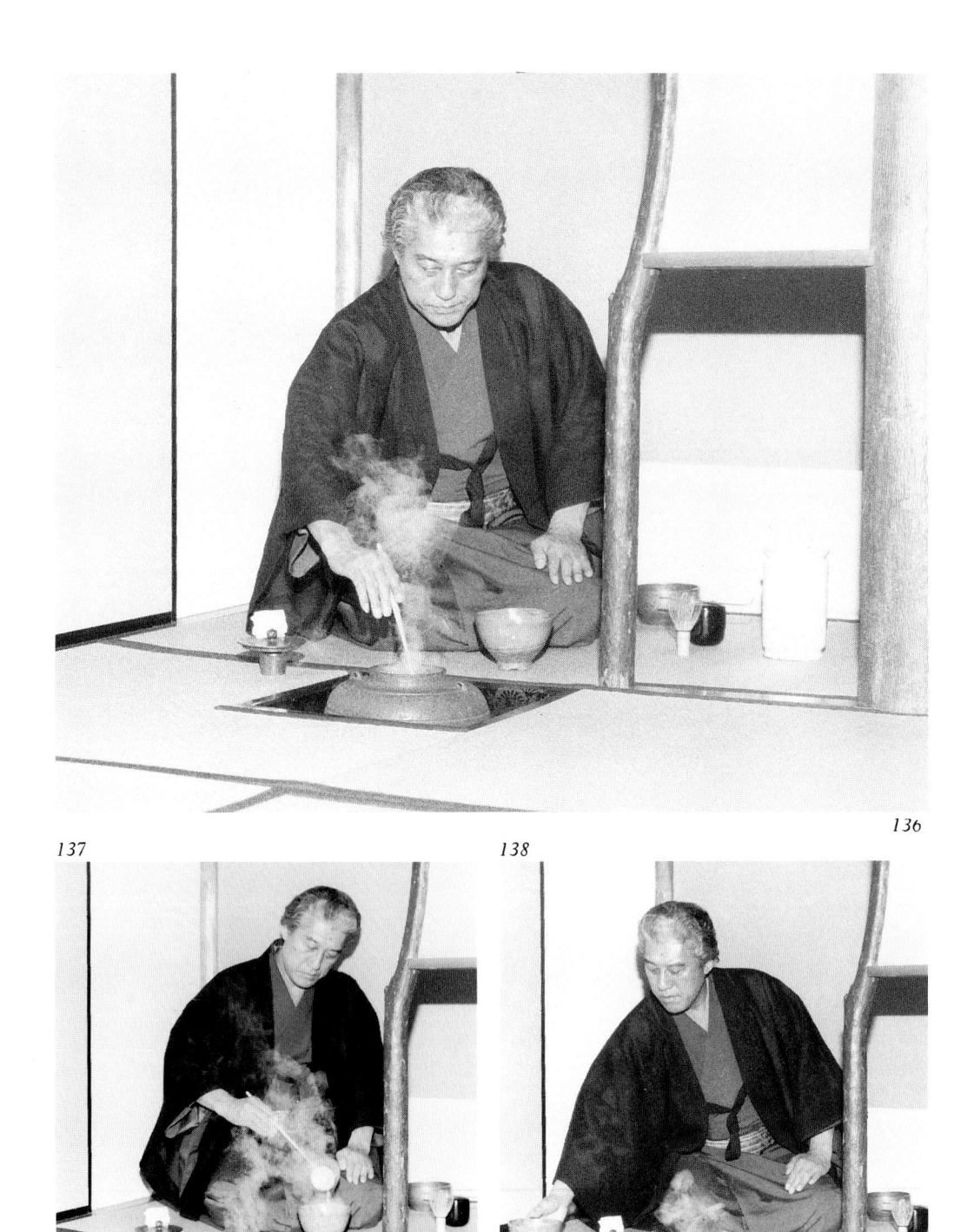

136–38. The host prepares thin tea.

140 CHAPTER SIX

139. The guests examine tea utensils and box inscriptions.

APPENDIX

Documents on the Urasenke Grand Masters

by Akio Tanihata

Calligraphic Transmission of Rikyū's Lay Name by Kokei Sōchin (Fig. 140) On the seventh day of the tenth month of 1585, Toyotomi Hideyoshi offered tea to the retired emperor Ōgimachi, the princes Higashinomiya Kazuhito (the crown prince) and Yōkōin Masahito, Lord Konoe Sakihisa, and two other guests in gratitude for his appointment to the position of *kampaku,* or regent. Hideyoshi himself was to host the imperial tea service in the Kikumi no Ma (Chrysanthemum-viewing Room) of the Kinri Gosho, the innermost quarters of the Imperial Palace in Kyoto, with Sōeki—as Rikyū was then known—as his assistant, after which Sōeki was to present tea to the other nobles in a nearby room. One technical problem, however, had first to be resolved: only nobles and members of the Buddhist clergy could be allowed into the imperial presence, and Sōeki was a commoner. The unprecedented solution was to have a priest formally bestow a Buddhist lay name upon him, and so his Zen master, Kokei Sōchin, wrote out the name Rikyū, under which he had already been training for years. The text of the transmission reads:

> Hōsensai Sōeki of Southern Izumi Province has been my student for thirty years. He has endeavored in Zen and tea. Recently he was honored by the emperor's order with the name and title of Layman Rikyū. Hearing of this auspicious enterprise, my joyful applause is endless, and composing this verse, I add my congratulations.
>
> Like Layman Pang, old author of miraculous powers.
> Eating rice when hungry, and drinking tea when it comes his way.
> Empty-minded, having passed the examination, he quietly looks—
> The flowers of seclusion, newly fragrant in the wind and dew.*

---

* Soshun Hamamoto, "Reflections on the Buddhist Name 'Rikyu'," translated by Dennis Hirota, *Chanoyu Quarterly*, No. 43 (Fall 1985), p. 11.

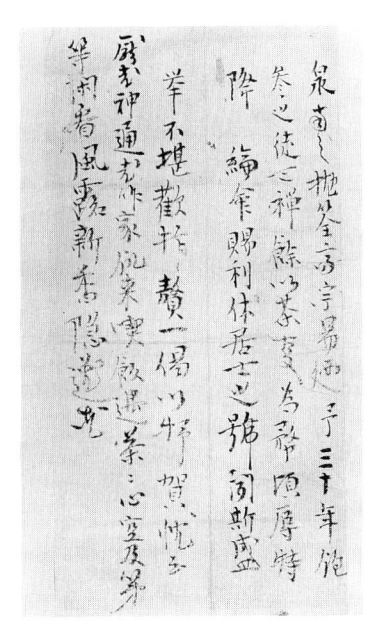

140. Calligraphic transmission of Rikyū's lay name by Kokei Sōchin.

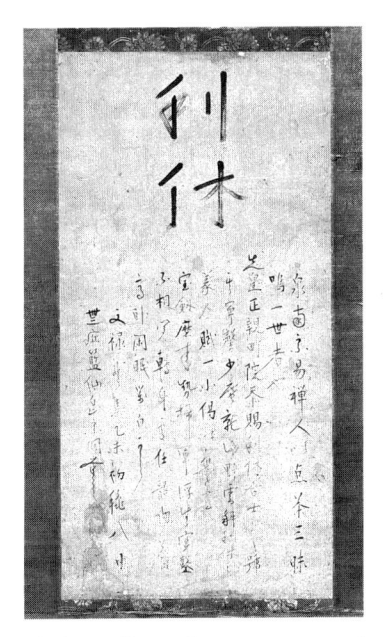

141. Calligraphic transmission of Rikyū's lay name by Sengaku Sōtō.

According to a firsthand account sent by Rikyū to his friend Shun'oku Sōen, abbot of Daitokuji, on the day of the tea service paintings by Ikushima Kyodō and the Southern Song artist Muqi hung in the tokonoma above a tea-leaf storage jar, while a plain wood *daisu* and chrysanthemum-crest *natsume* were used in the service. Rikyū went on to note that it was the most honorable event in his life.

Kokei Sōchin (1532–97), the one hundred eighteenth abbot of Daitokuji, was born into the Asakura clan of Echizen (present-day Fukui Prefecture). Upon entering Daitokuji, he trained under the one hundred eighth abbot, Shōrei Sōkin, as Shun'oku had earlier. Kokei's acquaintance with Rikyū went far back. When Rikyū's first patron, Oda Nobunaga, was assassinated in 1582, Nobunaga's successor, Hideyoshi, who revered Kokei, arranged for him to preside at the funeral. Kokei had close ties with a wide circle of tea connoisseurs. He may even have been responsible for persuading Rikyū to fund the construction work on the Daitokuji temple gate that led to the latter's downfall.

Calligraphic Transmission of Rikyū's Lay Name by Sengaku Sōtō (Fig. 141) This scroll was written in 1595 in answer to Rikyū's son Shōan's inquiry as to the meaning of his father's lay name. Shōan was around fifty at the time and had returned to Kyoto the previous year from exile in Aizu-Wakamatsu, Gamō Ujisato and Tokugawa Ieyasu having interceded with Hideyoshi in his behalf. At that point Hideyoshi returned to Shōan the various tea heirlooms of the Sen family and granted him a plot of land

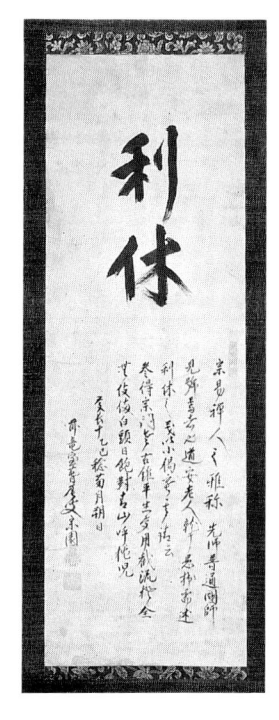

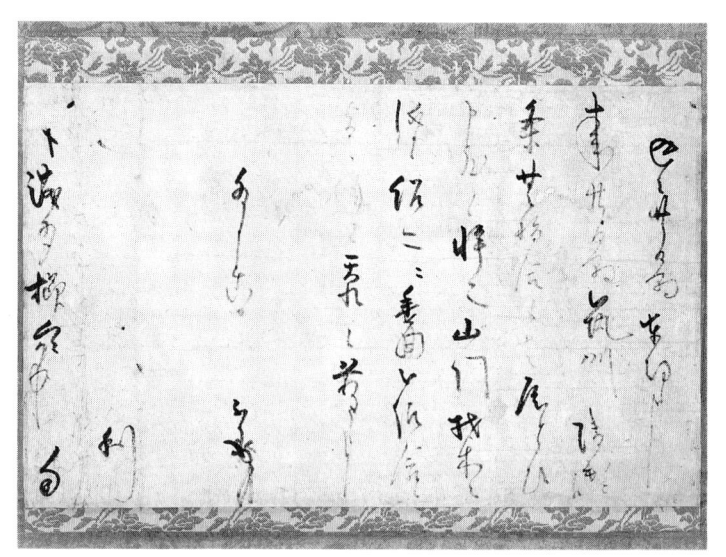

143. Letter by Rikyū concerning the Daitokuji temple gate, addressed to Asano Nagamasa, dated the eighteenth day of the fourth month.

142. Calligraphic transmission of Rikyū's lay name by Shun'oku Sōen.

next to Hompōji. With the Sen family thus on the road to recovery from the disgrace of Rikyū's enforced suicide, Shōan's inquiry probed the spiritual basis of the entire Sen tradition of tea.

Sengaku Sōtō (1545–95), the one hundred twenty-third abbot of Daitokuji, was the younger brother of the wealthy Sakai merchant Tani Sōrin. At the age of twelve he became a disciple of Dairin Sōtō, then of Shōrei Sōkin. Sengaku had been an old friend of Rikyū's, which no doubt prompted Shōan to approach him. The text of the transmission includes an explanation to the effect that Sōeki of Sakai, man of Zen, achieved fame throughout the realm by means of chanoyu. The retired emperor Ogimachi bestowed upon him the name Rikyū, of which Rikyū's son Shōan has come to inquire the meaning. In replay, Sengaku offered a poem that refers to one of Rikyū's farewell verses:

> Brandishing his polished jeweled sword against armies,
> Never a question that he'd penetrate the floating world,
> He let the sun's glory answer in his stead
> While he rested nobly among the clouds.

Calligraphic Transmission of Rikyū's Lay Name by Shun'oku Sōen (Fig. 142) This scroll was written in response to Rikyū's son Dōan's inquiry as to the meaning of the name Rikyū. Of the several extant documents concerning the name, this one is of the greatest interest because Shun'oku Sōen clearly indicates that Rikyū had been using the name prior to the Kinri Gosho tea service. The poem in the text also provides the clearest exposition of the meaning of the name Rikyū Koji, "Layman [*koji*] who puts Keenness [*ri*] to Rest [*kyū*]:

> The poetic name [Rikyū] was bestowed upon Sōeki, man of Zen, by his former teacher, Futsū Kokushi [Dairin Sōtō]. Old man Dōan has asked the meaning of the name Rikyū, and I reply in this short verse:
>
>> Sharpened over long years of spiritual training,
>> His skill attained a cutting edge in living.
>> By old age, he put all artifice behind him,
>> Satisfied to lie down in the green hills.

Letters by Rikyū Concerning the Daitokuji Temple Gate (Fig. 143)   Probably written a year or so before the completion of the Daitokuji temple gate addition in 1589, the first letter, addressed to Asano Nagamasa, expresses Rikyū's concern about the project as a whole and building materials in particular. The letter is dated the eighteenth day of the fourth month (no year is given). Its text reads:

> The morning of the twentieth, Maeda Toshiie Chikushū will be arriving, and I thought I would ask you to come, too, if you had no other plans. Also, as to the lumber for the temple gate, I understand that you have already discussed matters with Shōji. Thank you.

Shōji was Rikyū's son-in-law, son of the Sakai tea connoisseur Mizuochi Sōkei. Judging from the names that appear on an extant plaque on the gate itself, Rikyū mobilized all his family and friends for the project:

> Exalted Layman Rikyū and his associates Jōan, Sōan, Shōan, Shōji, Shimbō, Daizō, Gen'an; chief carpenters Kuwabara Jimbei Yoshiie and Kusunoki Kichibei Munetsugu, both nobles of the Fujiwara clan of Amagasaki; and plasterer Kojima Kichizaemon Masaji, also a noble of the Fujiwara clan. Noted the fifth day of the twelfth month of Tenshō 17 [1589] by old abbot Shun'oku Sōen.

The second letter is dated simply the seventh—no month or year is given.

> Concerning the work at Daitokuji, I have unofficially arranged for carpenters starting today. I fear I will inconvenience your work by using Tōgorō [but beg your indulgence].

Gion Festival Scene by Hasegawa Kyūzō; Colophon by Sōtan (Pl. 2)   Rikyū received from his first patron, Oda Nobunaga, a handscroll of twelve scenes of Kyoto's famous Gion Festival painted by Hasegawa Kyūzō (1568–93), son of the famous painter Hasegawa Tōhaku (1539–1610), who later painted Rikyū's portrait. The handscroll was cut up into individual scenes, which were mounted on the panels

144. Portrait of Dōan by Sōtan.

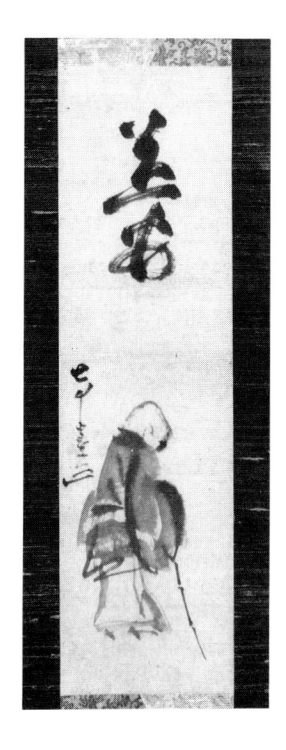

145. Calligraphic tramission of Dōan's art name Min'ō by Shun'oku Sōen.

of a folding screen. Sōtan later had the scenes removed from the screen and wrote a colophon for each. The inscription for this particular scene reads, "Presented by Lord Oda Nobunaga, heirloom of Rikyū." Other colophons include: "Article of [my] ancestor Rikyū Sōeki Koji"; "Article formerly owned by Lord Oda Nobunaga, presented to Rikyū Sōeki Koji"; and "Article of Rikyū Koji."

The present mounting of the scenes as hanging scrolls was the work of Gengensai, who used fabrics Sōtan had received from the empress Tōfukumon'in as a background. It is recorded that nine of the scrolls were formerly displayed together, presenting a lively panorama of the Gion Festival's parade, floats, and spectators.

Portrait of Dōan by Sōtan (Fig. 144) In this quick ink-wash study, the aged Dōan totters along with his cane under the bold two-character inscription of his name. The small inscription to the left, "By seventy-year-old Sōtan" (sixty-nine years old according to the Western system of reckoning age), dates the work to around 1647, some forty years after Dōan's death at the age of sixty-one.

Dōan was said to have had an "overpowering" manner in tea, as opposed to the gentler style of Shōan. According to the *Chawa Shigetsu Shū*, Dōan's prowess was such that he might easily have served tea before the Great Buddha of Tōdaiji, and indeed Rikyū recognized his skill. Was this image Sōtan's way of conjuring up the memory of his uncle, whose presence had been overshadowed by later developments in the Sen family tradition of tea?

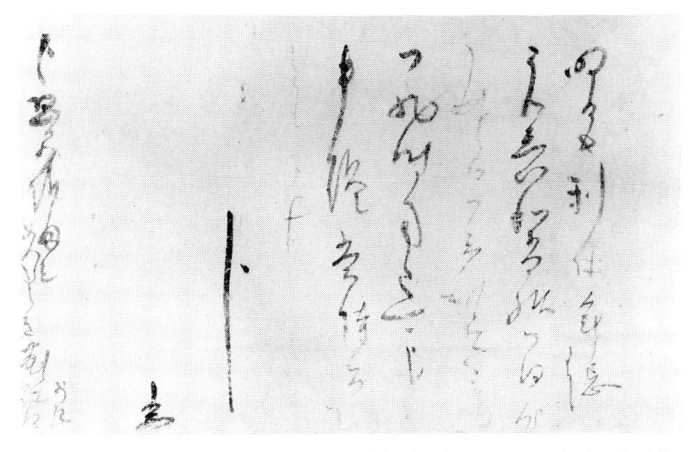

146. Letter by Shōan inviting the head priest of Soken'in to attend the Buddhist service in observance of what was probably the thirteenth anniversary of Rikyū's death (1603).

Calligraphic Transmission of Dōan's Art Name Min'ō by Shun'oku Sōen (Fig. 145) Dōan received the art name Min'ō in 1600 at the age of fifty-four. Having left Kyoto for the provinces immediately after Rikyū's death, Dōan was more than ready to lead a settled life in his later years, making his art name Min'ō—"Sleepy Old Man"—an apt choice. Shun'oku Sōen was Zen master to many renowned men of tea, including Furuta Oribe and Kobori Enshū, and no doubt was intuitively attuned to the subtleties of chanoyu. He was the ideal person to ask for an art name. The text of the transmission reads:

> The elderly Dōan has sent white *kōzo* paper from far Sakai, asking me to write an art name for him. Avoiding fixed ideas, I have come up with the name Min'ō, and beneath these two large characters I relate the meaning through this verse:
>
>> A hoary head finds a pillow indoors
>> To rest as things take their normal course;
>> The day has come for the old man to rest from labor,
>> Like a tired seagull asleep on the southern bay.

Letter by Shōan Regarding an Anniversary of Rikyū's death (Fig. 146) No verifiable date has been ascertained for this letter to Gyokuho Jōshō, the one hundred thirtieth abbot of Daitokuji, but from the mention of the one hundred forty-first abbot, Un'ei Sōi, who died in the tenth month of 1603, the memorial services mentioned appear to correspond to the traditionally observed thirteenth-anniversary services, which would have been held in the second month of that year. This would place the letter in the midst of the period when Shōan and his son Sōtan were struggling to put the Sen family back on its feet. Judging from the request to "bring flowers," Gyokuho was on very good terms with Shōan. The text reads:

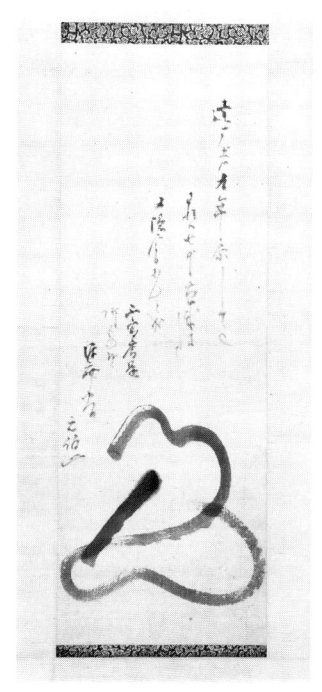

147. Bodhidharma *by Sōtan*.

Tomorrow memorial services for Rikyū will be held. I sincerely hope you will be able to attend, together with Abbot Un'ei. I will be prepared in either case. You may also invite those under you . . . Please bring some of your marvelous flowers.

Calligraphy by Sōtan, Reading "This Day" (Pl. 5)   A direct reference to Konnichian, "Hut of This Day," the two bold characters reading "This day" (*konnichi*) above Sōtan's diamond-shaped "weaver's spool" seal probably date from around the time of the completion of the tearoom in the spring of 1648.

Bodhidharma, Painted and Inscribed by Sōtan (Fig. 147)   This simple drawing of the Zen patriarch Bodhidharma, executed in two brushstrokes, bears the following inscription:

Bodhidharma spent nine years [staring at a wall]. I've spent seventy-six [seventy-five, by Western reckoning] years [at chanoyu] to come up with Yūin and Konnichian. Fushin'an—what to make of him?—for Gensai

Possibly produced in connection with the completion of the tearoom Yūin in 1653 and presented to Gensai—Sōtan's third son, Sōsa—the inscription seems to be saying that only in his retirement quarters Konnichian and Yūin did Sōtan feel he had attained his *wabi* ideal. The closing query, "Fushin'an—what to make of him?"

148   APPENDIX

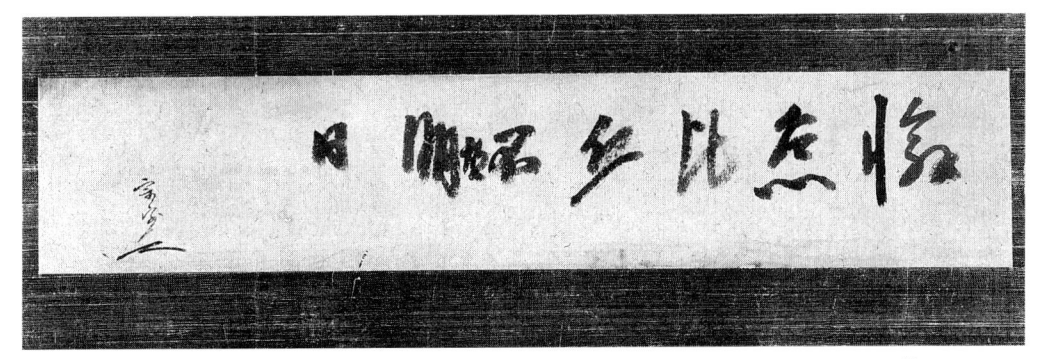

148. Calligraphy by Sensō, reading "The negligent monk expects no tomorrow."

is more problematic: does Fushin'an here refer to Rikyū, who built the tearoom of that name, or to Sōtan himself? If the former, Sōtan may be saying he has finally attained the state that Rikyū had; if the latter, Sōtan may be encouraging his son to equal or even surpass him in tea.

Calligraphy by Sensō, Reading "The Negligent Monk Expects No Tomorrow" (Fig. 148) These words, transcribed from a piece of writing by the one hundred seventy-first abbot of Daitokuji, Seigan Sōi, have behind them a story that led to the naming of Konnichian, "Hut of This Day." When construction of the tearoom was completed in 1648, Sōtan invited Seigan to come see the new tearoom and help think of a name for it. Sōtan waited long past the appointed hour, but there was no sign of Seigan. Finally he gave up and went out to do some errands. Eventually Seigan showed up, but now Sōtan was nowhere to be found. Seigan decided not to wait and, leaving behind a note of apology reading "The negligent monk expects no tomorrow," walked back to Daitokuji. When Sōtan returned and found the note, he felt ashamed at having gone out without leaving any message. He thereupon reinvited Seigan to the "Hut of This Day."

Another version of the story relates that Seigan named the room Konnichian and added the "negligent monk" comment in explanation. In response to this, Sōtan composed the phrase, "A fortuitous meeting with the monk waits not on the morrow." The original pieces of calligraphy by Sōtan and Seigan are preserved in the Urasenke collection.

Letter by Sensō Regarding the Centennial of Rikyū's Death (Fig. 149) This letter, dated the fifth day of the third month, was written in 1690 to Murai Izumo Tōjūrō, a general serving the Maeda clan of Kaga, as did Sensō. In the letter Sensō reports that the Rikyū centennial service held at Daitokuji went smoothly:

> I gratefully received your letter of the fourth and was happy to hear that [Lord Maeda Tsunanori] is doing well in Edo. Perhaps now, as you say, I will be allowed

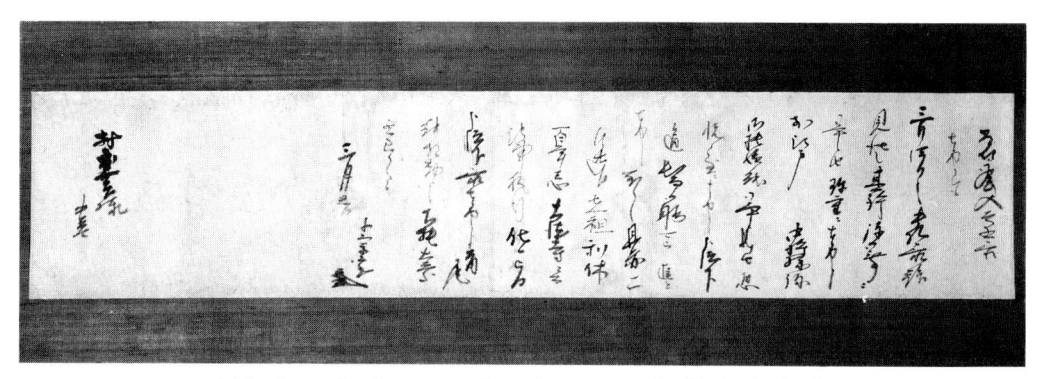

149. Letter by Sensō regarding the centennial of Rikyū's death.

to retire. As to the centennial memorial service for my ancestor Rikyū, held on the twenty-eighth of last month, I am happy to report that all went well from beginning to end.

Sensō's Farewell Verse (Fig. 150) Written in his own hand, Sensō's verse alludes to Sōtan's "Born out of thin air" farewell verse:

> If out of thin air
> Floating on thin air
> They came forth,
> So now echo back
> The bells of dawn.

Jōsō's Transcription of Sensō's Letter on the Wooden Statue of Rikyū (Fig. 151) This letter, dated the sixteenth day of the first month—no year is included—was written by Sensō to an unknown recipient. According to writings based on information from Gengensai, the head of the wooden statue of Rikyū originally installed in the Daitokuji temple gate was transferred to the Sen family by Kokei Sōchin and stored. The *Fuhaku Hikki* further reports that when Sensō sought to have the statue restored, he engaged the services of a descendant of the Buddhist statuary sculptor Intatsu, who had made the original statue. The text reads:

> I am most satisfied with the details you were able to supply on the prospects for the Rikyū statue and am encouraged to have the [restoration] work done. Once it is finished, I will make a place for it in the house. I only hope it can be enshrined during my lifetime. If need be, I will sell some of the family tea utensils to raise funds. I expect I will soon be contacting the people you indicated.

The two hundred sixteenth Daitokuji abbot, Denshin Sōteki, produced a scroll with a verse commemorating the completion of the Rikyūdō, the shrine housing the statue, on the seventh day of the first month of 1690:

150. Sensō's farewell verse, in his own hand.

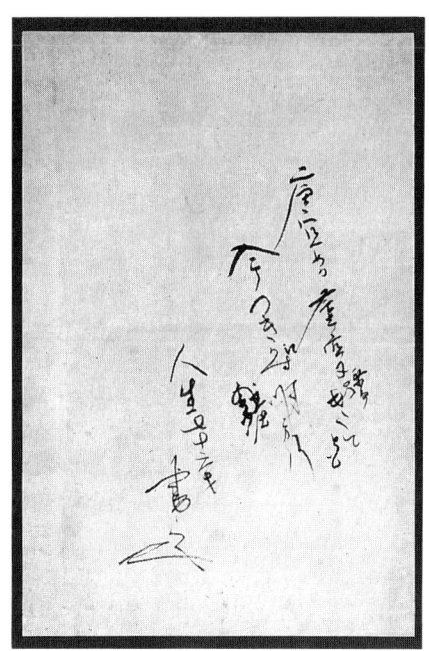

151. Jōsō's transcription of Sensō's letter concerning the wooden statue of Rikyū.

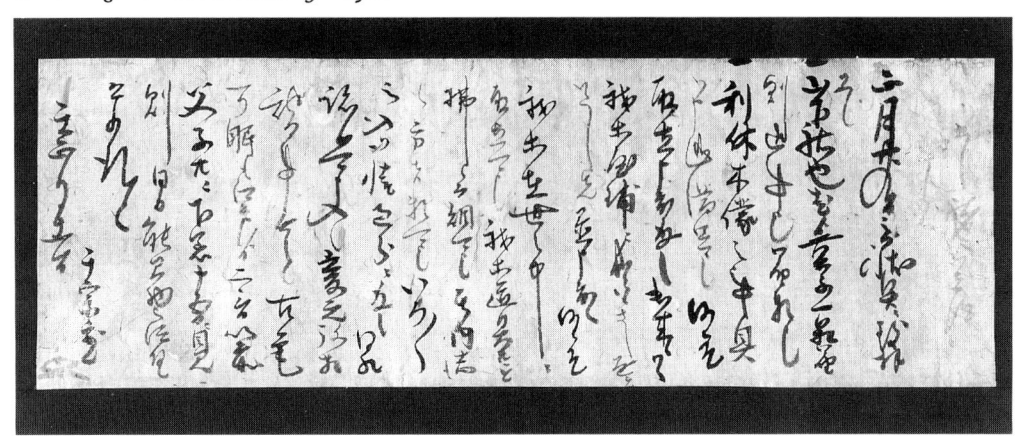

> After these hundred years the Sen family line
> Sees its descendants hold authority in tea
> And the new family shrine houses a statue
> With a countenance noble as an immortal's.

Jōsō's Transcription of the Lay and Art Names of Rikyū, Shōan, Sōtan, and Sensō (Fig. 152) Fifth-generation grand master Jōsō's writing of the names and death dates of his four predecessors, signed "Fifth generation, Jōsō Sōan," shows not only that the practice of counting out a generation-by-generation lineage existed in the

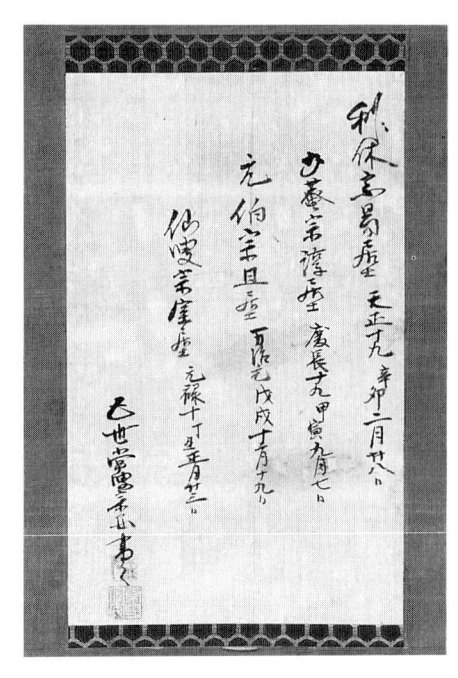

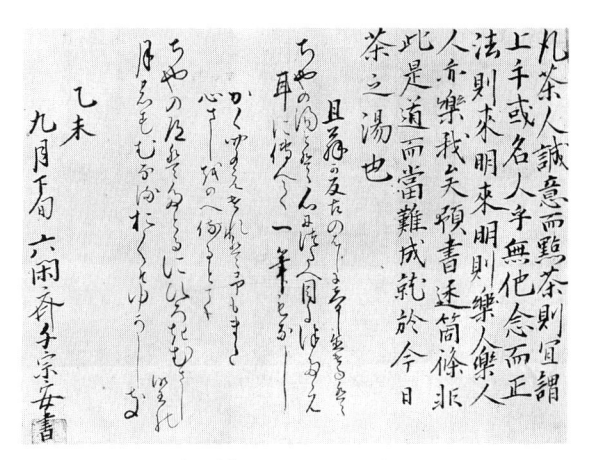

153. *Tan'ō Chanoyu Kyōji by Rikkansai.*

152. *Jōsō's transcription of the lay and art names of Rikyū, Shōan, Sōtan, and Sensō.*

Sen family by his time but also that Jōsō was keenly aware of his place in that lineage.

Tan'ō Chanoyu Kyōji (On Sōtan's Teachings in Chanoyu) by Rikkansai (Fig. 153)
This short document, dated the ninth month of 1715, is a heartfelt expression of the twenty-one-year-old Rikkansai's understanding of chanoyu. The piece has a strong Zen flavor: the emphasis on direct experience strongly echoes the Zen tenets of "transmission from mind to mind" (*ishin denshin*) and "no dependence on the written word" (*furyū monji*).

Grand masters of the Sen tradition from Rikyū on left written expressions of their insights. Included are *Rikyū Hyakushu* (One Hundred Verses of Rikyū) and Sensō's *Rikyū Chanoyu Hon'i*. The latter is similar in content to Rikkansai's document, which reads:

> Those who are able to prepare tea with all sincerity are to be called experts or masters. Ever attentive to the true practice of chanoyu, a practice identified with the guests, they put their guests at ease and, in so doing, put themselves at ease. It must be said that short of this it is difficult to call the practice a spiritual path. Sōtan noted his link with tradition thus:
>
> > That which is chanoyu
> > Is transmitted through the mind

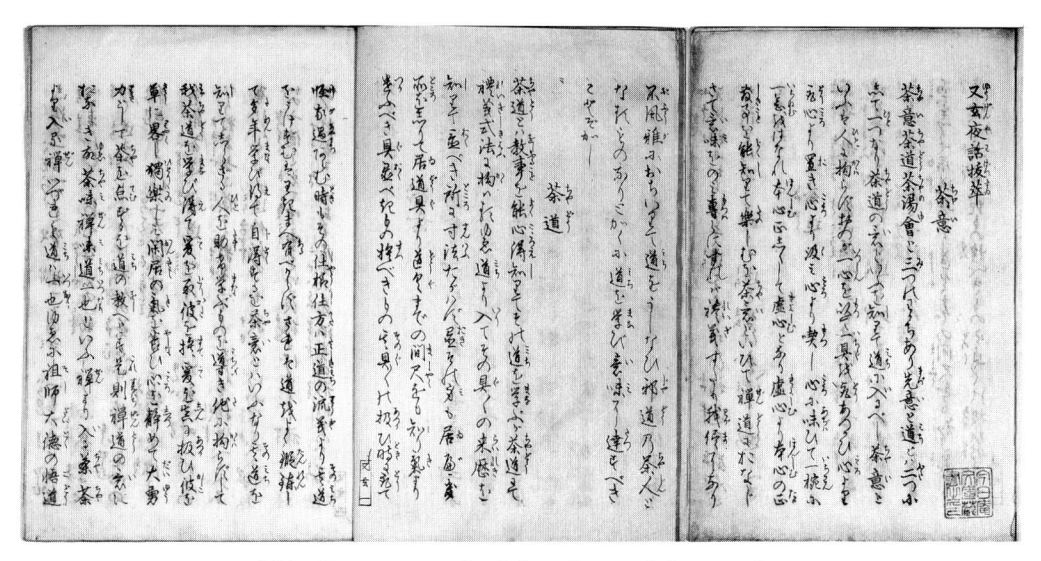

154. Opening page (right) and part of the text of an 1860 copy of the Yūgen Yawa Bassui *by Ittō.*

    Through the eyes
    Through the ears
    With not a single written word.

Hearing this, I too express my feelings:

    The further one fares
    On the Way of Tea, how vast,
    Like the Musashino plain
    Shown clear in the moonlight!
    How infathomably profound!

It is worth noting that the mention of the Musashino plain in connection with chanoyu is exceedingly rare. The simile probably only occurred to Rikkansai because he had to traverse the plain on the way to his post in Edo.

Yūgen Yawa Bassui (Extracts from "Night Talks of Yugensai") by Ittō (Fig. 154)   As the title indicates, this work is only a portion of Yūgensai Ittō's remarks on chanoyu. Even the edition of the *Yūgen Yawa* published in 1860 by Hishida Yūshōken Jitoku probably was not the complete work, since it was based on a 1787 text by Yūshōan Sōchi, who in turn had copied the original transcription of Ittō's words made by Yūrin'an Sōzai. An afterward to Sōchi's text identifies Sōzai as a disciple whom Ittō

156. Gengensai's record of a tea gathering commemorating the two hundred fiftieth anniversary of Rikyū's death.

155. Calligraphic transmission of Gengensai's art name Seichū by Kujō Hisatada.

taught while in Edo in the service of the Matsudaira clan and states that it was Sōzai who first compiled the contents under the title *Yūgen Yawa*. Unfortunately, Sōzai's original document has not been found, though a Meiji-era copy made by Norimasa Ikeda is extant. This copy consists of fifty-six folios in two volumes. Most of what is missing from the fourteen-folio *Yūgen Yawa Bassui* pertains to technique rather than the philosophy of tea.

Among other works which are credited to Ittō is the famous thirty-point treatise *Chadō Hama no Masago,* which covers the proper handling of tea articles, from the scrolls hung in the tokonoma to the silk cloths used for wiping utensils.

Calligraphic Transmission of Gengensai's Art Name Seichū by Kujō Hisatada (Fig. 155)
Gengensai first used the art name Seichū in 1859, having previously used such names as Fubō and Kyohaku. That year he also made the tea scoop "Five Constant Virtues" (Pl. 60) and signed the inner case Seichū Sōshitsu, which he claimed in the outer-box inscription was his "first writing" of this name.

The nobleman Kujō Hisatada was an illustrious figure in late-Edo-period politics, serving the three emperors Kōkaku, Ninkō, and Kōmei first as minister of the right, then as *kampaku*. The room-name plaque for the Rikyūdō is also in his hand, which probably means that he lent support for its reconstruction under Gengensai as an expression of the Kujō family's great expectations of Gengensai.

The scroll itself reads, "This art name granted to Gengensai," in small characters under the two bold characters of the name itself. According to Gengensai's own box inscription, the mounting was from a length of exquisite embroidered tie-dyed material presented to Rikyū by Hideyoshi and later made into curtains for the Rikyūdō. The borders above and below the calligraphy are fashioned from a length of plain gold material given to Gengensai by the wife of Matsudaira Sadamichi, lord of Matsuyama.

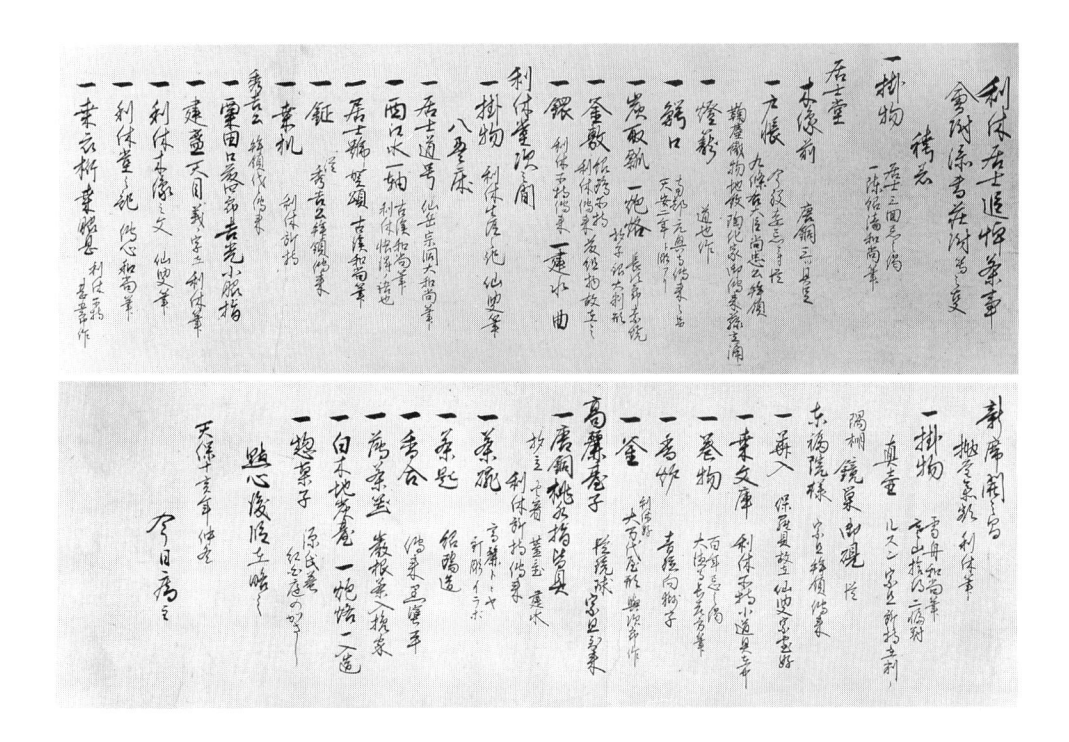

Gengensai's Record of a Tea Gathering Commemorating the Two Hundred Fiftieth Anniversary of Rikyū's Death (Fig. 156)   All three branches of the Sen family participated in the memorial service for Rikyū held at Daitokuji on the twenty-eighth day of the second month of 1840, the two hundred fiftieth anniversary of his death, though Gengensai made almost all the preparations. The commemorative tea gathering recorded here, also hosted by Gengensai, was held on the eighth day of the ninth month of the previous year for Minister of the Interior Konoe Tadahiro. About four hundred guests were invited to a series of seventy-nine tea functions, using all the tearooms in the Urasenke compound, in 1839 and 1840. During this period Gengensai also presented tea to the *kampaku*, Takatsukasa Masamichi, and to Kujō Hisatada at the *kampaku's* villa and attended tea functions hosted by the Omotesenke, Mushanokōjisenke, and Yabunouchi households. All this was followed by a week of the Seven Special Tea Exercises. Finally, Gengensai received formal greetings from his patrons—Lord Matsudaira; the warrior-class Tayasu family; Lords Konoe, Takatsukasa, and

DOCUMENTS ON THE URASENKE GRAND MASTERS   *155*

Kujō; Prince Arisugawa; and the head priest of Higashi Honganji—an indication of the breadth and stature of his circle of acquaintances. Gengensai's record of the tea service held for Konoe Tadahiro follows.

Rikyū Memorial Tea Function
Noting rooms and the articles displayed therein

Hakama-tsuke [Mushikiken]
　Scroll: Rikyū third-anniversary memorial verse by Abbot Ittō Jōteki Kojidō [Rikyūdō]
　　Three-piece bronze Buddhist altar setting before the wooden statue [of Rikyū]
　　Curtain presented especially for the present function by the minister of the right, Lord Kujō Hisatada; disk-pattern-weave fabric; an heirloom of his family
　　Wisteria in upright vessel
　　Lantern by Dōya
　　"Alligator Mouth" gong; a treasure of Gangōji temple, Nara; incised with the date Ten'an 2 [858]
　　Gourd charcoal container
　　Bisque-ware ash dish by [Raku] Chōjirō with silver ash spoon shaped like an oblong ōban coin
　　Kettle rest owned by [Takeno] Jōō; plaited rattan; an heirloom of Rikyū
　　Kettle rings: heirlooms of Rikyū
　　Bentwood waste-water receptacle
Room adjacent to Rikyūdō
　　Scroll: Record of Rikyū's life by Sensō
Eight-mat room [Totsutotsusai]
　　Scrolls: Rikyū's Buddhist name by Abbot Sengaku Sōtō; Xiang Xiao landscape by Abbot Kokei [Sōchin] with Rikyū's words of enlightenment; verse on Rikyū's lay name by Kokei
　　Gong: an heirloom presented by Lord [Toyotomi] Hideyoshi to Rikyū
　　Mulberry-wood desk presented by Lord Hideyoshi to Rikyū
　　Small sword by Awataguchi Tōshirō Yoshimitsu
　　Temmoku [tea bowl] with character *yoshi* [good] in Rikyū's hand
　　Letter by Sensō regarding the wooden statue of Rikyū
　　Record of the Rikyūdō by Abbot Denshin
　　Mulberry-wood kimono rack and mulberry-wood arm rest by [Hidari] Jingorō; heirlooms of Rikyū
Newly dedicated room [Hōsensai]
　　Plaque: "Hōsensai" by Rikyū
　　Scrolls: Pair of paintings of Hanshan and Shide by Abbot Sesshū
　　[Tea-leaf] jar: Luzon ware with Sōtan's cipher
　　"Mirror Case" inkstone, presented to Sōtan by the empress Tōfukumon'in, on adjacent shelf

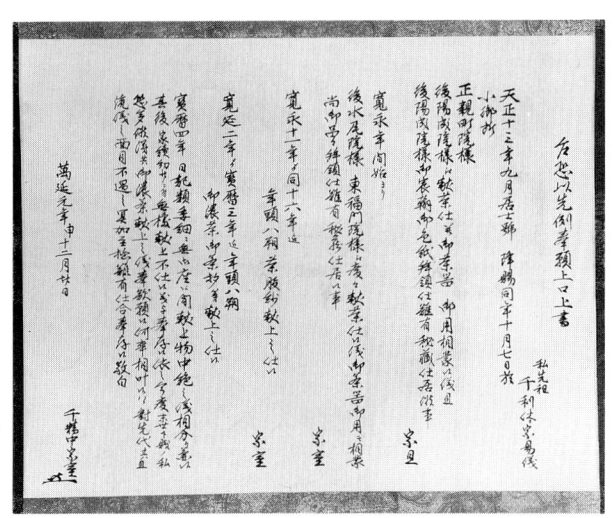

157. "Request Respectfully Submitted on the Basis of Predecessors' Words" by Gengensai.

    Flower container: conch shell favored by Sensō
    Mulberry-wood bookcase containing personal effects of Rikyū
    Handscroll: Rikyū centennial memorial verse by an elder of Daitokuji
    Celadon censer with lion ornaments
    Large Mozuya-style kettle by Yojirō, favored by Rikyū
    Korean-style *daisu* sent to Sōtan from the Ryūkyūs
    "Peach" bronze fresh-water container and matching utensils; heirlooms of
        Rikyū
        Ladle stand
        Fire chopsticks
        Kettle-lid rest
        Waste-water receptacle
    Tea bowls: Korean *totoya* ware; Korean *irabo* ware with sgraffito decoration
    Tea scoop by [Takeno] Jōō
    Incense container: heirloom, black-lacquered, flat shape
    Thin-tea container: *hikiya* case of tea caddy "Rock Cleft Roots"
    Unfinished-wood charcoal tray
    [Bisque-ware] ash dish by [Raku] Ichinyū
    Dry sweets: "Genji scrolls," red and white "garden flowers"
Tenshin repast and later proceedings omitted

Tempō 10 [1839], winter
Master of Konnichian

Gengensai's "Request Respectfully Submitted on the Basis of Predecessors' Words" (Fig. 157)
In the twelfth month of 1860 Gengensai submitted to the imperial household an

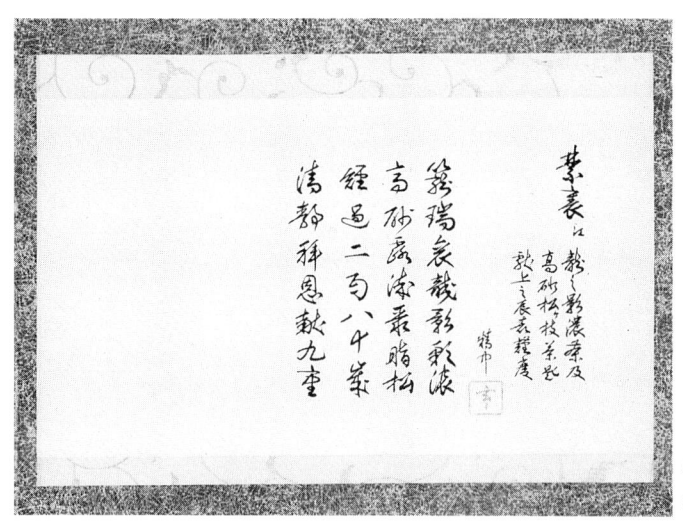

158. Verse by Gengensai commemorating a tea service for the emperor Kōmei in 1865.

official request to have the practice of presenting tea to the emperor reinstated. He cites many precedents, from Rikyū's presentation of tea to retired emperor Ogimachi in 1585, through Sōtan's association with Emperor Gomizunoo and Empress Tofukumon'in, and on through the following generations of grand masters. This practice came to a halt, however, in 1754, after which, for nine generations, the grand masters did not have the opportunity to offer tea to the emperor.

In the sixth month of 1865 Gengensai's request was granted. On the first day of the eighth month that year, he served thick tea with the poetic name "Dragon's Shadow" *(ryū no kage)* to the emperor Kōmei, using his tea scoop "Takasago." So elated was Gengensai that he commemorated the occasion with a verse that plays on the names of both the tea and the tea scoop and also alludes to the nine-generation hiatus (Fig. 158):

> The dragon's shadow darkly colors the water
> As the dew can be heard to settle on the Takasago pines,
> So after two hundred eighty years
> Its gratitude is returned ninefold.

A letter dated 1869 from Gengensai to Hayashi Kibei further reveals that, at least until the capital was moved to Tokyo, Gengensai continued to present tea to the emperor twice a year, in spring and autumn.

Gengensai's Record of a Tea Gathering Held in 1866 to Display Items Received from the Imperial Palace (Fig. 159) On the nineteenth day of the first month of 1866, the year after regular imperial tea presentations resumed, Gengensai celebrated their reinstatement with his disciples on the occasion of the first practice session of the year. At the gathering he displayed the chrysanthemums he had received from the emperor

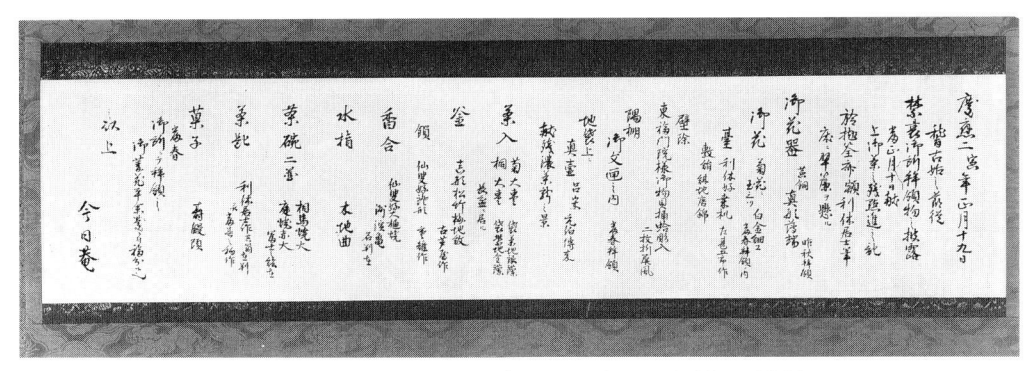

159. Gengensai's record of a tea gathering held in 1866 to display items received from the imperial palace.

at New Year's, arranging them in a brass vase received from the emperor the previous year. In place of a scroll he hung a green split-bamboo *misu* blind like the ones hung at the imperial palace, thus evoking the imperial presence. The writing box displayed on the corner shelf was also a New Year's gift from the emperor. Gengensai served two kinds of sweets, *hanabira mochi* (flower-petal rice cakes), now reserved for the first tea service of the year, and *kotobuki manju* (longevity cakes) to indicate his "double joy." Gengensai's record of the gathering follows.

Keio 2 [1866] Nineteenth Day of the New Year

On the occasion of the first tea practice of the year. Record of the display of items received from the imperial palace, and serving of the tea remaining from the presentation at the imperial palace that was held on the tenth day of the New Year.

In Hōsensai
Plaque: ["Hōsensai"] by Rikyū
Green *misu* blind hung in tokonoma
Flower container: brass, of formal shape with flaring lip, received last autumn
Flowers: chrysanthemums with three platinum-crafted globes, received this New Year
Stand: Mulberry-wood desk by Hidari Jingorō, favored by Rikyū
Spread: dark blue Chinese brocade
Two-panel screen inlaid with shells, formerly owned by the empress Tōfuku-mon'in, against the wall
Imperial writing box, received this New Year, on the corner shelf
Luzon-ware tea-leaf jar, heirloom of Sōtan, on built-in base cabinet

160. First issue of the Konnichian Geppō, *dated October 19, 1908; cover (right) and opening-page calligraphy by Ennōsai; publisher's statement on facing page (left).*

"Dragon Shadow" tea remaining from the imperial tea presentation
Tea containers: Chrysanthemum-motif large *natsume* with brown and silver brocade pouch; paulownia-motif large *natsume* with purple and gold brocade pouch; both on rectangular tray
Old Ashiya formal-shape kettle with "Pine, Bamboo, Plum" design
Chain [to hang the kettle]: stirrup shape, by Miyazaki Kanchi; favored by Sensō
Sensō's Ōhi-ware "Turtle on the Shoal" incense container, with name and cipher
Unfinished bentwood fresh-water container
Tea bowls: Large Sōma-ware bowl; large Red [Raku amateur] ware with design of Mount Fuji
Tea scoops: One by Rikyū with his cipher on the case; one the first [tea scoop] made this New Year
Sweets: "longevity" cakes; also "flower petal" cakes as a measure of my double joy at receiving these things from the imperial palace this New Year

First Issues of Urasenke Chanoyu Periodicals (Figs. 160-62)   In a sense the idea of the *Konnichian Geppō* (Konnichian Monthly), the first tea periodical, began with the two hundred fiftieth anniversary services for Sōtan in 1907. In the magazine's first issue, dated October 19, 1908, Ennōsai wrote in a publisher's statement: "On November 10 last year, on the occasion of the grand services observed at Jukōin in Kyoto, followers of the now nationwide tradition of this household gathered, drifting in like clouds from afar—even seventy- and eighty-year-old disciples from Gengensai's time mustering the strength to make their way here from far away."

161. First issue of the Chadō Geppō, *dated June 1922.*

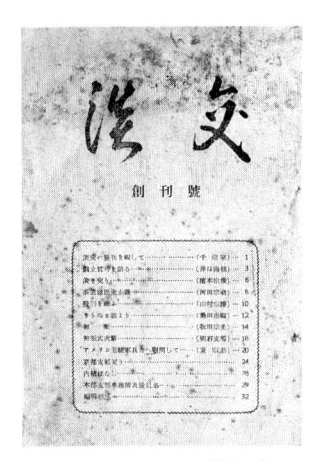

162. First issue of Tankō, *dated April 1947.*

Not everyone could manage to go to Kyoto, however. Instead, the Urasenke tradition would reach out through the printed word. This journal provided a vital forum for the rapidly growing number of tea enthusiasts. In June 1922, with the one hundred thirty-eighth issue, the journal was renamed the *Chadō Geppō* (Chadō Monthly) in recognition of the need to represent a total picture of the Way of Tea. Finally, in April 1947, it was reborn as the popular magazine *Tankō,* providing extended coverage not only of the Urasenke tradition but also of other traditional Japanese arts that share common borders with tea. Its readership now reaches beyond the shores of Japan.

INDEX

Aka hira mizusashi (Red Raku broad fresh-water container), 62; Pl. 26
"Ancient Sage" tea bowl (*hijiri chawan*), 60; Pl. 24
"Ant Hole" (*ari tōshi*) tea scoop, 93; Pl. 62
Arai Isshō, 54
Arare hyakkaigama ("Hundred Gatherings" hailstone-pattern kettle), 53–54; Pl. 16.
Ari tōshi ("Ant Hole") tea scoop, 93; Pl. 62
"Ariwara Narihira" tea scoop, 87–88; Fig. 68
"Asama" tea scoop, 85–86; Pl. 50
"Ascending Dragon" (*shōryū*) tea scoop, 91; Fig. 73
Ashiya kettles, 54
"Autumn Stream" tea utensil stand (*shūsendana*), 75–76; Fig. 54
"Awakened from Sleep" (*nezame*) tea scoop, 85–86; Fig. 66

Baigandō. *See* Yūgensai Ittō
Baigetsu ("Plum-Blossom Moon") *natsume*, 76; Fig. 55; Pl. 38.
Baishian. *See* Tantansai Sekisō
Bamboo (*take*) *natsume*, 58; Pl. 20
Basic Idea of Rikyū's Tea, The (*Rikyū Chanoyu Hon'i*), 82–83, 152
Basic Idea of the Way of Tea, The (*Chadō no Gen'i*), 47–48, 91; Pl. 59
Bodhidharma, 148–49; Fig. 147
Boki Ekotoba picture scroll, Fig. 4

Bronze "Peach" (*karakane momo*) fresh water container and matching utensils, 54, 157; Pl. 17
"Brushtip Persimmon" incense container (*fudegaki kōgō*), 71; Pl. 34
"Buddha Tetrad" (*shihōbutsu*) water basin, 112; Figs. 79, 96

Calligraphic Transmission of Rikyū's Lay Name: by Kokei Sōchin, 142–43; Fig. 140; by Sengaku Sōtō, 143–44; Fig. 141; by Shun'oku Sōen, 144–45; Fig. 142
"Camellia" scroll, 81–82; Pl. 45
"Carpenter's Workbox" shelf (*kugibakodana*), 41, 59, 110; Fig. 93
"Cast Fishtrap" Sanctuary. *See* Sanctuary of the Cast Fishtrap
Cha Jing (Classic of Tea), 3, 31
Cha suki (tea taste), 6, 8
Chadō Geppō (Chadō Monthly), 161; Fig. 161
Chadō Hama no Masago (Sand on the Beach), 44, 87, 154
Chadō Monthly, 161; Fig. 161
Chadō no Gen'i (The Basic Idea of the Way of Tea), 47–48, 91; Pl. 59
Chagō ("Tea Measurer") *natsume*, 60; Fig. 39
Chaji (tea function), 17, 68, 120–37; Figs. 105–39; Pls. 75–86
Charcoal baskets, 67, 70, 73; Fig. 49; Pls. 30, 36, 75
Chigaidana, 9, 10; Fig. 6

Chikusō Sōken, 43, 65–66, 86; Fig. 45; Pls. 28, 51, 52
"Chinese Brush Basket" charcoal baskets (*Tō-hitsu kago sumitori*), 73; Pl. 36
"Chinese Hat" flower basket (*tōjingasa hanaire*), 65; Pl. 28
Chōjirō, 27; Figs. 15, 16
Chōzaemon, 28, 41, 60; Pl. 24
"Chrysanthemum and Paulownia" *maki-e* tea scoop, 88; Pl. 54
"Clamshell" incense container with raised chrysanthemum pattern (*kiku okiage hamaguri kōgō*), 55; Pl. 18
"Clamshell" shelf (*hamaguridana*), 59, 108; Pl. 72
Classic of Tea (*Cha Jing*), 3, 31
"Coiled Thread" lacquer food-service set (*itome kaigu*), 68; Pl. 31
Cold Cloud Arbor (Kan'untei) tearoom, 40, 105–7, 111; Figs. 79, 90; Pl. 71
"Cold Cloud" (*kan'un*) *natsume*, 66; Fig. 45
Commentary of Yamanoue Sōji (*Yamanoue Sōji Ki*), 18, 20, 21–22, 37; Fig. 13
"Compact" Chrysanthemum *maki-e* incense container (*kiku maki-e tokigata kōgō*), 56; Fig. 35
"Crane alights . . ." calligraphy, 92–93; Pl. 61
"Crane at dawn" calligraphy, 87; Pl. 53
"Crane in Rice Field" (*tazuru*) tea scoop, 86; Pl. 52

Daikoku Black Raku tea bowl, Fig. 16
Dairo no Ma (Great Hearth Room), 46, 114–15, 116, 117; Figs. 79, 100
Daisu, 11, 54
Daitokuji temple, 44, 77–78, 145, 150–51
Dancha, 3
Dōan, 25–26, 37, 79, 146; Figs. 144, 145
Dōbōshū, 10; Fig. 7
Dōgen, 7
Dōjinsai (Sanctuary of Equal Benevolence), 14–15; Fig. 10
Downtown (*shimoryū*) tea school of Kyoto, 30–31

"Eggplants" scroll, 80; Pl. 43
Eisai, 4–5
Endō Genkan, 32
Ennōsai Tetchū, 49, 74–75, 93–94, 160; Figs. 53, 76, 160; Pls. 37, 64
Enshū (Kobori), 25, 53
"Evening Bell from a Temple in the Mist," Pl. 7

"Feather Brushes" scroll, 87; Fig. 67
"Feather Cloak" (*hagoromo*) *natsume,* 71; Pl. 33
"Feather Cloak" incense container, Pl. 14
"First Blossom" (*hatsuhana*) tea scoop, 89; Pl. 56
"First Carving" (*hatsu kezuri*) tea scoop, 95; Fig. 78
"Five Constant Virtues" (*gojō*) tea scoop, 91, 154; Pl. 60
"Flaming Jewel" incense container (*hōju kōgō*), 60; Fig. 38
Flower containers, 52–53, 57, 59, 65, 122; Pls. 15, 23, 28, 83
"Flower Raft" hearth frame (*hana ikada robuchi*), 58–59; Pl. 22
Fudegaki kōgō ("Brushtip Persimmon") incense container, 71; Pl. 34
Fujimura Yōken, 30, 39; Fig. 24
Fukensai Sekiō, 44–45, 68–69, 88–89, 110–11, 113; Figs. 47, 69, 70; Pls. 10, 31, 55, 56
"Fukurokuju" scroll, 93; Fig. 75
"Fukurokuju" tea scoop, 90; Pl. 58
Fukutomi Zōshi, Fig. 12
Fukyūsai Jōsō, 42, 62–63, 83–84, 151–52; Figs. 40, 41, 62–64, 151, 152; Pls. 26, 47, 48
Further Retreat (Yūin) tearoom, 40, 102–5, 111–12, 117; Figs. 79, 86–88; Pl. 70
Furuta Oribe, 23–24; Fig. 18
Fushin'an (Hut of Uncertainty), 29, 39, 40

Gamō Ujisato, 23, 25, 37; Fig. 20
Ganro, 11; Fig. 8
Geiami, 10
Gempaku Sōtan, 26–27, 29–30, 37, 38–40, 56–59, 80, 88, 98–104, 112, 122, 146, 148–49; Figs. 29, 36, 58, 59, 95, 144; Pls. 4, 5, 20–22, 39, 43, 44, 72, 83
Gengensai Seichū, 45, 46–48, 54, 70–72, 91–92, 96, 114–17, 123, 155–60; Figs. 50, 51, 73, 74, 156, 157, 159; Pls. 13, 33–35, 60, 85
Genshitsu. See Fukensai Sekiō
Genshitsubō ("Master Genshitsu") bamboo flower container, 88–89, 122; Pl. 83
Ginkakuji temple, 14
"Gion Festival Scene" scroll, 145–46; Pl. 2
"Girl's Day Dolls" scroll, 85; Pl. 49
"Give thanks for tea" scroll, 95; Pl. 65
Gojō ("Five Constant Virtues") tea scoop, 91, 154; Pl. 60
Gomizunoo, Emperor, 26–27, 57, 146, 158; Fig. 23
"Gourds" scroll, 81–82; Fig. 61
Grand Kitano Tea Gathering, 36, 103

"Grass, Man, Tree" (*Sōjimboku*), 32; Fig. 28
Great Hearth Room (Dairo no Ma), 46, 114–16; 117; Figs. 79, 99, 100
"Great Rectitude" (*taishō*) tea scoop, 93; Pl. 64
Gyōki, 4

Hagoromo ("Feather Cloak") *natsume*, 71; Pl. 33
Hakkaku kōgō (octagonal incense container), 68; Pl. 10
Hakuun chawan ("White Cloud" tea bowl), 63–64; Fig. 42; Pl. 27
Hall of the Honorable Ancestor (Rikyūdō), 31, 41, 59, 105, 107–9, 113, 114; Figs. 79, 91; Pls. 72, 73
Hamaguridana ("Clamshell" shelf), 59, 108; Pl. 72
Hana ikada robuchi ("Flower Raft" hearth frame), 58–59; Pl. 22
"Hare's-fur" *temmoku* tea bowl, Fig. 9
Hasegawa Kyūzō, Pl. 2
Hasegawa Tōhaku, Pl. 1
Hatsu kezuri ("First Carving") tea scoop, 95; Pl. 78
Hatsuhana ("First Blossom") tea scoop, 89; Pl. 56
Hayami Sōtatsu, 44
Hearths, 11–12, 58–59, 127–28; Fig. 9; Pl. 22
Helmet Gate (*kabuto mon*), 96–97, 114; Fig. 79; Pl. 67
Hideyoshi. *See* Toyotomi Hideyoshi
"*Higaki*" tea scoop, 80; Fig. 59
Higashiyama culture, 12; Fig. 12
Hijiri chawan ("Ancient Sage" tea bowl), 60; Pl. 24
Hiki Ikkan, 57, 58
History of Kiyomizudera Picture Scroll (*Kiyomizudera Engi Emaki*), Fig. 1
Hizumi chawan (warped tea bowl), 24
Hōju kōgō ("Flaming Jewel" incense container), 60; Fig. 38
"Homecoming" (*satogaeri*) tea scoop, 80–81; Pl. 46
Hon'ami Kōetsu, 60, 80
Hōsensai (Sanctuary of the Cast Fishtrap), 46, 114, 117; Figs. 79, 102
Hosokawa Sansai, 24; Fig. 19
Hōunsai Sōshitsu, 51, 120, 123–37; Pl. 86
"Hundred Gatherings" hailstone-pattern kettle (*arare hyakkaigama*), 53–54; Pl. 16
Hut of This Day (Konnichian) tearoom, 29, 39, 40, 98–101, 111–12, 113, 148–149; Figs. 81–85; Pl. 69

Hut of Uncertainty (Fushin'an) tearoom, 29, 39, 40
Hut of Vigilance (Taian) tearoom, 21, 77; Fig. 17

Iemoto system, 33–34
Imai Sōkyū, 17, 19–20, 23
Incense containers, 55, 56, 60, 68, 71; Figs. 35, 38; Pls. 10, 18, 21, 34
Incha, 4
International Chadō Cultural Foundation, 50
Ise Grand Shrine, 50
Itome kaigu ("Coiled Thread" lacquer food-service set), 68; Pl. 31
Ittō. *See* Yūgensai Ittō
"Ivy" (*tsuta*) *natsume*, 64; Pl. 32

"Jeweled Hare" (*tama usagi*) tea scoop, 95; Pl. 66
"Jeweled Orb" kettle (*manjugama*), 63; Fig. 41
Jian ware (*temmoku*), 7; Fig. 9
Jitsuzan (Tachibana), 31–32
Jōchi (Yabunouchi), 30, 31
Joshinsai Tennen, 43–44
Jōsō. *See* Fukyūsai Jōsō

Kabuto mon (Helmet Gate), 96–97, 114; Fig. 79; Pl. 67
Kaibara Ekiken, 33
Kaiki (Tea-gathering records), 17–18, 121–23
Kaiseki meals, 18, 68, 121–23, 130–35
Kaisho (meeting places), 8, 9; Figs. 4, 6
Kamiryū (uptown) tea school of Kyoto, 30–31
Kanchi kettle foundry, 28, 41
Kanō Sōboku, 44
Kan'un ("Cold Cloud") *natsume*, 66; Fig. 45
Kan'untei (Cold Cloud Arbor) tearoom, 40, 105–7, 111; Figs. 79, 90; Pl. 71
Karakane momo mizusashi kaigu (bronze "Peach" fresh-water container and matching utensils, 54, 157; Pl. 17
Karamono (continental tea utensils), 8
Katagiri Sekishū, 25
Kawakami Fuhaku, 27
Kenkei, 31
Kenkōsō chawan ("Suspended Light Piebald" Red Raku tea bowl), 72; Fig. 51; Pl. 35
Kettles, 53–54, 59, 60, 63, 73; Figs. 36, 39, 41, 52; Pls. 16, 25
Kiku maki-e tokigata kōgō ("compact" chrysanthemum *maki-e* incense container), 56; Fig. 35

INDEX *165*

Kiku okiage hamaguri kōgō (clamshell incense container with raised chrysanthemum pattern), 55; Pl. 18
Kirimon konatsume (small *natsume* with paulownia crest), 54–55; Fig. 34
Kissa Ōrai (Letter on Tea Drinking), 8, 11, 17–18
Kiyomizudera Engi Emaki (History of Kiyomizudera Picture Scroll), Fig. 1
Kizō ("Tortoise Constellation") *natsume*, 74–75; Fig. 52
Kōaka chaki (red-topped thin-tea container), 42, 62; Fig. 40
Kobori Enshū, 25, 53
Kokei Sōchin, 142–43
Kokoro no Fumi (Letter of the Mind), 12–13, 23
Koma meimeibon ("Spinning Top" individual serving trays), 68–69; Fig. 47
Koma mon ("spinning top" crest) of Sen family, 59
Konnichian Geppō (*Konnichian* Monthly), 49, 160–61; Fig. 160
Konnichian (Hut of This Day) tearoom, 29, 39, 40, 98–101, 111–12, 113, 148–49; Figs. 81–85; Pl. 69
Kōtō (Red Raku tea bowl), Fig. 15
Kuchikiri ("Opening the Tea Leaf Jar") tea scoop, 80; Pl. 44
Kugibakodana ("Carpenter's Workbox" shelf), 41, 59, 110; Fig. 93
Kujō Hisatada, 154–55; Fig. 155
Kumesaburō. *See* Fukensai Sekiō
Kurezome Sanrokuan, 32
Kusumi Soan, 25, 28, 30, 39
Kutsugata chawan (shoe-shaped tea bowl), 24
Kuwayama Sōsen, 25
Kyōto Chaen Teishitsu Zu (Plans of Tea Gardens and Arbors in Kyoto), 112–13; Fig. 97

Lacquered bentwood fresh-water container (*nuri mage mizusashi*), 69–70; Fig. 48
Lacquered-paper (*urushibari*) *natsume*, 64–65; Fig. 44
Letter of the Mind (*Kokoro no Fumi*), 12–13, 23
Letter on Tea Drinking (*Kissa Ōrai*), 8, 11, 17–18
Letter with Verses on Snow (*Yuki no Utairi no Fumi*), 77; Pl. 40
"Light Autumn Leaves" (*usumomiji*) tea scoop, 89; Fig. 70
"Long Abalone Strip" (*naganoshi*) tea scoop, 90; Fig. 72
Lu Yu, 3, 31

Makimura Hyōbudayū, 24
Mamemaki ishi (scattered-bean stepping stones), 112; Fig. 95
Manjugama ("Jeweled Orb" kettle), 63; Fig. 41
"Master Genshitsu" (Genshitsubō) bamboo flower container, 88–89, 122; Pl. 83
Matcha (powdered tea), 4
Matsuya Hikki (Matsuya Family Records), 24
Matsuya Kaiki, 17, 20
"Matsuyama" charcoal basket (*matsuyama kago sumitori*), 70; Fig. 49
Meals, at tea functions, 8, 17–18, 68, 130–35; Figs. 123–26; Pls. 76–82
Miyake Bōyō, 28, 39; Fig. 25
Miyazaki Kanchi, 28, 60; Pl. 25
Mizusashi. *See* Water containers
Momo kōgō ("Peach" incense container), 58; Pl. 21
"Mount Asama" tea scoop, 85–86; Pl. 50
Mount Fuji scroll, 90; Fig. 71
Mugensai. *See* Tantansai Sekiso
Murata Shukō, 13, 19, 23
Murata Sōshu, 15
Mushanokōjisenke school of tea, 27, 30, 40
Mushikiken (Shelter of No Colors) vestibule, 43, 59, 109–11, 113; Figs. 79, 92–94; Pl. 74
Myōe, 5

Naganoshi ("Long Abalone Strip") tea scoop, 90; Fig. 72
Nakamura Sōtetsu, 57, 58–59, 60, 65, 66, 69, 71
Nambō (Takayama Ukon), 23
Nambō Sōkei, 31–32
Nampō Roku (Record of the South), 31–32; Fig. 27
Naorai banquets, 4, 17
Natsume, 54–55, 57, 58, 60, 64–65, 66, 67–68, 69, 71, 76; Figs. 34, 39, 44–46, 53, 55; Pls. 19, 20, 32, 33, 38
"Nestled Rice Fields" (*taori*) tea scoop, 81; Fig. 60
New Again (Yūshin) tearoom, 118, 119; Figs. 79, 104
Nezame ("Awakened from Sleep") tea scoop, 85–86; Fig. 66
"Night Cherry Blossom" (*yozakura*) *natsume*, 56; Pl. 19
Night Talks of Yūgensai (*Yūgen Yawa*), 87, 153–54; Fig. 154
Nijiriguchi (crawl-in entrances), 22; Fig. 112

Nintokusai Hakusō, 45–46, 69–70, 90; Figs. 48, 49, 71, 72; Pls. 11, 12, 32, 57, 58
Nishimura Dōya, 59
Nōami, 10, 11, 13
Nobunaga. *See* Oda Nobunaga
Nuri mage mizusashi (lacquered bentwood fresh-water container), 69–70; Fig. 48

Ōchamori (great tea bowl) ceremony, 4; Fig. 2
Octagonal incense container (*hakkaku kōgō*), 68; Pl. 10
Oda Nobunaga, 19–20, 35, 145–46
Ōhi kiln, 28, 42, 60
Ōhi ware, 60; Pls. 6, 24
"Old Zen abbot . . ." scroll, 85; Fig. 65
Ōmizuya preparation room, 114, 116; Figs. 79, 101
Omotesenke, 27, 29, 30, 32, 40, 42, 43
On Sōtan's Teachings in Chanoyu (*Tan'ō Chanoyu Kyōji*), 152; Fig. 153
"One iron bar, . . ." scroll, 92; Fig. 74
"One Thousand Autumns, Ten Thousand Years" (*senshū banzai*) tea scoop, 83–84; Figs. 63, 64
"Opening the Tea Leaf Jar" (*kuchikiri*) tea scoop, 80; Pl. 44
Oribe (Furuta), 23–24; Fig. 18
Oshiita (inset display boards), 9, 100–101

"Peach" incense container (*momo kōgō*), 58; Pl. 21
Plans of Tea Gardens and Arbors in Kyoto (*Kyōtō Chaen Teishitsu Zu*), 112–13; Fig. 97
Pleasant Surprise Sanctuary. *See* Sanctuary of Pleasant Surprise
Plum Well (*ume no i*), 114; Figs. 79, 99
"Plum-Blossom Moon" (*baigetsu*) natsume, 76; Fig. 55; Pl. 38
Poetry gatherings, and tea, 3, 6, 8
Powdered tea (*matcha*), 4

"Rabbit Lugs" fresh-water container (*usagi mimi mizusashi*), 71–72; Fig. 50
Raku ware, 21, 57, 62, 63, 72; Figs. 15, 16, 43; Pls. 13, 26, 27, 35
"Raven in the Cold" scroll, 83; Pl. 47
Record of the South (*Nampō Roku*), 31–32; Fig. 27
Red Raku broad fresh-water container (*aka hira mizusashi*), 62; Pl. 26
Red-topped thin-tea container (*kōaka chaki*), 42, 62; Fig. 40
Renga gatherings, 6, 8

"Rice-Cake Mortar" fresh-water container (*usu mizusashi*), 66–67; Pl. 29
Rikkansai Taisō, 42–43, 63–65, 84–86, 152–53; Figs. 42–44, 65, 66, 153; Pls. 7, 27, 49, 50
Rikyū Chanoyu Hon'i (The Basic Idea of Rikyū's Tea), 82–83, 152
Rikyū Kōji. *See* Rikyū Sōeki
Rikyū shichitetsu (Seven Sages of Rikyū), 23–25
Rikyū Sōeki, 10, 19–23, 28, 31–32, 35–37, 52–55, 77–79, 142–45; Figs. 21, 34, 56, 57, 140–43; Pls. 1, 3, 15–18, 39, 40
Rikyūdō (Hall of the Honorable Ancestor), 31, 41, 59, 105, 107–9, 113, 114; Figs. 79, 91; Pls. 72, 73
Roji (tea gardens), 24, 97, 111–13, 127; Figs. 94–97; Pl. 68
Ryūrei (tabletop tea service), 48, 71, 118; Fig. 104

Sadō (tea advisers), 19–20; Fig. 14
Saidaiji temple, 4; Fig. 2
Sakai, 15–16, 19–20
"Salt Basket" charcoal basket (*shiokago sumitori*), 67; Pl. 30
"Salt-maker's Hut" kettle (*shioyagama*), 60; Pl. 25
Sanctuary of Equal Benevolence (Dōjinsai), 14–15; Fig. 10
Sanctuary of Pleasant Surprise (Totsutotsusai) tearoom, 46, 114–16, 117; Figs. 79, 99, 100
Sanctuary of the Cast Fishtrap (Hōsensai), 46, 114, 116–17; Figs. 79, 102
Sand on the Beach (*Chadō Hama no Masago*) tearoom, 44, 87, 154
Sansai (Hosokawa), 24; Fig. 19
Sarei (tea etiquette), 6
Satogaeri ("Homecoming") tea scoop, 80–81; Pl. 46
"Scattered Bean" stepping stones (*mamemaki ishi*), 112; Fig. 95
"Scooping up water" scroll, 86; Pl. 51
Seigan Shōtetsu, 12
Seki Sōchō, 57, 60
Sen Rikyū. *See* Rikyū Sōeki
Sen'ami, 10, 35
Sen-family crest, 59; Pl. 6
Senshū banzai ("One Thousand Autumns, Ten Thousand Years") tea scoop, 83–84; Figs. 63, 64
Sensō Sōshitsu, 28, 30, 31, 38, 40–41, 59–60, 80–83, 108, 109, 149–50; Figs. 30, 38, 39,

INDEX *167*

60, 61, 93, 148–50; Pls. 6, 23–25, 39, 45, 46, 72
Seta Kamon, 24
Seven Sages of Rikyū (Rikyū shichitetsu), 23–25
Seven Special Tea Exercises (shichiji shiki), 44, 66, 116, 155
"Shakuhachi" bamboo flower container (shakuhachi take hanaire), 52–54; Pl. 15
Shelter Facing the Stream (Tairyūken) tearoom, 117; Figs. 79, 103
Shelter of No Colors (Mushikiken) vestibule, 43, 59, 109–11, 113; Figs. 79, 92–94; Pl. 74
Shibayama Kemmotsu, 24
Shichiji shiki (Seven Special Tea Exercises), 44, 66, 116
Shihōbutsu ("Buddha Tetrad") water basin, 112; Figs. 79, 96
Shimoryū (downtown) tea school of Kyoto, 30–31
Shin'ō (Yabunouchi), 31
Shinsein (Yukako), 48–49
Shiokago sumitori ("Salt Basket" charcoal basket), 67; Pl. 30
Shioyagama ("Salt-maker's Hut" kettle), 60; Pl. 25
Shōan Sōjun, 25–26, 37, 55–56, 79–80, 147–48; Figs. 35, 146; Pls. 19, 42
Shoe-shaped tea bowl (kutsugata chawan), 24
Shoin-style architecture, 9–10, 105–7, 117; Fig. 5
Shoin-style chanoyu, 10–12
Shōryū ("Ascending Dragon") tea scoop, 91; Fig. 73
Shukō (Murata), 13, 19, 23
Shūsendana ("Autumn Stream" tea utensil stand), 75–76; Fig. 54
Small natsume with paulownia crest (kirimon konatsume), 54–55; Fig. 34
Smoking sets, 57
Sōami, 10
Sōan. See Fukyūsai Jōsō
Sōan-style chanoyu, 12–19, 22–23
Sōchō (Seki), 57, 60
Sōeki. See Rikyū Sōeki
Sōhen (Yamada), 28–30, 39, 59
Sōjimboku (Grass, Man, Tree), 32; Fig. 28
Song-dynasty influences on tea, 6–8
Sōsa, 28, 30, 38, 39
Sōsetsu, 27, 38
Sōshitsu Sen. See Hōunsai Sōshitsu
Sōshu, 28, 30, 38
Sōtan. See Gempaku Sōtan

"Spinning Top" individual serving trays (koma meimeibon), 68–69; Fig. 47
"Spreading Fortune" (suehiro) tea scoop, 84; Pl. 48
"Square" kettle (yohōgama), 59; Fig. 36
Suehiro ("Spreading Fortune") tea scoop, 84; Pl. 48
Sugiki Fusai, 28, 29–30, 39; Fig. 26
"Sumiyoshi Shrine" kettle (Sumiyoshigama), 73; Fig. 52
"Suspended Light Piebald" tea bowl (kenkōsō chawan), 72; Fig. 51; Pl. 35

Tabimakura take hanaire ("Wayfarer's Pillow" bamboo flower container), 59; Pl. 23
Table-top tea service (ryūrei), 48, 71, 118; Fig. 104
Tachibana Jitsuzan, 31–32
Taian (Hut of Vigilance) tearoom, 21, 77; Fig. 17
Tairyūken (Shelter Facing the Stream) tearoom, 117; Figs. 79, 103
Taishō ("Great Rectitude") tea scoop, 93; Pl. 64
Takayama Ukon, 23
Take (Bamboo) natsume, 58; Pl. 20
Takeno Jōō, 15, 19, 22, 23, 25, 35; Fig. 11
Tama usagi ("Jeweled Hare") tea scoop, 95; Pl. 66
Tanaka Sōeki. See Rikyū Sōeki
Tankō, 161; Fig. 162
Tan'ō Chanoyu Kyōji (On Sōtan's Teaching in Chanoyu), 152; Fig. 153
Tantansai Sekisō, 49–51, 75–76, 94–95, 117–18; Figs. 54, 55, 77, 78; Pls. 14, 38, 65, 66
Taori ("Nestled Rice Fields") tea scoop, 81; Fig. 60
Tazuru ("Crane in Rice Field") tea scoop, 86; Pl. 52
Tea advisers (sadō), 19–20; Fig. 14
Tea bowls, 21, 24, 60, 63–64, 72; Figs. 9, 15, 16, 43; Pls. 13, 24, 27, 35
Tea gardens (roji), 24, 97, 111–13, 117–18, 127; Fig. 98; Pl. 68
"Tea Measurer" (chagō) natsume, 60; Fig. 39
Tea plants, history of cultivation in Japan, 3, 5–6
Tea scoops, 78–95; Figs. 57, 59, 60, 64, 66, 68, 70, 72, 73, 78; Pls. 39, 42, 44, 46, 48, 50, 52, 54, 55, 58, 60, 64, 66
Tea-gathering records (kaiki), 17–18, 121–23
Tearooms, 10–16, 21–22, 24, 28–29, 38, 39–40,

44–45, 46, 50, 52, 96–119; Figs. 6, 10, 17, 79–99; Pls. 67–74
Temmoku (Jian ware) tea bowls, 7; Fig. 9
Temmon-era chanoyu, 16–19
Three Sen families, the (san Senke), 30–31, 40
Tōcha competitions, 6
Tofukumon'in, Empress, 26–27, 57, 146, 158; Fig. 22
Toganoo tea, 5–6
Tōgudō (Hall Facing East), 14; Fig. 10
Tōhitsu kago sumitori ("Chinese Brush Basket" charcoal baskets), 73; Pl. 36
Tōjingasa hanaire ("Chinese Hat" flower basket), 65; Pl. 28
Tokonoma, 9
Torii Insetsu, 19
"Tortoise Constellation" (kizō) natsume, 74–75; Pl. 53
Tosa Mitsusada, 89; Pl. 55
Tosa Mitsuzane, 90; Fig. 71
Toshikazu (Shibayama Kemmotsu), 24
Totsutotsusai (Sanctuary of Pleasant Surprise) tearoom, 46, 114–16, 117; Figs. 79, 98, 100
Toyotomi Hideyoshi, 20–21, 23, 35–37
Tsubotsubo natsume, 67–68; Fig. 46
Tsuda Sōgyū, 20, 23, 36
Tsuji Yojirō, 54; Pl. 16
Tsukeshoin, 9, 10, 117; Fig. 6
Tsuta ("Ivy") natsume, 69; Pl. 32
"Twin Leaves" Red Raku tea bowl, Pl. 13

Uji tea, 6
Ume no i (Plum Well), 114; Figs. 79, 99
Uptown (kamiryū) tea school of Kyoto, 30–31
Urasenke compound, 44–45, 96–119; Figs. 79–104; Pls. 67–74
Urasenke Foundation, 50
Urushibari (Lacquered-Paper) natsume, 64–65; Fig. 44
Usagi-mimi mizusashi ("Rabbit Lugs" fresh-water container), 71–72; Fig. 50
Usu mizusashi ("Rice-Cake Mortar" fresh-water container), 66–67; Pl. 29
Usumomiji ("Light Autumn Leaves") tea scoop, 89; Fig. 70
Utensil stands, 74, 75–76; Fig. 54; Pl. 37

Wabi, 14, 22–23, 39, 59, 77, 80
Waka, 8, 22
Warped tea bowl (hizumi chawan), 24
Water containers (mizusashi), 52, 54, 62, 66–67, 69–70, 71–72; Figs. 48, 50; Pls. 3, 17, 26, 29
"Wayfarer's Pillow" bamboo flower container (tabimakura take hanaire), 59; Pl. 23
"White Cloud" tea bowl (hakuun chawan), 63–64; Fig. 42; Pl. 27

"Xiang Xiao" Landscape, 94–95; Fig. 77

Yabunouchi Chikushin, 31
Yabunouchi Kenchū Jōchi, 30, 31
Yabunouchi Shin'ō, 31
Yamada Sōhen, 28–30, 39, 59
Yamanoue Sōji, 18
Yamanoue Sōji Ki (Commentary of Yamanoue Sōji), 18, 20, 21–22, 37; Fig. 13
Yohōgama ("Square" kettle), 59; Fig. 36
Yojirō (Tsuji), 54; Pl. 16
"Yoshino" tea utensil stand (yoshinodana), 74; Pl. 37
Yotsugashira no chakai (four-headed tea gathering), 7–8; Fig. 3
Yozakura ("Night Cherry Blossom") natsume, 56; Pl. 19
Yūgen Yawa Bassui (Extracts from Night Talks of Yūgensai), 153–54; Fig. 154
Yūgensai Ittō, 43–44, 66–68, 87–88, 153–54; Figs. 46, 54, 67, 68; Pls. 9, 29, 30, 53, 54
Yūin (Further Retreat) tearoom, 40, 102–5, 111–12, 117; Figs. 79, 86–88, 95, 96; Pl. 70
Yukako, 48–49
Yuki no Utairi no Fumi (Letter with Verses on Snow), 77; Pl. 40
Yūmyōsai Jikisō, 48–49, 73, 92–93; Figs. 32, 52; Pls. 36, 61, 62
Yūshin (New Again) tearoom, 118, 119; Figs. 79, 104

Zashiki kazari, 10; Fig. 6
Zen Buddhism, 4–5, 6–7, 23, 39, 66
"Zen in one taste" scroll, 83; Fig. 62

A NOTE ON JAPANESE USAGE

Long vowels in Japanese words are indicated by macrons except in the case of well-known place names (Tokyo, Kyoto, Osaka, Kyushu) and words that are included in standard English dictionaries (shoji, shogun). All Japanese words are italicized except for names and other proper nouns, words that appear unitalicized in English dictionaries, and the word *chanoyu*. The romanization of Chinese words follows the pinyin system.

The names of Japanese people active before the Meiji Restoration of 1868, which marks the beginning of the modern period of Japanese history, follow the Japanese custom of giving the family name first. The names of modern Japanese follow the Western convention, family name last.

Premodern Japanese dates are also handled somewhat differently from those in the modern period. Because a lunar calendar was used until 1872, the first month of the year did not always correspond to January. For this reason all premodern dates in the book specify months by number rather than name: "the third day of the fifth month," not "May 3."

Until the Restoration each emperor's reign was divided into a number of *nengō*, or "eras," which were used for dating. While all dates in the book have been converted to the Western system, it has occasionally been necessary to refer to *nengō* that are important in the history of tea, such as the Temmon era (1532–55) and the Genroku era (1688–1704).

Traditionally, the Japanese consider a baby to be one year old at birth. The ages of all people mentioned in this book have been adjusted to conform to the Western system, but in a few instances, as when a person's age is mentioned in a poem, the age is necessarily given in Japanese style. In all such cases the equivalent age in Western terms is also noted.

Likewise, traditionally the computation of the years that have passed since a person's death includes the year of death. Thus, Sen Rikyū died in 1591, and the centennial of his death was commemorated in 1690, not 1691.

A slight discrepancy also exists between the way in which the Japanese traditionally count the successive generations of Buddhist abbots and the accepted Western practice. In Japan, the founder of a temple is not regarded as the first abbot. That designation belongs to his successor, who would be known as the second abbot in most Western-language sources. The Western system has been adopted here.

The "weathermark" identifies this book as a production of John Weatherhill, Inc., publishers of fine books on Asia and the Pacific. Editorial supervision: Jeffrey Hunter. Book design and typography: Miriam F. Yamaguchi. Production supervision: Mitsuo Okado. Layout of illustrations: Yutaka Shimoji. Composition: Samhwa Printing, Seoul. Platemaking and printing: Nissha Printing, Kyoto. Binding: Makoto Binderies, Tokyo. The typeface used is Monotype Perpetua.